CONTENTS

Rome & the Apennines → p. 106

Southern Italy → p. 122

Road atlas → p. 176

DID YOU KNOW?

MAPS IN THE GUIDEBOOK

(178 A1) Page numbers
and coordinates refer to
the road atlas
(O) Site/address located
off the map
Coordinates are also given for
places that are not marked
on the road atlas
(U A1) Coordinates refer to the
street map of Rome inside
the back cover

**INSIDE BACK COVER:
PULL-OUT MAP →**

PULL-OUT MAP 📖

(📖 A–B 2–3) Refers to the
removable pull-out map
(📖 a–b 2–3) Refers to the
additional inset map on the
pull-out map

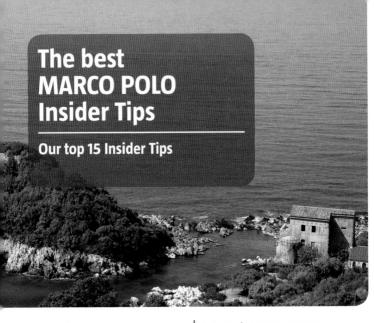

The best
MARCO POLO
Insider Tips

Our top 15 Insider Tips

BEST OF ...

● *Sound of the Dolomites*
Soloists from the Berlin Philharmonic Orchestra or Italy's famous cellist Mario Brunello shoulder their instruments and hike to cave and mountain venues in the Trentino Dolomites. Accompany them, and you can enjoy marvellous renditions by professional musicians completely free of charge → p. 60

● *Cascata del Molino hot springs*
Spa resorts have the monopoly on most of Italy's thermal springs, but in some areas such as *Saturnia* in Tuscany, you can still enjoy a hot spring in natural surroundings (photo) → p. 104

● *Magna Graecia in Metaponto*
Along the coast of Southern Italy, you can visit the archaeological sites of ancient towns built by the Greeks in the 8th century BC during their colonisation of Italy. The ruins of the ancient city of *Metapontum* are particularly impressive → p. 132

● *Cavern town of Matera in Basilicata*
You do not have to pay a penny to enjoy history and marvel at how people manage to create living space when you wander the streets, terraces and stairs carved into the rock of the ancient *sassi* settlement → p. 131

● *Via Appia Antica in Rome*
The ancient route led from Rome to the Adriatic. This Roman road in the large archaeological park is a fine example of the Roman Empire's excellent road network – and there is no entrance fee → p. 116

● *Trasporto della Macchina di Santa Rosa*
Traditional festivals – such as the festival in honour of Santa Rosa in *Viterbo* in September – offer a free display of Italian joie de vivre, in the form of open-air concerts, fireworks and a magnificent procession → p. 161

●●●● Dots in guidebook refer to 'Best of ...' tips

● *Gran Paradiso National Park*

Italy not only has the longest marine coastline (7600km/4722mi in total) in Europe but also the highest Alps, one example being the protected *Gran Paradiso* massif in the Aosta Valley (4016m/13,180ft high peak) and inviting mountain valleys and forests bursting with wildlife → p. 39

● *By the lake*

The lakes in northern Italy are so beautiful that you may find it difficult to decide which of these jewels with their mild climate, verdant vegetation and spectacular waterside villas is the most beautiful. Perhaps *Lago di Como* with its enchanting little lakeside towns such as Bellagio and Varenna? → p. 76

● *Cucina Italiana*

You can experience the diversity of Italian cuisine at its best at *Eataly*. Serving delicious ravioli from the north or crispy pizza that even Naples could not beat, this modern chain from Turin is in the process of conquering the market all the way to Bari → p. 47

● *I rolli – magnificent palaces*

The powerful maritime republics accumulated great wealth, and their legacy includes the *rolli,* the magnificent palazzi in Genoa, unique examples of fine architecture, which can still be admired today (photo) → p. 39

● *Art and faith in Assisi*

In the homeland of the great saints, art has also taken its inspiration from faith, as is clearly visible in Giotto's frescos about the life of the patron Saint Francis of Assisi in the *Basilica di San Francesco* → p. 96

● *Ostia Antica*

2000 years ago the harbour of Rome; today this ruined city in the shade of large pines gives you a taste of ancient times → p. 119

● *Val d'Orcia*

When you think about the Italian landscape, classic Tuscany immediately springs to mind. These scenes are particularly beautiful in *Val d'Orcia* south of Siena with its gently rolling hills, olive groves and lines of cypresses → p. 149

ONLY IN

BEST OF ...

RAIN

● *In the dripstone caves*
It is cold and damp below the Earth's surface, but you will not get wet during your excursion deep below the rocks. There are large dripstone caves all over Italy with fascinating formations of stalactites and stalagmites; the largest cave is the *Grotta Gigante* near Trieste → p. 61

● *Aquarium in Genoa*
The diverse underwater world in the country's largest aquarium provides a perfect excursion when it is raining on the Ligurian coast – sharks and penguins will provide hours of entertainment (photo) → p. 156

● *Galleria Vittorio Emanuele II. in Milan*
Under the glass-domed roof of Italy's largest and most elegant shopping arcade, you can wander over skilfully laid marble floors past elegant boutiques and bookstores and then enjoy a view of the cathedral square as you sip on an espresso → p. 72

● *Rome's main churches*
Rome's four main churches, which naturally include *St Peter's Basilica*, are so large and packed with art treasures that you can use the rainy weather to explore them at your leisure → p. 114

● *Napoli Sotterranea*
The city of Naples is built on tuff (volcanic) stone. Over the centuries, its inhabitants have created an underground world of cellars, large cisterns, subterranean places of worship and catacombs, and today these offer a fascinating experience → p. 140

● *Designer outlet centre Serravalle*
Searching for a bargain in the rain? Spend a relaxing day exploring the more than 170 shops in the country's largest outlet village → p. 31

● *Hay bath in Fiè allo Sciliar*
Lie down in the warm, damp hay! At *Hotel Heubad*, essential oils extracted from the mountain herbs that grow on the Seiser Alm in South Tyrol penetrate the body, and relax and refresh you in a most agreeable way → **p. 54**

● *On the Brenta Canal to magnificent villas*
An opportunity to relax and see something at the same time? Then take the 'Burchiello' excursion boat from Padua to Venice and cruise past the beautiful Venetian villas that line the water's edge → **p. 56**

● *On the piazza*
Where better to relax than in a pavement café on an Italian piazza – sip an espresso and watch the hustle and bustle in front of the breathtaking palazzi and church architecture, e.g. in *Cremona* or *Ascoli Piceno* → **p. 80, 92**

● *On the seafront promenade in Reggio di Calabria*
It is the chaotic town of Reggio di Calabria of all places that has one of Italy's most beautiful *lungomare*: enjoy the sunset! → **p. 134**

● *Fango therapy in the Euganean Hills*
Owing to their past volcanic activity, the hills of Padua are rich in minerals and mud that has healed and relaxed many generations over the centuries. Now it is your turn – in the *Abano Terme* → **p. 57**

● *An inspiring trail*
There is hardly any other trail that provides such a breathtaking panorama as pleasantly and easily as that offered by Trieste's rocky coast → **p. 61**

● *On the Cilento beaches*
In June, you can enjoy the beautiful sandy beaches along this piece of very unspoilt coastline just south of Naples → **p. 145**

INTRODUCTION

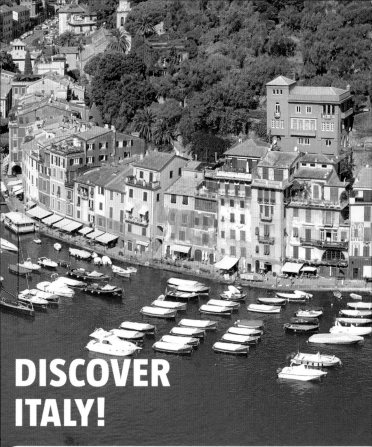

DISCOVER ITALY!

When you arrive in Italy, the first thing you should do is to go to the piazza; it is the sitting room, hub of urban life and private stage all rolled into one. Sit down in the café with the best view, order a cappuccino, a Campari or even a local aperitif and simply watch the Italians. You will no doubt see a few elderly men standing talking with great gusto about everything and anything (football included of course). And if it is market day in winter, there will a lot of ladies in mink intent on creating a *bella figura*, which is far higher up their list of priorities than animal rights. Groups of young people will go past, gesticulating wildly, all fashionably dressed and clutching the ubiquitous *telefonino*.

The Italians have a high standard of living and so a trip to Italy can be an expensive pleasure. The prices for hotels, restaurants, museums and for the beach are often hefty. Nonetheless, the present economic crisis has its benefits: hotel and restaurant prices have essentially stagnated. Many restaurants have introduced inexpensive lunch menus, and flexible online booking makes it possible to find reasonable rates

Photo: Liguria, Portofino harbour

Probably the most famous steps in Rome: Scalinata Trinità dei Monti (Spanish Steps)

in what are otherwise high-priced hotels. What is more, in the last few years – if one ignores the usual rip-offs and poor service that can be experienced anywhere in the world – hotels and restaurants have improved. A lot has happened in the hospitality industry: in coastal towns and in the medieval hamlets, *locande,* small, individually run and tastefully furnished guest houses are opening; while in the large cities, there is a choice between charming boutique hotels, chic design hotels or comfortable B & B rooms, often in beautifully restored town houses.

In the evening, people meet for an aperitif at the bar, in the town quite often in the luxury hotels, in the summer by the sea in beach areas that turn into lounge bars when the sun goes down or provide DJ facilities for the beach party. New stylish shops selling clothes, shoes and original designer pieces are opening up everywhere; they often use the spectacular setting provided by an old town palazzo.

From 1000 BC
Highly developed art and technology of the Etruscans

8th–5th century BC
Greeks establish over 40 towns in the south of Italy

4th–1st century BC
Rome rules throughout Italy and in the Mediterranean region

5th century
Teutons, Lombards, Vandals and Huns invade Italy

11th century
The Normans capture Campania, Apulia and Sicily

14th/15th century
Formation of independent duchies, town and maritime

There is always a good reason to improve and renovate districts and buildings that have seen better days. For the holy millennium year 2000, half of Rome was given a facelift and the infrastructure modernised for the millions of pilgrims. Cities like Rome, Naples and Venice saw some new additions as well, such as contemporary art projects, ultra-modern museums and exhibition facilities. In Turin, once dominated by Fiat, there have been successful efforts made to bring the town into the post-industrial era with ambitious cultural projects. This was helped by the Winter Olympics in 2006 and Italy's 150-year anniversary as a nation state in 2011, which is visible in the rejuvenated museums, the improved infrastructure and restoration work that has been carried out. In the fascinating harbour city of Genoa, many of the palazzi and magnificent museums have been spruced up. This attention to old town centres contrasts with the sometimes almost depressing sprawl of the suburbs and the often surprisingly crude architecture. And despite the fact that Italians are taking environmental protection more seriously, for example by introducing better sewage plants, setting up nature reserves and increasingly bringing agriculture in line with the criteria of organic farming, it is still shocking to see the rubbish left behind on some beaches, in the woods and by the rivers – especially, but not only, in the south.

> **In the evening people meet for an aperitif in the bar**

It is the Italians themselves that criticise their country the most, especially when things do not work as they would like them to. Traffic chaos, lack of parking space in

republics of the Kingdom of Naples/Sicily and the Papal States

1556–1799
Division of Italy between the Bourbons, Habsburgs and France

1848–71
Italian reunification *Risorgimento* into a single state with Rome as the capital

1915
Italy goes to war against Austria and Germany in the First World War

1919
As part of the Treaty of Versailles, Italy receives South Tyrol, Trentino, Trieste and Istria

the cities, bad service, crowded trains. The Italians can despair about themselves and their country. As when the factories close in August, and with them a lot of the restaurants and businesses in the large towns, and all of Italy sets off for the seaside. Chaos and high prices are the inevitable result. Naturally, there are reserves that provide service to those who do not go off on holiday and for the solitary, intrepid tourists. And, of course, it is lovely to be able to enjoy these hot, deserted towns without all the traffic and noise.

This provides the cue for why people love to keep going back to Italy: the leaning tower of Pisa, shimmering olive groves, Michelangelo's David, the gondola ride along the Canal Grande, romantic coastlines such as the Cinque Terre or the Costa Amalfitana... The Italians continue to be friendly, generous and open people, even if their life is by no means full of the pleasure and indulgence expressed in the famous dolce vita! In fact, statistics show that they actually work more than the English, French and Germans.

Italy is predominantly a mountainous country

Italy is essentially a mountainous country and has to accommodate almost 58 million people in its hills and valleys. In the north, much of the Alps belong to Italy: the south-facing massifs of the Central and Western Alps, whose foothills run down to the large lakes, and the Southern Limestone Alps which include the Dolomites. In 2009, Unesco declared the latter a World Heritage Site because of its unique scenic beauty. Bordering this area is the Po Valley, a broad plain, which stretches from Piedmont down to the Adriatic coast around Rimini. Italian travellers tend to pass through here quickly. Flat, humid and plagued with mosquitoes, it is not your typical Italian landscape, yet towns such as Parma, Mantua and Ferrara are well worth a visit. Poplars and dykes line the Po River, which flows into a nature reserve at the delta leading to the Adriatic – a place of great beauty with its ponds, tributaries, sand dunes and many different bird species.

In terms of climate, northern Italy has a predominantly continental climate, which means that in winter Turin and Milan can often be just as cold as London or New York, although the proximity to the south is evidenced by the higher summer temperatures. The Riviera sheltered by the Maritime Alps and the Ligurian Apennines is well known for its mild winters. Behind Liguria, the Alps meet the Apennines,

1922–1943
Fascist dictatorship under Benito Mussolini

1946
Italy becomes a republic

1992–94
Bribery scandals, mafia murders, collapse of the traditional parties

2008
Right-wing populist Silvio Berlusconi is elected Prime Minister for the third time

2009
Severe earthquake in Abruzzo

2013
Leader of the coalition, Enrico Letta, is sworn in as Italy's 55th Prime Minister

Umbria, the 'green heart' of Italy: a kind of Tuscany for insiders

which run over 1200km/ 746mi to the southern tip of Calabria. In the south, the Apennines even offer an active volcano –

The Apennines extend 1200km/ 746mi across the country

Vesuvius near Naples, and while it does not smoke, is still not extinct.

Italy covers a total area of around 116,000 square miles. About a sixth of this and half of its 760km/4,722mi coastline belong to the islands. This travel guide only covers the mainland, however there are separate MARCO POLO guides available for Sicily, Sardinia, and Naples and the Amalfi Coast.

The diversity in the country's geography and climate, with its Alpine summits, river plains, densely forested highlands, Mediterranean hillscapes and coastline is in keeping with the multifariousness of Italy's past. Thus each town, each province and each island has its own history. Greeks and Etruscans were – after the large migration around 1000 BC – the first to leave their mark on the culture and history of Italy. From the 8th century BC, the Greeks founded over 40 towns in the south of Italy. The Etruscans, who mainly settled in the north of Lazio, in Tuscany and the Po Valley, were people with highly advanced skills in handcrafts and art. Thanks to their surprisingly cheerful approach to death, numerous examples of their expressive art have been preserved. Their burial towns, the necropolises, especially those in Lazio, are key tourist attractions.

During the 4th and 3rd century BC, Rome controlled all of Italy and, during the subsequent century, set about building a powerful empire in the Mediterranean area, in Asia Minor and Europe. Imposing buildings still bear witness to the representative ambitions of this former world power. They include the Colosseum that was inaugurated in AD 80 with 100 days of continuous tournaments, the gigantic Hadrian villa in Tivoli, the Baths of Caracalla in Rome, which could accommodate up to 1600 bathers, and Verona Arena with space for 22,000 spectators.

In the 5th century, Ravenna became the residence of the West Roman Emperor

The fall of the Roman Empire took hundreds of years. Already under threat from the Alemanni, the Franconians, the Visigoths and Ostrogoths, the Huns and the Teutons, the empire was divided into a West and East Roman Empire, the latter having its capital in Constantinople. In the 5th century, Ravenna became the residence of the West Roman Emperor, which is why today it is one of the main cities to see in Italy. New nations invaded Italy and dissolved the Roman centralism by setting up independent duchies. During the Middle Ages, the Arabs, Normans and the Hohenstaufens controlled southern Italy. Impressive cathedrals and fortresses date from the Norman and Hohenstaufen period, especially in Apulia.

From the 10th to 13th centuries, the Holy Roman Emperors and their rivalries with the popes of Italy left their mark on the Italy of the Middle Ages. The harbour towns prospered as a result of the crusades and trade with the orient. Even today, stately palaces in the towns testify to the self-confidence of the communities, which became independent town states in the 13th century.

In the 14th and 15th century, local duchies developed, with powerful families like the Visconti and Sforza in Milan, the Scaligeri in Verona, the Este in Modena and Ferrara, the Gonzaga in Mantua, the Malatesta in Romagna, the Montefeltro in the Marche region, but especially the Medici in Tuscany. Besides the church, they were the major art patrons driving the Italian Renaissance. Their art and culture became the measure for Europe as a whole. They enabled outstanding art geniuses such as Masaccio, Piero della Francesca, Brunelleschi, Donatello, Leonardo da Vinci, Michelangelo, and Botticelli to develop. The Catholic Counter-Reformation encouraged the emergence of the Baroque period, which can be particularly admired in Rome and Naples. In subsequent centuries, major European powers fought for supremacy in 'the boot'. This ended in 1861 with the creation of the Italian national state.

Italy's rich and eventful history has resulted in the country's vast array of art treasures and cultural assets — but what an enormous task it is to look after them. The Italian passion for gambling helps in this respect as a significant percentage of the state lottery profits flows into the upkeep of historical monuments. Museums have long since had longer opening times to enable more people to visit them. EU citizens under 18 and over 65 years of age do not have to pay for their ticket at the large state museums and those aged 18 to 25 only pay half price. And many towns have introduced tickets enabling the holder to enter the various sights and museums at a discounted price as well as to travel free on public transport.

Yet Italy's magic is by no means limited to the fine arts. Whilst in one respect the gastronomy sector is not soaring quite as high, a lot of dedicated young chefs are now encouraging a return to local specialities. Organic farming, organic grocery shops and farmer's markets all support this trend. Italy's Slow Food movement has played a leading role in this respect. At home and abroad, it actively promotes the preservation of local products, culinary traditions and environmentally conscious food production. Environmental organisations and the state are also investing an increasing amount of energy into protecting nature. The first large nature reserves were created at the beginning of the 20th century, such as the Alpine national park Gran Paradiso between the high peaks of the Aosta Valley and the Parco Nazionale dell'Abruzzo with its wild Apennine Mountains in the south

Museo Archeologico Nazionale: Greek gold in Tarento

that is home to wolves and bears. In the 1990s, the government allocated new protected areas, and today ten per cent of Italy's landscape and coastal areas are under conservation. Tourist authorities provide maps of the nature reserves, hiking and bicycle trails. Even those who enjoy more extreme sports will find challenging playgrounds in the mountains and the sea, ranging from rock climbing in the Alps and Apennines to biking and surfing as well as rafting down wild mountain streams. Beautifully located farmhouses offer holiday accommodation, often with horse rides, swimming pool and guest bicycles as well as home-produced food. This rural option, called *Agriturismo*, offers a relaxing contrast to the sightseeing tours – and it is becoming increasingly popular with holidaymakers.

Agriturismo enjoys growing popularity

Thus the chances of having an exciting and enjoyable trip to Italy, a country that can boast beautifully preserved old towns, growing rural conservation and seemingly endless coastlines, are now even better than ever.

WHAT'S HOT

1 Remodelled

Where to stay In Italy, you can stay in an old flour mill with a beautiful view *(Molino Stucky, Giudecca 810, Venice, photo)*, a former pasta factory *(AC Torino Hotel, Via Bisalta 11, Turin)* or what was once a tobacco factory *(Il Tabacchificio, Via San Antonio 33, Gagliano del Capo)*. The facilities were simply converted into hotels when they reached the end of their industrial life. Where people used to toil, there are now penthouse terraces with a swimming pool, and former offices have been turned into stylish hotel rooms.

New masters

Art The art scene is in constant flux, sometimes focusing on video installations, then on the classic canvas and paintbrush. The main objective of *Pescara Electronic Artists Meeting (www.artificialia.com/peam)* is to promote digital art. There are a wide range of very different contemporary works on view in the *Museo Laboratorio d'Arte Contemporanea (Piazzale Aldo Moro 5, Rome)*. Turin's international fair *Artissima* provides a good overview of what is going on in the art world *(www.artissima.it, photo)*.

3 Like the ancient Romans

On the beach Luxury laps at the gates of Rome. Guests relax on lounge chairs or in hammocks on Fregene's beaches. They can also chill in *Shilling (Piazzale Cristoforo Colombo)* in Ostia's yoga and massages areas. Further south, too, dolce vita holds sway at the beach pools. The guests of the *Bagno Elena (Naples, www.bagno elena.it)* feel like they are in holiday heaven. On a wooden terrace overlooking the sea, you can sunbathe while you surf the internet and drink *prosecco* cranberry on ice.

Adventurous excursions

Volcano trekking Inquisitive travellers can learn why it is best not to wear synthetic socks if you are a volcanologist and what makes lava soil so fertile during a special guided tour to Vesuvius and. The certified experts from *Guide Vesuvio (Via San Vito, 151, Ercolano, www.guidevesuvio. it)* lead the way to the crater of the active volcano. With *Vesuvio Trekking (www. vesuviotrekking.com, photo)*, it is not just about destination but also about the journey. Vesuvius fans will love the guided hike through the surrounding park. Those who would prefer to explore the caves at the foot of Mount Etna or watch small eruptions at sunset, should contact *Volcano Trek (www. volcanotrek.com)* or *Etna Experience (www. etnaexperience.com)* in Sicily.

Wind and water

Active Until now Lake Garda has been the Mecca of Italy's water sports fans. The steady breeze attracts kite surfers to Malcesine or Riva del Garda. Now, other locations are making a name for themselves as destinations for water sports. The still undeveloped south, in particular, offers fantastic conditions for the fast-paced sport. *BuenaOnda (Arango-Magliacane, www.buenaondasurf. it)* in Calabria's Catanzaro provides not only kite surf courses but also wakeboard lessons. Approximately 80km/50mi further north *Kitesurf Crotone (Via delle Conchiglie, Crotone, www.kitesurfcrotone.it)* on Gabella beach is popular with kite surfers and those who want to learn. The wind also blows on the other side of the peninsula: Gizzeria is the home of the *Hangloose (www.hangloosebeach.it, photo)* kite surfing school.

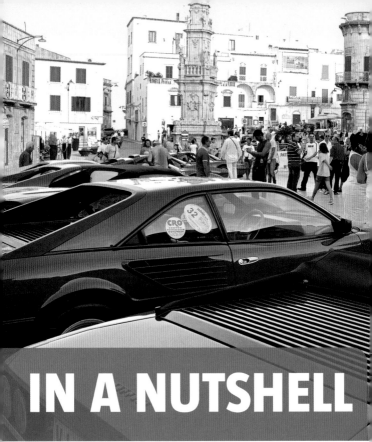

IN A NUTSHELL

A MORE

The Latin lover has lost his lustre, or so it would seem; these days cosmopolitan young men on Italian beaches excite at best a grin. Perhaps their irresistibility was just a bit of wishful thinking, which the Italians wanted to believe as much as everyone else. Even though for centuries it has been an Italian girl whose romantic tale has fired the imagination of people around the world: the tragic heroine Juliet, Romeo's star-crossed lover from Verona – who is even on the Internet these days: *www.julietclub.com*, a site which awards an annual prize for the most beautiful love letter. A romantic trip to Verona on Valentine's Day is also an eloquent expression of love: *www.veronainlove.it*. Perhaps it is the Italian language that makes languishing sound so beautiful, which is why the best troubadours continue to be the Italians: the melancholy Paolo Conte for the ladies and sexy Eros Ramazzotti for the girls.

B AR

The bar opens at the crack of dawn with the fragrance of fresh *cornetti* (croissants) and *cappuccini*. During the day, housewives, school children, manual workers, office employees, and passersby pop in. In the afternoon, youngsters plan

Photo: Ferrari Festival in Brindisi

Slow Food, the Mafia and saints: notes on the culture, daily life and politics of a multifaceted country

what they are doing in the evening while the older generation play endless games of cards. In the towns, the cocktail hour marks the day's climax; in the villages, the men return to the bar for a last chat after dinner. In the summer, guests watch the activities on the piazza from their seats in front of the bar. From sober to shabby (sometimes quite kitschy) but nowadays also increasingly very trendy, the bar is the Italian's second home and visitors are also made very welcome.

CARS AND MOTORBIKES

High speeds appeal to the temperament of the Italians; only they could invent sleek cars such as the blazing red Ferrari from Modena. Motorcycle fans swear by the Italian cult brand Ducati from Bologna, and little girls swoon for the unbeatable racing driver Valentino Rossi. And like buzzing swarms, Vespas whizz through the narrow streets of the Italian towns. Despite the high motorway tolls and the traffic chaos in the towns, the Italians still enjoy driving. They have a nippy, nimble style, but can also be impatient and aggressive. That can be rather intimidating for foreign drivers at first so the best thing to do is to throw yourself into the fray and trust the lightening reactions of the other drivers. Anyway the fun element is not what it was, since the once typical statistics for Italy – a lot of vehicle damage but few road casualties – is no longer true. Smog has led to many of the large cities closing off their town centres to vehicles, including tourist cars. But it is possible to rent a bicycle in almost all of the town centres, generally in the vicinity of the station. Environmental awareness is thus also picking up speed on Italy's roads; driving with low-emission fuel is very widespread, car sharing is no longer a foreign concept and taxi companies use the hybrid cars Prius.

ECONOMY

In the second half of the 20th century, Italy developed from a rural, agricultural country into a highly developed industrial nation. Tourism dominates the service area while important industries include mechanical engineering, the packaging industry and food production. Traditional sectors, such as the textile and shoe industry, also play a key role in Italy's economy. These benefit from the creativity of the world-famous Italian fashion designers, but also from the successful structure of Italian business, which is dominated by highly specialised small to medium-sized often family-run companies. They are mainly based in the north and centre of Italy and, as flexible family-run corpora-tions, often play an essential supporting role to the few large companies such as Ferrero (Nutella, Kinder), Benetton, Barilla and Fiat. However, things are not as good as they were. Relocation of production facilities to low-wage countries is also affecting Italy and bureaucracy, national debt and taxes are causing a heavy burden. There is a lack of investment in education and research, and the opportunities for young people are correspondingly poor. They represent 36 per cent of the 10 per cent unemployment. Despite years of subsidies, the south also continues to lag behind the rest of the country. A major problem is the widespread informal economy, illegal employment. Yet numerous reforms have recently been launched.

FAMILY

The Italian family still exists. However, it is no longer the large patriarchal family with several generations under one roof, but has split up into single and small family households. Added to this, the nation famous for being fond of children has seen an astounding decrease in its birth rate – and with statistically about one child per family, holds the European record for producing the fewest children. Today, immigrants from Africa, Asia and Eastern Europe help to ensure that Italy's own ageing population does not tip the pyramid on its head. The family continues to exist as a unit providing mutual support dealing with unemployment, finding work, coping with housing problems, looking after older members of the family and helping out when kindergarten spaces are not available. In the family, you can always find handymen, a doctor, a lawyer and an inexpensive fur coat. That may in part explain why many Italians can live beyond their means despite high prices and often low wages – and why many youngsters would find it difficult to move into a home of their own.

GIOTTO

Of the many artist geniuses that Italy has produced, the painter and master builder Giotto di Bondone (1266–1337), son of a farmer from a village near Florence, has earned a very special place. During the period of powerful cities like the Florence of the 13th and 14th century, Giotto developed a new painting style, far removed from the schematic representation of Byzantine art, popular in the

the Cappella degli Scrovegni in Padua and the frescoes depicting the life of St Francis in the *Basilica of St Francis* in Assisi.

IMMIGRATION

The Italians find it hard to regard their country as a 'promised land' for immigrants. The idea is too deeply ingrained in their mind that you have to leave Italy to find opportunities and from 1876 to 1976, a whopping 24 million Italians actually did leave for different parts of the world. Yet, like every large industrial nation, the country has long become a goal for people

Worship of Padre Pio: false piety or fervent belief?

Middle Ages. Perspective, colour variations, motion, human characterization – in short realism. His painting thus became the starting point for the development of a typically Italian painting tradition, which led out of the 'international' Middle Ages. In the Uffizi in Florence, it is easy to see this innovation when comparing Giotto's 'Maestà' with that of Cimambue, Giotto's teacher who was a generation older. Giotto's masterpieces are the frescoes in

from less prosperous nations, as is more than obvious from the overcrowded vessels found making their way to the south coast: 7.5 per cent of the Italian population today comes from Romania, Albania, Africa, Pakistan and China. It would be difficult to imagine the economy and the social fabric of Italy without them. The immigrants look after Italy's elderly and their children, run small corner shops and market stalls, work in the hospitals, trattoria kitchens and for the waste disposal companies. The factories in the north and the tomato fields in the south would have to shut down or lie fallow without the African workers.

LANGUAGES

Italy is a country of linguistic diversity. Apart from Italian and its dialects, ten other independent languages are spoken: Ladin in Friuli and the Dolomite valleys, German in South Tyrol (where it is ranked equally with Italian) and in Trentino. In some of the villages in Sicily and southern Italy, the locals speak Albanian, a legacy from the Albanian settlers of the 14th century. In Apulia and Calabria, there are villages where you will hear remnants of Greek. In the northern Italian border provinces of Trieste, Gorizia and Udine, the Italians speak Slovene and in some villages in Molise in southern Italy Serbo-Croat. Catalan has survived in Alghero on Sardinia, as has Franco-Provençal in the north-western regions of Aosta Valley and Piedmont. French is even the second official language in the Aosta Valley. Sardinian is also an independent language and not a dialect. The still highly acclaimed and much cited national poet Dante Alighieri from Florence (1265–1321) provided the basis for standard Italian with his 'Divine Comedy', with its 15,000 verses. Since the 20th century, however, schools and television have ensured that the multilingual Italians can all understand each other.

MAFIA

In Italy alone, the Mafia makes around 100 billion euros a year, mainly through protection rackets, 'tribute' money, drugs and more recently waste disposal. The fact that their operations stretch beyond the borders of Italy became all too clear with the murders in Germany 2006.

Yet there are constantly successful results in the quest to catch the 'untouchable' mob bosses, and even the civilian population is contributing to the efforts. That is why the *Addiopizzo* movement (goodbye to protection money) is making itself felt in Sicily even in tourist hotels and restaurants, where the owners are bravely resisting the extortion rackets. In Calabria, the *Ammazzateci tutti* (kill us all) movement is growing in strength with campaigns to raise public awareness of legality. Organic oil, wine and pasta, produced on land confiscated from the mafia are now being sold under the label *Libera Terra (www. liberaterra.it)*. However, it is not without reason that the mafia is called *piovra,* octopus, because it constantly develops new tentacles.

MUSICA ITALIANA

The music scene is as rich and diverse as the countryside. The north has produced incredibly popular old rockers, such as Vasco Rossi, Zucchero, Ligabue and Gianna Nannini. Genoa has a reputation for producing fine songwriters, the most famous of whom include Gino Paoli and the late Fabrizio De André, who is still worshipped by his fans. A different music trend has developed in the south, a mixture of the rhythms of traditional folk music – predominantly *pizzica taranta* from Apulia – and modern sound. Vanguards include Teresa De Sio and Edoardo Bennato, and the next generation includes groups such as Sud Sound System. Pino Daniele mixes jazz, pop and Neapolitan dialect. Anyone looking for the *canzoni napolitane* should listen to Roberto Murolo. And the Italian charts? Young Italians listen to melodic pop of the Subsonica, Le Vibrazioni and Negroamaro. Unconventional pop bards include Tiziano Ferro, Sergio Cammariere, Simone Cristicchi as well as – on the female side – Carmen Consoli,

National poet Dante: highly respected as a pioneer of the Italian language

Laura Pausini, Giorgia and the young Malika Ayane. Many of these artists give live concerts at the numerous summer festivals and piazza events that take place throughout Italy.

SAINTS

Over 90 per cent of Italy's population are Roman Catholics. The Pope, the supreme pastor of the church, lives in the centre of the capital in his Papal state of the Vatican. Particularly in the south, priests continue to have tremendous influence on politics and elections. Much of the population relies on an army of innumerable saints to give them support in their daily struggle for survival. Worth special mention is Naples's St Januarius. In May and in September, the devout meet in his cathedral for the 'Miracle of the Blood', praying for as long as it takes for a vial of the saint's blood to liquefy. Millions of admirers have already made a pilgrimage to San Giovanni Rotondo in

Apulia to pay their respects to the miracle healer Padre Pio (1887–1968) who was only recently declared a saint.

SLOW FOOD

Italians guard their culinary traditions in much the same way as they do their art treasures. That is shown by the success of the Slow Food movement initiated in 1986, which began fighting against the fast food industry by promoting restaurants that serve carefully prepared local specialities and organising 'taste education' campaigns and regional food markets. Met with some disdain to begin with, Slow Food has long since proved that good taste and the conscious selection of food from the vicinity and from local producers goes hand in hand with environmental protection and social responsibility. There are now Slow Food supporters in over 130 countries (for more information about events, markets and fairs in Italy, see *www.slowfood.it*).

FOOD & DRINK

Few countries can match the global popularity of Italian food. Children in the western world grow up with spaghetti and ravioli, and in the international arena the pizza is the only serious competitor of the hamburger.

The *salumerie,* the cheese shop, and the food markets will have your mouth watering within seconds. However, it is the simple, but ingenious, durum wheat flour pasta that is the traditional mainstay of Italian cuisine. The imagination and creativity of the Italians have produced around 250 different types of pasta, first and foremost spaghetti, 'strings of pasta' in numerous widths. In southern Italy, *maccheroni*

holds sway, either thick or thin, smooth or ribbed, and also called *tubetti, rigatoni* or *penne*. Then, there are the more typically northern Italian pasta, *tagliatelle, fettuccine* or *pappardelle,* and finally the filled pasta made of egg and flour dough in many forms and with different fillings, *ravioli, agnolotti, cappelletti, tortellini, tortelloni, cappellacci.* Many pasta dishes are traditionally topped with grated cheese, *parmigiano* (cow's milk, predominantly in the north) or *pecorino* (sheep's milk, generally in central and southern Italy). A meal begins with *antipasti,* which include starters such as salami, ham, pickled onions, aubergines, artichokes or seafood;

Pasta is the traditional mainstay of Italian food – and each region produces the right wine to accompany it

this is followed by the *primo* (first course), a pasta dish, soup or risotto; the *secondo* (main course) is braised or grilled meat, or fish, also often simply grilled, and a choice of vegetables *(contorno).* Vegetables provide the cue for the south, which is where the tomatoes taste particularly good as do the aubergines, artichokes, fresh *fave* (green, sweet broad beans), hearty leaf vegetables, such as *cicorie,* *cime di rape, friarielli* and broccoli. The meal culminates with creamy desserts such as *tiramisu, zabaione* or *zuppa inglese* as well as biscuits which you dunk into sweet fortified wines. In the south, people like to use the mild cream cheese *ricotta* in their desserts.

Ristorante, trattoria, osteria and *locanda* are words that will help you choose a restaurant, although these days it is

LOCAL SPECIALITIES

▶ **agnello** – lamb (photo left) served as a roast *(al forno)* or as a grilled chop *(alla griglia)*

▶ **arrosto di maiale/di cinghiale** – roast pork is popular throughout Italy; central Italy also has wild boar

▶ **bollito misto** – various cuts of stewed meat: beef, tongue, chicken, sausage, served with a green sauce *salsa verde* or fruit mustard *(mostarda)*

▶ **brasato** – roast beef braised in red wine, typical in the north of Italy; it is usually served with polenta (a side dish made of finely ground cornmeal)

▶ **(insalata) caprese** – the classic summer snack: tomatoes, mozzarella (preferably made of buffalo milk), basil

▶ **coniglio** – roast rabbit, which you can buy almost everywhere

▶ **fritto misto di pesce** – battered, deep fried fish, squid rings, seafood

▶ **gnocchi** – tiny potato flour dumplings served, like pasta, as a *primo* with a *sugo* (photo right)

▶ **insalata di frutti di mare** – a seafood salad with a lemon, olive oil, garlic and parsley dressing comprising of chopped squid, octopus and mussels.

▶ **ossobuco** – braised veal or beef shanks in a tomato sauce, typical for Lombardy

▶ **pesce alla griglia** – fresh grilled fish: bream *(dorata)*, dentex *(dentice)*, sea bass *(spigola)*, mullet *(triglie)*, plaice *(sogliola)*, sardines and mackerel *(pesce azzurro)*

▶ **(alla) pizzaiola** – stewed in tomato sauce, typical for the south

▶ **porchetta** – a suckling pig roasted on the spit and seasoned with herbs

▶ **spaghetti alle vongole/allo scoglio** – spaghetti with clams or seafood

▶ **zabaione** – light and fluffy custard cream with wine, originally from Piedmont

often better just to look at the ambience and menu as well as the guests eating there (are they Italians?). The once traditional *osteria* now calls itself an *enoteca* or, when in a more international vein, a wine bar. Fine wines are served in a *calice* (goblet) and cost from 2.50 to 10 euros

a glass including cheese and charcuterie specialities.

The invoice includes the *coperto,* the price for bread and cover (1–5 euros), which is always indicated on the menu. The service, unless specifically indicated as *non compreso*, is included in the price. The restaurant kitchen tends to open between 12.30pm–2pm and 7.30pm–10pm. Pizzerias usually keep their ovens running until midnight. Anyone feeling peckish during the day, can buy *panini* (sandwiches), *tramezzini* (toasted sandwiches) and sweet pastries in a bar. Restaurants in the towns now often offer a quick meal – very urban and not at all Italian – for lunch. Locals like to go to self-service restaurants or *rosticceria* at lunchtime, where you can generally buy surprisingly tasty regional dishes. There are snack bars selling pizza everywhere, and kebab shops have also been around for a while. Italy is a haven for connoisseurs, producing as it does a wide choice of delicious and very varied wines. Besides the international varieties, Italian vineyards also cultivate their own regional varieties, even in the alpine Aosta Valley where both dry white wine and good reds are produced. Italy's best red wines come from Piedmont, including the famous Barola. Crisp white wines flourish on Liguria's terraced slopes. First-rate Lombard wine comes from Oltrepò, Franciacorta and Valtellina while Emilia-Romagna produces more wine than any other region in Italy. South Tyrol and Trentino focus on red wines while Friuli, especially Collio, is known for its excellent white wines. Veneto is renown for having Italy's most copious wine drinkers! Of particular note are the white Soave, the red Valpolicella and the *prosecco*, which is especially good from the area around Conegliano and Valdobbiadene.

The famous wine region of Chianti is in Tuscany; the noble Brunello grows near Montalcino. Of the Umbrian wines, the white Torgiano deserves special mention. The Verdicchio from Jesi and Macerata in the Marche region go well with fish. The *osteria* and *trattoria* in Lazio serve the white Frascati and wines from Castelli Romani. Abruzzo is home to the red Montepulciano d'Abruzzo and the white Trebbiano d'Abruzzo, and the Biferno and Pentro are pressed in Molise.

Apulians are rightly proud of their rosé wines. The light sparking red Aglianico from Basilicata still comes from vines that the Greeks planted in southern Italy in

It need not be the 1979 vintage: Barolo

400 BC. The white Greco di Tufo grape was already grown in ancient Pompeii; on Mount Vesuvius lava slopes it is called Lacryma Christi. Calabria has strong red wines and excellent dessert wines, including the Moscato di Saracena. In the north, the Italians round off a lavish meal with a *grappa,* in the south, they tend to opt for the fruity lemon liqueur *limoncello*.

SHOPPING

The Italians display their exquisite taste in fine food and wine, sophisticated fashion and accessories as well as traditional craftsmanship in the country's many ateliers, markets and elegant shops.

DELICATESSEN & WINE

Culinary specialities make ideal souvenirs, e.g. extra virgin olive oil *(olio d'oliva extra-vergine),* or wine bought directly from the wine dealer, vineyard or local supermarket. A nice accompaniment is air-dried salami, pickled wild boar sausage, a thick slab of vacuum-packed Parmigiano-Reggiano, dried porcini, top-quality charcuterie like the *culatello,* balsamic vinegar and grappa ... Recommended from the south: the lemon liqueur *limoncello*, sundried tomatoes and the *vasetti* with pickled vegetables such as aubergine and artichokes in vinegar or oil, especially the little Mediterranean onions *lampascioni,* a speciality from Apulia. One souvenir tip from Calabria is the *'nduja*, a fiery *peperoncino* pork sausage, which keeps well and adds real spice to a pasta sauce.

FASHION & SHOES

Top of the list are the big fashion names such as Armani, Dolce & Gabbana, Prada, Versace, Max Mara, followed by the more casual brands such as Benetton, Stefanel and Diesel. Look out for the sales *(saldi)* if you want to avoid high prices; they often start in the summer. Otherwise go to the outlet centres, which also stock the main brands. They are laid out like villages and located near the motorway, e.g. the largest ● *Serravalle Designer Outlet* in Serravalle Scrivia near Alessandria in Piedmont *(Via della Moda 1 | www.mc arthurglen.it)* with over 170 shops, in Lombardy near Brescia in Rodengo Saiano the *Franciacorta Outlet Village,* in Emilia-Romagna near Fidenza the colourful *Fidenza Village,* in Tuscany in Mugello the *Barberino Designer Outlet,* near Rome the *Designer Outlet Vastel Romano*. Under the name 'Diffusione Tessile', the Max Mara brand sells high-quality goods from the previous season for half the price: *www.diffusionetessile.it.* The manufacturers' outlets *(spaccio aziendale)* are more difficult to find; the tourist offices

Cuisine, clothing and crafts: there is something for everyone in the markets, fashion boutiques and outlet centres in *bella italia*

can help with addresses. The regularly updated **INSIDER TIP** *'Lo Scopri-occasioni'* provides information in Italian, and an aid in English is: *www.factory-outlet-italy. com/en/FO/index.php.*

HANDICRAFTS

Tourism can be thanked for its role in helping to preserve local craft traditions. Even young people are now learning the old crafts and combining them with attractive new design ideas. Woodcarving work can be found in the South Tyrolean Val Gardena and Aosta Valley. Murano is famous for its mouth-blown glass and nearby Venice does a flourishing trade in handmade masks and marbled paper. Handmade paper can also be found in Fabriano and Amalfi. Drive to Impruneta for the nicest terracotta pots or for rustic Mediterranean ceramics to the Amalfi

coast, Vietri sul Mare or Apulia in Grottaglie. Lecce's speciality is papier-mâché figurines of saints and for nativity scenes.

MARKETS

Practically every town has a market. There you will find the *moka* for making espresso, the milk frother for the cappuccino, the cheese grater, the truffle slicer, the mortar in marble or olive wood, the vinegar and oil set – all things that have been available at home for a long time, but which acquire an additional local flair when you buy them in Italy. There is an increasing number of farmer's markets in the large towns bearing the motto 🙂 'Bio Okm'. And at the weekly markets, every kind of clothing is for sale, including surprisingly high quality items at reasonable prices.

THE PERFECT ROUTE

LAKES, VILLAS AND METROPOLISES IN THE NORTH

Near the Swiss border at Bellinzona or Lugano you enter the ① *Italian Lake District* → p. 76, at Lago Maggiore in the west and Lago di Como in the east. On the western shore, the route takes you past wonderful villas in the Lombardy Alps and through the Camonica Valley with its famous prehistoric rock art to Lago d'Iseo and into the wine-growing region of Franciacorta. Old towns such as Brescia and Bergamo are along the way to the north Italian city of ② *Milan* → p. 71. From there, you travel via Vigevano to ③ *Turin* → p. 46, the elegant capital of Piedmont, with the Savoy castles in the surrounding areas, and Alba and Asti providing the good food and wine.

MOUNTAINS, COASTS AND ANTIQUITY

Once over the Apennines, you arrive in Liguria and the spectacular harbour town of ④ *Genoa* → p. 39. Magnificent hiking areas open up at ⑤ *Cinque Terre* → p. 43 and join up with the Versilia coast of Tuscany, which has top-class seaside resorts that include Forte dei Marmi and Viareggio. In ⑥ *Pisa* → p. 105, you should not miss the opportunity to climb up the leaning tower. Travel on to ⑦ *Florence* → p. 85. From there, head south to the little town of ⑧ *Assisi* → p. 96 before journeying through green Umbria and the central mountain region of Lazio to reach the seething city of ⑨ *Rome* → p. 112. From here, you can take excursions to the Etruscan towns and to ancient Ostia.

TEMPLES, A VOLCANO AND SAND BAYS

The route now goes via Capua and Caserta to ⑩ *Naples* → p. 138 and the Gulf of Naples (and Mount Vesuvius) and the Amalfi coast. The Cilento, a mountainous region with an unspoilt coast and beautiful seaside resorts begins with the ancient temple city of Paestum. This is followed by the Golfo di Policastro and Calabria's coastal hotspots such as ⑪ *Tropea* → p. 136, and on the Ionian side such ancient Greek sites as Locri and Sibari. Winding streets lead up to the rugged mountain area of ⑫ *Aspromonte* → p. 135.

BAROQUE, ORIENTAL FLAIR AND CASTLES

On the north of the Gulf of Taranto, the route takes you to ⑬ *Matera* → p. 131, the 'cave town' in the Basilicata. The heel of the Italian boot is Salento in Apulia, with little seaside towns, such as Gallipoli, that exude an oriental flair, the south-eastern extremity Santa Maria di Leuca, the scenic road up to Otranto and the enchanting Baroque town of ⑭ *Lecce* → p. 136, which you must not miss. On your way north, you go through the Trulli countryside, past Romanesque churches such as the cathedral in Trani, and castles dating back to the Hohenstaufen such as ⑮ *Castel del Monte* → p. 126.

ADRIATIC, ABRUZZO AND VENETIAN FLAIR

The Adriatic coast meanders through the woods and cliff villages of the Gargano region to old harbour towns. Inland, Abruzzo's impressive mountains rise up in front of you. Attractive little towns border the Marche coast, two of which are San Benedetto del Tronto and Fano as well as ⑯ *Conero* → p. 94 (photo), a lovely part of the Adriatic south of Ancona, with superb conditions for diving and swimming. After famous seaside resorts with names like Riccione and Rimini, it is the turn of the towns in the Po Valley such as ⑰ *Ferrara* → p. 71. Across the Po delta you reach the lagoon landscape on the northern Adriatic coast and its highlight ⑱ *Venice* → p. 62. This includes discovering the villas of the Venetian aristocracy, e.g. on the trip across the Brenta Canal to Padua. Via ⑲ *Verona* → p. 64 you go to Lake Garda, before your journey through Italy comes to an end.

4780km/2970mi. Driving time: 10 days
Recommended trip length: 4 weeks
Detailed map of the route on the back cover, in the road atlas and the pull-out map

THE NORTH-WEST

Italy's 'boot' starts on the south side of the Alps and anyone travelling by sea has to traverse the mountains. The passes used by the Romans, Alpis Poenia and Alpis Graia, are now called the Little and Great St Bernhard passes, and they connect Italy to France and Switzerland.

Mountains dominate the three regions in north-west Italy. The Aosta Valley and the 100km/62mi-long plain through which the Dora Baltea River flows, are lined by mountain ranges that are among the most magnificent the Alps have to offer. In the north, one can see the east face of Mont Blanc (4810m/15,780ft), the Matterhorn (4478m/14,690ft, ital. Cervino) and the Monte Rosa (4634m/15,200ft), whilst towering in the south is the Gran Paradiso (4061m/13,320ft), a ski and hiking paradise. Providing a backdrop to Turin, capital of the Piedmont region, are the snow-covered peaks of the Piedmont Alps in the north and west, and in the south the Apennine hills of Monferrato, Roero and Langhe, well known for their mushrooms, truffles and excellent red wines.

The Maritime Alps in the north-west and the Apennines in the south-east help foster the mild climate of the Riviera on the Ligurian coast. Though providing a stunning backdrop for the Ligurian seaside resorts, the mountains have obliged

Photo: View of Alassio

Alps and Riviera: the Aosta Valley's mountains, Piedmont's gourmet paradise and Liguria's seaside resorts

Genoa, the large harbour town, to expand 35km/21mi along the coast.

AOSTA

(178 B2) *(𝄞 C2)* **Aosta (pop. 35 000) is also called 'the Rome of the Alps'. The well-preserved city gate Porta Pretoria, an equally intact Arco di Augusto, and** especially the 22m/72ft high stage wall of the Roman theatre look impressive against the backdrop of the snow-covered peaks.

This picturesque town with its lively old quarter, ideal for shopping and browsing, is the logistic and geographic centre of the Aosta Valley, the smallest Italian region with the statute of autonomy, and officially bilingual (Italian and French).

Porta Praetoria: old town remains from the Roman period

dating back to the Carolingian age. On the south side, between the church and the priory house decorated with terracotta is the wonderful ⭐ *cloister* (1133), with 40 Romanesque marble columns displaying fine stone masonry work around the capitals. Its imposing presence underlines the former importance of the cloister in the Alpine region, one of the main stops on the Via Francigena. *Oct–Feb daily 10am–12.30pm and 1.30pm–5.30pm, Sun to 6.30pm, March–Sept daily 9.30am–12.30pm and 2pm–6pm*

FOOD & DRINK

OSTERIA DELL'OCA
A courtyard leads to this friendly local restaurant. In summer, it is lovely to sit outside; besides regional dishes such as polenta and game ragout, the restaurant also serves pizza. *Closed Mon | Via Aubert 15 a | tel. 01 65 23 14 19 | www.ristoranteosteriadelloca.com | Budget–Moderate*

PAM PAM TRATTORIA DEGLI ARTISTI
Great atmosphere and good food (e.g. crêpes with mountain cheese, *crespelle*) at this popular restaurant in the old town. *Closed Sun/Mon | Via Maillet 5–7 | tel. 0 16 54 09 60 | Moderate*

SHOPPING

An original souvenir from the Aosta Valley is the *grolla*, a round wooden vessel with several spouts, from which locals drink a kind of coffee punch in the winter. On Jan 30/31 and in mid Aug, the *Sagra di Sant'Orso* takes place, Italy's oldest arts and crafts market. The valley's craft products can be bought all year round from the *IVAT (Institut Valdôtain de l'Artisanat de Tradition)* in the town hall *(Piazza Chanoux 11)*.

Mining, energy generation (water), woodworking and the summer and winter tourism have made the Aosta Valley into one of the most affluent areas in Italy. The valley and town also thrived during the time of the Roman Empire, because of their strategic importance for protecting the Po Valley in the north-west and as the starting point for the conquest of the Gauls.

SIGHTSEEING

SANTI PIETRO E ORSO
The cloister complex includes a late Gothic church of Romanesque origin with a crypt

WHERE TO STAY

B & B AMBROSIA ♨ ☼

Two attractive rooms in an eco house. Sumptuous breakfast and gorgeous view of Aosta. *fraz. Arpuilles 94/H | tel. 33 95 74 95 94 | www.bedbreakfastaosta.com | Budget*

MILLELUCI

Slightly further out, in the Porossan Roppoz district. Romantic rooms and health centre. *31 rooms| tel. 0165 23 52 78 | www.hotel milleluci.com | Moderate–Expensive*

INFORMATION

Piazza Chanoux 2 | tel. 0165 23 66 27 | www.regione.vda.it/turismo, www.natur aosta.it

WHERE TO GO

BREUIL-CERVINIA (178 C2) (*ω C2*)

The special appeal of this internationally renowned ski region in the Aosta region is no doubt explained by the fact that it lies at the foot of the imposing Matterhorn (4478m/14,690ft) in Valtournenche. A large ski area of 350km/217mi connects it to the Swiss side around Zermatt. Offering an amazing view and great summer skiing is the ♨ *Plateau Rosà* glacier at 3480m/11,420ft, which you can reach with a cable car (all year round). Relaxed elegance and excellent service make the *Hermitage (36 rooms| Via Piolet 1| tel. 0166 94 89 98 | www.hotelhermitage.com | Expensive)* the region's finest hotel.

Down in Valtournenche near *Antey Saint-André*, there is a charming hotel in an old farmhouse: INSIDER TIP *Maison Tissière (14 rooms | Petit Antey 9 | tel. 0166 54 91 40 |www.hoteltissiere.it |Moderate)* with a spa and a good restaurant. *www.cervinia.it*

FORTRESSES AND CASTLES
(178 C2) (*ω C3*)

There are over 130 in the Aosta Valley. Among the most important are the ♨ 14th century *Verrès* castle *(Fri–Wed 10.30am–12.30pm and 1.30pm–6pm, in winter to 4.30pm)* perched on a steep cliff and *Issogne* castle, which has a richly ornamented interior, painted Renaissance courtyard and the famous fountain in the form of a pomegranate tree. *Fénis* awaits you with a medieval knight's castle and the *MAV handicraft museum (Chez Sapin 86 | Tue–Sun 10am–5pm)*. The imposing fortified complex *Forte di Bard (Tue–Fri 10am–6pm, Sat/Sun 10am–8pm)* houses

---

MARCO POLO HIGHLIGHTS

★ **Cloister**
Fine stonemasonry in the Santi Pietro e Orso cloister in Aosta → p. 36

★ **Mont Blanc Crossing**
Across the glacier in a cable car → p. 38

★ **Genoa's old town**
A fascinating mix of dark alleys and magnificent palaces → p. 39

★ **Cinque Terre**
Five picturesque – and car-free – Ligurian cliff villages → p. 43

★ **Reggia di Venaria Reale**
The Savoy castle near Turin is regarded as the Italian 'Versailles' → p. 51

★ **Sacri Monti**
Colourfully arranged figures in the Baroque pilgrimage chapels in Piedmont → p. 51

a modern designed and fascinating *Alpine museum. Fenis and Issogne: March–June and Sept daily 9am–6.30pm, July/Aug 9am–7.30pm, Oct–Feb 10am–noon and 1.30pm–4.30pm, in winter Fénis closed Tue, Issogne closed Wed*

COURMAYEUR (178 B2) (*∅ C2*)

At the foot of Mont Blanc, this town has been a summer resort since the 19th century, as is evident from the beautiful old chalets. Today Courmayeur *(www.courmayeur.it)* together with its French counterpart Chamonix offer some of the most challenging ski pistes in the Alps. The Mont Blanc tunnel connects the two resorts as does a cleverly designed series of cable cars: the famous ★ 🔆 *Mont Blanc Crossing* (valley station in La Palud, 3.5km/2mi from Courmayeur, *www.montebianco.com*). For one and a half hours you glide over the breathtaking silent white peaks and glacier landscape. Experience the exclusive atmosphere of Courmayeur in the elegantly comfortable chalet hotel

L'Auberge de la Maison (33 rooms | Via Passerin d'Entrèves 16 | tel. 0165 86 98 11 | www.aubergemaison.it | Expensive) which has a fine restaurant, sauna and gym; the *Meublé Berthod* is more basic *(25 rooms | Via Mario Puchoz 11 | tel. 0165 84 28 35 | www.hotelberthod.com | Budget–Moderate)*.

Val Veny (with a camping site) and Val Ferret (with a golf course), the two lateral valleys, bring you closer to this magnificent mountain world. Arnouva, a village in Val Ferret, is ideal as a starting point for hikes and mountain bike tours to *Chalet Val Ferret,* which is only open in the summer *(7 rooms | tel. 0165 84 49 59 | www.chaletvalferret.com | Moderate)* with a restaurant in a former barn. Courmayeur's famous guides organise adventurous mountain tours *(tel. 0165 84 20 64 | www.guidecourmayeur.com).* The old *thermal baths (Allées des Thermes | tel. 0165 86 72 72 | www.termedipre.it)* in Pré-Saint-Didier have been elegantly restored – and are now a popular health oasis.

Anyone who finds hiking dreary has never been to the Gran Paradiso National Park

GRAN PARADISO NATIONAL PARK ●
(178 B–C 2–3) (ᗰ C3)

Early in the morning, ibex – the emblem of this magnificent nature reserve in the south of Aosta – appear at the tree line. Even golden eagles and wolves live here below the powerful Gran Paradiso (4061m/ 13,320ft). The biodiversity is thanks to King Victor Emmanuel II; in the 19th century, this alpine region was already his protected hunting reserve. In this hikers' paradise, you will find camping sites in the middle of the countryside with a wonderful mountain backdrop, for example in Valsavarenche at the 1800m/5906ft high *Camping Gran Paradiso (8 wooden bungalows | Plan de la Pesse | tel. 0165 90 58 01 | www.campinggranparadiso.it | Budget)*. In the charming main town of *Cogne*, with its attractive hotels, the art of bobbin lace making continues to this day. *www.pngp.it, www.cogne.org*

GRESSONEY VALLEY
(178 C2) (ᗰ C 2–3)

The scenically varied valley extends towards the Monte Rosa massif. It was from the other side of Monte Rosa that a group of immigrants came from the Swiss canton of Wallis 750 years ago. They settled here and in some of the neighbouring valleys in Piedmont. Their legacy includes the Walser-German dialect and a distinctive style of architecture. You will come across the old INSIDER TIP ► Walser houses at the end of Valsesia, Val di Gressoney, Val d'Ayas and Valle Anzasca. They are tall constructions; the first floor has walls of roughly hewn stone and above it is dark weathered wood. In *Gressoney-Saint-Jean* an old Walser house has been converted into a charming hotel *La Gran Baita (12 rooms | Strada Castello Savoia 26 | tel. 0125 35 64 41 | www.hotelgranbaita.it | Moderate)*. The beautiful valley offers skiing, golf, trekking and rafting and is par-

ticularly popular with people from Milan. *www.gressoneymonterosa.it*

PONT SAINT-MARTIN
(178 C2) (ᗰ C3)

The excellently preserved Roman arch bridge (100 BC) spans the Lys mountain stream.

GENOA (GENOVA)

(179 D4–5) (ᗰ D4) **A (possible) son of this town, Christopher Columbus, discovered America in 1492, yet his 'conquest' marked the beginning of Genoa's decline. La Superba (the proud) lost its central trading role as an international maritime power to Mediterranean harbours in north-west.**

In 1992, by means of an Expo celebrating the 500-year anniversary of his discovery, Columbus was commandeered into helping Genoa (pop. 620,000) to recover after being badly affected by decreasing port activities and the crisis in heavy industry. The old harbour was revitalised, and many palaces were restored as was the Teatro Carlo Felice which had been destroyed during the Second World War.

For Genoa's role as the European Capital of Culture in 2004, many buildings in the ★ old town were restored and Liguria's once typical painted façades refreshed. Wander around the lively tangle of streets and also cross the Baroque avenues of *Via Garibaldi* and *Via Balbi* to see the wonderful palaces – once residences of wealthy shipbuilders, merchants and bankers from Genoa's golden age in the 16th and 17th century – now full of art collections. Numerous aperitif bars and hip restaurants are located in the walls of the old town. 42 of them, called ● *Palazzi dei*

Baroque palazzi are a familiar sight on the large boulevards in the centre of Genoa

Rolli, are listed as Unesco World Heritage Sites *(www.irolli.it)*. You reach the ⬈ upper part of the town with funiculars and lifts. The ⬈ roof terrace of the maritime museum in the old harbour area offers probably the most beautiful view of the town, the harbour and the sea. Genoa is one of Italy's most appealing travel destinations.

SIGHTSEEING

CATTEDRALE SAN LORENZO
It took centuries to complete Genoa's largest sacral building, extending from the early Christian period to the Renaissance; the *Museum of the treasury* is well worth a visit *(Mon–Sat 9am–noon and 3pm–6pm). Piazza San Lorenzo*

LANTERNA ⬈
One of Europe's oldest lighthouses (dating from the 12th century, 117m/338ft) stands in the south-west section of the old harbour and can be reached using the new promenade. History buffs will enjoy

the small *city museum* at the base of the lighthouse. *Both Sat/Sun 10am–7pm*

MUSEI DI STRADA NUOVA
A newly arranged museum complex consisting of three old palazzi teeming with art treasures (Rubens, Dürer, Veronese, Van Dyck, Caravaggio and many more), precious fabrics and furnishings: *Palazzo Bianco, Palazzo Rosso, Palazzo Doria Tursi* on the boulevard Via Garibaldi. *Tue–Fri 9am–7pm, Sat/Sun 10am–9pm | www.museidigenova.it*

PALAZZO DUCALE/PIAZZA MATTEO
The square is the focal point of the Genoa district once controlled by the merchant family Doria. It is here on the *Piazza Matteo* that you will find many of the family's palazzi and the Romanesque, black and white striped church containing the tomb of Andrea Doria. The *Palazzo Ducale (www.palazzoducale.genova.it)*, once the exclusive residence of the doge, is now a central meeting place with exhibitions, restaurants, cafés and bookstores.

PALAZZO REALE

The magnificent furnishings of this 17th century Savoy palace testify to the luxury of times gone by. Wonderful ☆ hanging gardens. *Tue/Wed 9am–1.30pm, Thu–Sun 9am–7pm | Via Balbi 10 | www.palazzo realegenova.it*

PORTO ANTICO

The old harbour area has become a popular place for a walk, with cafés, a swimming pool, skating rink and museums such as the maritime museum ☆ *Galata Museo del Mare* containing Italy's largest submarine *(March–Oct daily 10am– 7.30pm, Nov–Feb Tue–Fri 10am–6pm, Sat/Sun 10am–7.30pm)* and the famous aquarium (see 'Travel with kids').

INSIDER TIP ▸ VIA DEL CAMPO 29: ROSSO

In the old town in Via del Campo, at number 29, you will find a piece of Italy's musical soul: the legendary record shop Gianni Tassio with its huge selection of songs by Genoan songwriters – first and foremost the cult figures Fabrizio De André and Gino Paoli – is now a *music museum*. *Tue–Sun 10am–7pm | www.via delcampo29rosso.com*

FOOD & DRINK

INSIDER TIP ▸ BAGNI SANTACHIARA

Sunbathe during the day, in the evening happy hour and fresh light cuisine not far from the town's little fishing village of Boccadasse. *June–Sept daily | Via Flavia 4 | Capo Santa Chiara | tel. 33 98 61 71 67 | Moderate*

LA CUCINA DI GIUDITTA ☺

In this light and friendly restaurant in the old town, the chefs prepare the food using fresh organic vegetables, and everything is delicious. *Closed Sun and evenings except Fri, Sat | Piazza Valoria 11 r | tel. 01 02 77 00 94 | www.lacucinadigiudita. it | Budget–Moderate*

YZ PANINO D'AUTORE

Delicious *panini* with Slow Food products. Superb sandwich bars *(Gran Ristoro and Colombo 92)* also in the Sottoripa colonnade on the way to the old harbour. *Closed Sun | Via XX Settembre 68 r | www. ilpaninogenova.it | Budget*

TRATTORIA ROSMARINO

Lovely modern trattoria in the town centre near Piazza De Ferrari; the kitchen offers typical Ligurian cooking that is fresh and creative. *Closed Sun | Salita del Fondaco 30 | tel. 01 02 51 04 75 | www.trattoria rosmarino.it | Moderate–Expensive*

SHOPPING

You will find a selection of shops and arts and crafts in the narrow streets of the old town and elegant fashion along the *Via XX Settembre, Via Roma, Via XXV Aprile.* You should pop in to admire the abundance on display in the market hall of the INSIDER TIP ▸ *Mercato Orientale (Via XX Settembre).*

ENTERTAINMENT

Happy hour in the trendy bars in the old town, e.g. on the Piazza delle Erbe, and in Porto Antico, e.g. in *Banana Tsunami*, or along the Via Garibaldi in the museum cafés; in summer along the Corso Italia by the sea. Operas in *Teatro Carlo Felice (www.carlofelice.it).*

WHERE TO STAY

HOTEL METROPOLI

Tastefully renovated and conveniently situated. *48 rooms | Piazza Fontane Marose/*

Via XXV Aprile | tel. 01 02 46 88 88 | www.
bestwestern.it/metropoli_ge | *Moderate*

HOTEL VERONESE
Hospitable, simple and neat, near the
aquarium. *19 rooms | Vico Cicala 3 | tel.
0 10 25 10 77 | www.hotelveronese.com |
Budget–Moderate*

WWW.COLUMBUSVILLAGE.COM
Website with numerous, often very charming bed and breakfast offers in the centre
of Genoa. *Budget–Moderate*

LOW BUDGET

▶ The grand finale of the *Bataille
des Reines* takes place in the Aosta
arena on the third Sunday in October.
Throughout the summer, you can
watch the exciting qualifying rounds
between the strong black cows in the
meadows and farms free of charge.
www.amisdesreines.it

▶ Street food in Liguria: *farinata*,
the flat loaf is made with chickpea
flour, or the *focaccia* filled with
cheese, fish or vegetables, e.g. at
*Antica Sciamadda (Via San Giorgio
14 r | closed Sun)* in Genoa.

▶ For those who enjoy good, reason-
ably priced fish, the *Sagra del Pesce*,
possibly Italy's most famous food
festival, is held on the second May
weekend in the seaside town of
Camogli, in Liguria.

▶ On dark winter evenings the installations of well-known artists, the *luci
d'artisti*, light up the streets of Turin –
an impressive spectacle that is free.

INFORMATION

Via Garibaldi 12 r | tel. 01 05 57 29 03; info
kiosk in Porto Antio | Piazza Caricamento |
tel. 01 05 57 42 00 | www.turismo.comune
-genova.it

RIVIERA DI LEVANTE

(179 D–E5) *(\varphi D–E 4–5)* **The east coast
of Liguria between Genoa and Tuscany
is rocky and often steep; picturesque villages squeeze themselves into small
spaces, which makes this stretch of coast
even more attractive.**

WHERE TO GO

CAMOGLI (179 D5) *(\varphi D4)*
The tall, sunny yellow houses, some of
them displaying Liguria's typical trompe
l'oeil windows, stretch along the craggy
cliff walls while flights of stairs in between
entice you to wander round. This attractive
little coastal town (pop. 6000) was home
to Italy largest merchant fleet until the
19th century. In the summer, people come
to savour the Ligurian fish dishes on the
idyllic terrace of *La Cucina di Nonna Nina
(closed Wed | Via Molfino 126 | tel. 01 85
77 38 35 | Budget–Moderate)* in the higher
lying district of San Rocco. You need to
reserve in advance. By taking one of the
boats that leave every hour (or on foot
from San Rocco further up from Camogli),
you can visit the headland *Punta Chiappa*
with its beautiful beaches as well as an
idyllically situated monastery INSIDER TIP
San Fruttuoso directly by the sea, which
you can also reach from Portofino by taking a lovely walk via Monte Portofino. If
you want to try the local culinary speciality *focaccia*, a flat pizza-style bread with

herbs, go to nearby *Recco,* where you can enjoy this delicious titbit in restaurants and snack bars or on the fourth Sunday in May at the gourmet food festival INSIDER TIP *Sagra della Focaccia.*

Riomaggiore keep the confined village pleasantly free of cars, but it is still better and easier to visit them by train. At the village stations, information offices provide the addresses of hotels and private rooms

Camoglic: a pretty little seaside town at the foot of the Portofino Peninsula

CINQUE TERRE ⭐
(179 E5) (*ω E5*)

These five fishing villages are situated on one of Liguria's most gorgeous stretches of coastline, high on the cliffs (Corniglia) or at the sea set against the steep rock walls: *Monterosso,* the only village with a large beach, *Vernazza,* the largest village, *Corniglia, Manarola* and *Riomaggiore.* Above them, ripening on the steep hillside terraces, are the grapes of the DOC white wine and the heavy dessert wine Sciacchetrà. The protected mountain landscape of Cinque Terre is very popular with hikers. In the summer, the car parks located just outside Monterosso and

as well as details regarding the Cinque Terre Card (a form of visitors' tax) and the hiking routes: *www.parconazionale5terre.it* Located just in front of the Cinque Terre on a broad sandy beach is the delightful coastal town of *Levanto.* From here, there is a particularly nice 8km/5mi ☀️ *coastal path* offering a fantastic view of Monterosso, the first of the Cinque Terre villages. On the way, in a beautiful location, you pass a small hotel with 12 pretty rooms – each with its own terrace – the hotel also has a swimming pool and serves a good breakfast: ☀️ *La Giada del Mesco (Via del Mesco 16 | tel. 01 87 80 26 74 | www. lagiadadelmesco.it | Moderate–Expensive).*

Sestri Levante offers a stunning location for a swim in the sea

GOLFO DI LA SPEZIA

(179 E5) (*E5*)

The modern harbour town La Spezia – badly damaged during the Second World War – located on the gulf cut deep into the coast now has some very interesting museums: in the ⚡ castle buildings of Castello San Giorgio there is the *Museo Archeologico (Wed–Mon 9.30am–12.30pm and 3pm–6pm, June–Sept 5pm–8pm)* containing the mysterious **INSIDER TIP** stone stelae found near the coast; in the town centre is a collection of old masters in the *Museo Amedeo Lia (Tue–Sun 10am–6pm | Via Prione 234)*. The old town is ideal for shopping. Along the waterside promenade, at *Dai Pescatori*, you can buy nicely prepared fresh fish – caught by local fishermen *(daily | Banchina Revel/Viale Italia | tel. 34 02 50 89 24 | Budget)*. The tourist office is located directly opposite. On the ⚡ headland, protecting the gulf from the open sea, the enchanting little seaside town of *Portovenere* and the near-

by islet *Palmaria* await you. On the east coast of the gulf is the exclusive *Lerici* on the idyllic bay *Golfo dei Poeti,* which was a Mecca for poets and artists in the 19th century. Further along, take time to wander round the ruggedly romantic cliff villages of *Fiascherino* and *Tellaro.*

SANTA MARGHERITA LIGURE AND PORTOFINO (179 E5) (*D4*)

On the Gulf of Rapallo bordering the Monte Portofino headland, there are some first-class resorts. The largest is *Santa Margherita Ligure;* its *Piazza Martiri della Libertà* is crowded with pubs and restaurants, and in the summer offers some of the area's best nightlife. *Portofino,* a little car-free fishing village, is one of Italy's most exclusive and expensive places. A luxury hotel par excellence in a magnificent location: *Splendido (64 rooms | Dépendance Splendido Mare 16 rooms | Viale Baratta 16 | tel. 01 85 26 78 01 | www.hotelsplendido.com | Expensive)*

SESTRI LEVANTE
(179 E5) (*Ⓜ E4*)

The small town on the coast greets you with two enchanting sandy bays, the *Baia delle Favole,* which fans out in front of the colourful houses, as well as the more serene and expensive *Baia del Silenzio.*

VARESE LIGURE
(179 E5) (*Ⓜ E5*)

The village, 45km/28mi inland in the mountains, is popular owing to the intact old town and its reputation as a 😊 model ecological village that strives to promote organic agriculture and alternative energy (*www.valledelbiologico.it*). Here, accommodation may be simple, but the food more than makes up for it: *Amici (closed Wed | 28 rooms | Via Garibaldi 80 | tel. 0187842139 | www.albergoamici.com | Budget*).

RIVIERA DI PONENTE

(178–179 C–D 5–6) (*Ⓜ C–D 4–5*) **One seaside resort after another dots the shore as it curves round between Genoa and the French border at Ventimiglia.**

The wonderful climate initially saw elegant resorts here with parks, palm-lined avenues and luxury hotels in towns like Bordighera and San Remo. Later on, the cut flower industry and mass tourism arrived. But there are still lots of pretty towns to discover, such as *Celle Ligure, Varigotti* and *Laigueglia; Cervo, Noli* and *Albenga* have lovely old districts, while *Finale Ligure* attracts the younger generation with its outdoor activities. And up through the olive groves and chestnut woods are the tranquil mountain villages of *Dolceacqua, Apricale* and *Triora.* The hiking trail ⚡ *Alta Via (www.altaviadeimontiliguri.it)* is well marked and has places to stay; it is 440km/273mi from Ventimiglia to La Spezia. A 24km/15mi INSIDER TIP ▶ bicycle track runs from Ospedaletti to Sanremo and on to Imperia, and offers a ⚡ panoramic view of the coast. For bike rental facilities and picnic places, see (*www.pistaciclabile.com*). *www.visitrivieradeifiori.it*

WHERE TO GO

ALASSIO
(178 C5) (*Ⓜ C5*)

Of the small towns along the coast of western Liguria, it is Alassio (pop. 12,000) with its long sandy beach that best represents the mild, floriferous character of a Ligurian summer. Package tourists like it here, but so do VIPs, as shown by the signatures written in ceramic on the famous *muretto* (wall) in the town centre. One of the many excursions nearby includes the *Toirano caves* to admire the stalagmites and stalactites.

INSIDER TIP ▶ BUSSANA VECCHIA AND BUSSANA MARE (178 C6) (*Ⓜ C5*)

Reduced to a pile of stones by an earthquake in 1887, *Bussana Vecchia* situated north of San Remo became an artists' colony in the 1960s, and is now full of interesting ateliers and workshops (*www.bussana.com*). Offering a nice contrast, *Bussana Mare* on the coast, has two restaurants which specialise in beautifully prepared fish dishes: *Gente di Mare (daily June–Sept | Via Bussana Mare 26 | tel. 0184 514992 | Moderate)* and *La Kambusa (daily June–mid Sept | Via al Mare 87 | 0184 514537 | Moderate–Expensive).*

SAN REMO
(178 C6) (*Ⓜ C5*)

Members of the English aristocracy used to stay here in splendid luxury hotels. One of Europe's most famous casinos opened in the town (pop. 60,000) in 1906 *(www. casinosanremo.it)* and still draws the crowds today, although now the most glamorous event is the Italian pop festival in spring. Stroll through the winding streets of the old town, called *La Pigna* – it is well worth it. People like to meet on the *Piazza Bresca* with its many restaurants and cafés. In *Bordighera* 10km/6mi to the west, a good place to eat is the *Osteria Magiargè (closed Mon/Tue and July/Aug noon | Piazza Giacomo Viale | tel. 0184 26 29 46 | www. magiarge.it | Budget–Moderate)*, a Slow Food tip – thanks to its delicious regional and seafood cuisine.

VILLA HANBURY ☼ (178 C6) (*Ø C5*)
The Giardini Botanici Hanbury with its stunning terraced gardens – a prime example of Liguria's rich flora – is close to the French border in La Mortola near Ventimiglia. *March–mid June and mid Sept–mid Oct, daily 9.30am–5pm, mid June–mid Sept 9.30am–6pm, mid Oct–Feb Tue–Sun 9.30am–4pm | www.amici hanbury.com*

TURIN (TORINO)

(178 C3) (*Ø C3*) **The city, traversed by the Po, is marked by the wide, straight avenues, with arcades full of inviting fashion boutiques and fragrant coffee houses (*Corso Vittorio Emanuele*): elegant-bourgeois flair.**

Turin (pop. 1 million), once royal seat of the House of Savoy, became home to a huge wave of Italians from the south when the Fiat car factory was founded (1899) and a symbol of industrialised Italy. Now it represents post-industrial Italy and has blossomed into a centre for major sports events (Winter Olympics 2006)

WHERE TO START?
The city's core artery Via Roma starts at the train station **Porta Nuova** and links up the main squares and many good shops. West of the Via Roma is the Quadrilatero Romano, which traces the chessboard layout of the former Roman settlement. Today, much of it is pedestrianised and teeming with bars and shops. From Palazzo Reale or from Piazza Castello the route continues eastwards towards the river, past the Mole Antonelliana to the Piazza Vittorio Veneto – a popular meeting place in summer – and to the Po waterfront.
A large underground car park is near Piazza Castello: *Parcheggio Roma-Piazza San Carlo-Piazza Castello (2.50 euros/hr)*.

and modern lifestyles. Locals meet in the bars and restaurants of the former storerooms on the Po riverbank walls, called *murazzi*, in the town centre the *Quadrilatero Romano* district south of Porta Palatina as well as the spacious *Piazza Vittorio Veneto*. In addition to important art galleries, private foundations also display the town's interest in modern art. These include the *Fondazione Sandretto Re Rebaudengo (Fri–Sun noon–7pm | Via Modane 16 | www.srr.org)* or the *Fondazione Mario Merz (Tue–Sun 11am–7pm | Via Limone 24 | www.fondazionemerz.org)*.

SIGHTSEEING

CATTEDRALE SAN GIOVANNI BATTISTA
The Baroque *Cappella della Santa Sindone* belongs to the cathedral complex and the only Renaissance building in the town. It is here that the Turin Shroud is kept

which came into the possession of the House of Savoy in the middle of the 15th century and is now only shown on special occasions. Visitors can see infrared photographs of the image. *Piazza del Duomo*

INSIDER TIP ▶ **EATALY** ●

The modern food centre in a former factory in Lingotto is truly a feast for the eyes: you can shop for Italian culinary delights and can eat them in the *ristorantini* or in *Casa Vicina Guidopereataly (closed Sun evening and Mon | tel. 01119 50 68 40 | Expensive)*, regarded by many as Turin's best restaurant. *Daily 10am–10.30pm | Via Nizza 230 | www.torino.eataly.it*

GALLERIA SABAUDA

You can admire the rich art collections of the Savoy monarchs in the Baroque palace *Palazzo dell'Accademia delle Scienze* on the *Via Roma. Tue, Fri, Sat, Sun 8.30am–2pm Wed/Thu 2pm–7.30pm*

LINGOTTO

An example of how to modernise former industrial buildings: today – in the old Fiat factory from the 1920s with the legendary futuristic test track on the roof – there is now an elegant hotel, a concert hall, trade fair facilities, shops and, on the roof, the *Pinacoteca Agnelli (Tue–Sun 10am–7pm | www.pinacoteca-agnelli.it)* with works by artists such as Canaletto, Tiepolo and Picasso. *Via Nizza 262*

MOLE ANTONELLIANA ☼

Turin's landmark building is a large domed edifice from 1863. At 67m/549ft, it is Italy's tallest architectural monument and towers above the otherwise rather flat town. From the roof there is an exceptional panoramic view of the town and mountain backdrop. The celebrated museum of cinema **INSIDER TIP** ▶ *Museo Nazionale del Cinema (Tue–Sun 9am–8pm, Sat until 11pm | www.museonazionaledel cinema.org)* has a spectacular interior. *Via Montebello 20*

INSIDER TIP ▶ **MUSEO DELL'AUTOMOBILE**

Vintage cars, legendary models such as Topolino and Giulia, as well as luxury cars – the museum has had a facelift and the

The Mole Antonelliana dominates the Turin skyline

exhibits are well presented. *Mom 10am–2pm, Tue 2pm–7pm, Wed, Thu, Sun 10am–7pm, Fri, Sat 10am–9pm | Corso Unità d'Italia 40 | www.museoauto.it | Via Roma*

MUSEO EGIZIO
One of the world's leading museums for Egyptian art, accommodated as the Galleria Sabauda in the Palazzo dell' Accademia delle Scienze. *Tue–Sun 8.30am–7.30pm | www.museoegizio.org | Via Roma*

PARCO VALENTINO
This lovely urban park stretches along the left bank of the Po. *Corso M. D'Azeglio*

PIAZZA CASTELLO AND PIAZZA REALE
Right in the heart of Turin is the Piazza Castello and is the imposing *Palazzo Madama (Tue–Sat 10am–6pm, Sun until 8pm),* once a medieval fortress, later a Baroque residence belonging to Madama Cristina of the Savoy dynasty, now a museum for ancient art and crafts; on the adjacent square is the palace of the Savoy kings, the majestic *Palazzo Reale (Tue–Sun 9am–7.30pm)* from 1660.

FOOD & DRINK

CAFÉS
Turin has the oldest and most beautiful cafés in Italy, e.g. the elegant *Torino* and *San Carlo* on the large Piazza San Carlo, the wonderfully ornate little *Mulassano (Piazza Castello 15),* the art nouveau café *Platti* on Corso Vittorio Emanuele 72, and in *Al Bicerin (Piazza Consolata 5)* you receive the famous little glass of *bicerin* with coffee, chocolate and cream.

PASTIS
Restaurant, street café and artists' haunt in the trendy Quadrilatero Romano. *Closed Sun–noon | Piazza Emanuele Filiberto 9 b | tel. 0115 21 10 85 | Budget*

PORTA DI PO
Fine Piedmontese cuisine in an elegant and contemporary setting on one of Turin's most beautiful squares. *Closed Mon afternoon and Sun | Piazza Vittorio Veneto 1 | tel. 01 18 12 76 42 | www.portadipo.it | Moderate–Expensive*

DAI SALETTA
The rusic family style trattoria Dai Saletta, a Slow Food recommendation, is famous for Turin specialities such as *vitello tonnato. Closed Sun | Via Belfiore 37 | tel. 01 16 68 78 67 | www.ristorantedaisaletta.com | Moderate*

SHOPPING

You can buy the Turin speciality *gianduiotti* (nougat) in the time-honoured patisserie *Baratti & Milano* on the Piazza Castello. The huge **INSIDER TIP** *market* – Italy's largest – on the *Piazza della Repubblica/Porta Palazzo (Mon–Fri 8am–1pm, Sat 8am–5pm)* mirrors the ethnic diversity of the population. On *Sat afternoon* the *El Balon* flea market takes place in the nearby *Via Borgo Dora* and every second Sunday in the month the *antiques market El Gran Balon*.

WHERE TO STAY

COLAZIONE DI PIAZZA CASTELLO ☺
Centrally located B & B in the stylish space of a palazzo, 2 rooms and organic breakfast. *Piazza Castello 9 | tel. 01 12 07 69 83 | www.colazioneinpiazzacastello.it | Budget–Moderate*

TOWN HOUSE 70
Comfortable city hotel in central location with pleasant décor and excellent breakfast buffet. *48 rooms | Via XX Settembre 70 | tel. 0 11 19 70 00 03 | www.townhouse.it/th70 | Moderate–Expensive*

URBANI

Near the train station, a nice clean hotel for budget travellers. *44 rooms | Via Saluzzo 7 | tel. 0116 69 90 47 | www.hotel urbani.it | Budget*

INFORMATION

Piazza Castello/Via Garibaldi, at Porta Nuova station and at the airport | tel. 0 11 53 51 81 | www.turismotorino.org, www.extratorino.it, piemonteitalia.eu

WHERE TO GO

ALBA AND ASTI (178 C4) *(ⵍ C–D 4)*

These two old towns have attractive centres and dominate the horizon of the Monferrato, Roero and Langhe hills to the south-east of Turin, where the wonderful red wines of Piedmont grow. These are celebrated in the Barolo castle: in the *enoteca* you can try the different wines before choosing the ones you want to buy, as well as visit the modern wine museum *WiMu (Fri–Wed 10.30am–7pm | www. wimubarolo.it)*. In autumn and winter, the connoisseurs flock to these hills for the truffle season in *Alba* (pop. 30,000). There is a truffle market in October. *Casetorri,* tower houses dating back to the Middle Ages are a typical sight in Alba's old town centre. The larger town *Asti* (pop. 79,000) centre of Monferrato, also has a large medieval centre with stately squares, houses and churches.

In this famous gourmet area around Asti and Alba, you have the choice between numerous first-class gourmet establishments and a number of good trattorias. As recommended by the Slow Food movement, most of them use quality regional ingredients, such as meat from the local beef *fassone* and the good Piedmont cheeses. In Alba, for example, you can choose between the friendly *Osteria dell'*

Vine-covered hills and castles: on the road in the wine and truffle paradise of the Langhe

Arco (closed Sun/Mon | Piazza Savona 5 | tel. 0173 36 39 74 | www.osteriadellarco. it | Budget–Moderate) or one of the very top restaurants of Piedmont the *Piazza Duomo (closed Sun evening and Mon | Piazza Risorgimento 4 | tel. 0173 36 61 67 | www.piazzaduomoalba.it | Expensive)*, in *La Piola (Budget–Moderate)*, on the ground floor, delicious Osteria cuisine by the same manager.

Having a nice room to go to is the perfect way to follow a perfect meal, for example *del Maiale Pezzato (9 rooms | Via Carlo Coccio 2 | Sinio | tel. 0173 26 38 45 | www. maialepezzato.it | Moderate)* with pool. It is even more rural in the B & B  *La Luna Buona (Via Lavezzato 4 | Vesime | tel. 34 86 55 95 54 | www.lalunabuona.it | Budget)* 36km/22mi south-east of Alba with three pleasantly nostalgic rooms and a substantial organic breakfast. The goat herd next door produces the milk for the delicious cheese. The *All'Enoteca (closed Mon noon and Sun | Via Roma 57 |*

The deer on the roof gives it away: the Palazzina di Stupinigi is a hunting lodge

in the *Locanda del Boscogrande (closed Tue | Messadio district | tel. 0141 95 63 90 | www.locandaboscogrande.com | Budget–Moderate)* approx. 12km/7.5mi south of Asti in Montegrosso d'Asti with seven comfortable rooms *(Moderate)* and a swimming pool. In Langhe 10km/6mi south of Alba, you can eat (e.g. specialities from the establishment's own pig farm), drink and sleep in a sophisticated country house style surrounded by the vines in the *Osteria*

tel. 0173 95 85 7 | www.davidepalluda.it | Expensive) in *Canale* 15km/9.3mi north of Alba in the wine-growing area of Roero is regarded as a top address by insiders.

BAROQUE BUILDINGS OF THE HOUSE OF SAVOY (178 C3) (𝖔 C3)

Famous court architect Filippo Juvara also built Baroque and Rococo buildings in the immediate vicinity of Turin for the House of Savoy. Enthroned on a hill in the east of Turin is the monumental *Basilica di Superga (daily 9am–noon and 3pm–6pm, in the winter until 5pm),* which guards the tombs of the Savoy kings. The hunting lodge *Palazzina di Stupinigi (daily 10am–5pm)* 10km/6mi south-west of Turin is a stunning example of rococo architecture. The 'Versailles' of the Savoys, the magnificent ⭐ *Reggia di Venaria Reale (Tue–Fri 9am–6pm, Sat/Sun 9am–8pm | www.lavenaria.it)* 5km/3mi north of Turin, was completed in its present form in 1728, and is also the work of Juvarra. You can visit the 50 rooms of the restored complex and the magnificent park. The Savoy castle *Castello di Rivoli (Tue–Fri 10am–5pm, Sat/Sun 10am–7pm | www.castellodirivoli.org)* 15km/9.3mi to the west is a renowned exhibition centre for contemporary art, and the avant-garde gourmet restaurant *Combal.Zero (closed Sun/Mon | tel. 0119 56 52 25 | www.combal.org | Expensive).* Finally, 35km/22mi to the south is the richly decorated *Castello di Racconigi (Tue–Sun 9am–6.30pm, with tours through the beautiful park every 90 minutes | www.ilcastellodiracconigi.it).*

LOMELLINA
(179 D3) (*m* D3)

Stretching between Vercelli, Novara and Pavia is the Lomellina plain. In the spring, the water-logged rice fields look as smooth as glass. You can try biodynamic rice at, e.g. the 🕓 INSIDER TIP *Azienda Agricola Cascine Orsine (www.cascinaorsine.it)* in *Bereguardo* in the *Valle del Ticino* nature reserve. Other sources of good risotto rice are: the *Azienda Agricola Tenuta Castello (www.tenutacastello.com)* with the restaurant *Ozyra* and eight rooms in *Desana.* Delicious risotto is also served 9km/5.5mi south-west of Vercelli in *Da Balin (closed Sun evening and Mon | tel. 0 16 14 71 21 | www.balinrist.it | Budget–Moderate)* in *Castell'Apertole* in Livorno Ferraris.

SACRI MONTI ⭐ ∿

I Sacri Monti (the sacred mountains) Baroque pilgrimage sites were built in the 16th and 17th century as a bulwark against the dangerous ideas of the Reformation. They are right out in the countryside, on forested hills and mountain tops, one chapel after the other containing life-size statues enacting scenes from the lives of Christ, Mary and St Francis of Assisi. Local craftsmen made these silent yet dynamic figures out of painted plaster, clay and wood. The most beautiful pilgrimage sites are the *Sacro Monte* in *Varallo* (178 C2) (*m* D2) with 44 chapels, the *Sacro Monte* overlooking the picturesque *Lago d'Orta* (179 D2) (*m* D2) with 20 chapels dedicated to the life of St Francis, plus in the north of Biella the *Santuario di Oropa* (178 C2) (*m* C3), a devotional complex with 19 Mary chapels. All of them have an excellent position with fantastic views and were recently added to the Unesco list of World Heritage Sites.

SESTRIERE AND SUSA
(178 B3–4) (*m* B–C3)

Enthroned above the entrance to the Susa Valley – site of the 2006 Winter Olympics – is the impressive monastery ∿ *Sacra di San Michele* with its wonderful Romanesque stonework on the church portal (sign of the zodiac) and a breathtaking panorama. *Susa* (pop. 7000) is a picturesque little town surrounded by high mountains. The main sights include a castle, a Romanesque-Gothic cathedral and a Roman Arch of Augustus. The most popular and modern ski resort in Susa Valley is *Bardonecchia* (1312m/4304ft), but winter sports fans particularly like the pistes of *Sestriere* in the neighbouring Chisonetal. On the way through the valley, you will be impressed by the *Fenestrelle,* the 4000 steps leading up to the Napoleonic fortress.

THE NORTH-EAST

The Brenner Pass, the busiest crossing into Italy, is also known as the gateway to the south. At an elevation of 1370m/4495ft, the pass opens up the main Alpine ridge between Austria and Italy. In the pale limestone of the Dolomites, mild breezes and verdant vegetation announce the arrival of the south. Through the passes and valleys, the roads lead down as always to the Adriatic and the once legendary maritime Republic of Venice.

Throughout history, the borders in north-east Italy have been pushed back and forth. That is why people speak German in South Tyrol whilst on the other side of Trieste, the locals speak Slovenian.

BOLZANO

(180 C2) *(ₘ F2)* **Waltherplatz/Piazza Walther** is the centre of this vibrant provincial capital (pop. 101,000) in South Tyrol. Visitors sit in the elegant street café with a cappuccino and apple strudel and gaze at the beautiful late Gothic *cathedral.* Other sites include the impressive frescoes in the chapel of St John (14th century) and the cloister (15th century) of the *Dominican monastery (Mon–Sat 9.30am–5.30pm | Dominikanerplatz)* and the famous *carved altar* (around 1475) by Michael Pacher in the parish church in the Gries district. And

Photo: Seiser Alm alpine meadow

Italy's gateway: castles and mountains in South Tyrol, central Europe in Friuli, and villas and waterscapes in Veneto

naturally 'Ötzi', the leathery mummy from Similaun in the *Museum of Archaeology* (see 'Travel with Kids'). Great shopping is possible in the centre's arcades and at the market on Obstplatz. For delicious South Tyrolean cuisine visit *Vögele (closed Sun | Goethestr. 3 | tel. 04 71 97 39 38 | www. voegele.it | Budget–Moderate)* in the centre. A pleasant family hotel is the *Magdalener Hof (39 rooms | Rentscherstr. 48 | tel. 04 71*

97 82 67 | www.magdalenerhof.it | Moderate) on the eastern outskirts of Bolzano in the countryside. Information: *Pfarrplatz 11 | tel. 04 71 99 99 99 | www.suedtirol.info*

WHERE TO GO

BRIXEN (BRESSANONE) (180 C1) (*Ø G2*)
About 50km/31mi to the north is Brixen, a cheerful little episcopal and commercial

town (pop. 16,000). It has a beautiful medieval centre and a magnificent Baroque ⭐ *cathedral* with a *cloister (daily 9am–noon and 3pm–6pm)* decorated with frescoes depicting Biblical scenes (done between 1390–1510); the episcopal *Hofburg* (court palace) contains an interesting Diocesan museum *(mid March–Oct,*

heubad.com | *Moderate–Expensive)*, also available to non-resident guests.

North of Bolzano, in the *Eisacktal/Valle Isarco*, the route branches off at Waidbruck opposite the magnificent *Trostburg* (family seat of Oswald von Wolkenstein, *Easter–Oct, tours daily 11am, 2pm, 3pm, 4pm)* to the Grödnertal valley *(www.groednertal.*

In South Tyrol, wearing national costume is a natural part of everyday life

Tue to Sun 10am–5pm, nativity museum Dec/beginning of Jan daily 10am–5pm).

SOUTH TYROLEAN VALLEYS
(180 B–C 1–2) (*ഡ F–G 1–2*)

The picturesque 🔆 *Ritten* plateau is the summer getaway for Bolzano's middle classes, as is the *Seiser Alm*, Europe's largest high-alpine pasture (approx. 23mi²), a floral paradise set against the magnificent backdrop of the *Schlern/Sciliar* mountain, Bolzano's landmark. Enjoy the health benefits of an invigorating hay bath e.g. in *Völs am Schlern* in the hotel ● *Heubad (43 rooms | tel. 04 71 72 50 20 | www.hotel*

com), leading on to well known ski resorts such as *St Ulrich* (Ortisei), also famous for its woodcarving. Travelling via the Sella Pass past the magnificent pale grey limestone of the Sellastock massif, you arrive at the ⭐ 🔆 *Great Dolomite Road,* one of Italy's most beautiful panoramic routes. It begins in Bolzano, continuing via the narrow *Eggental/Val d'Ega* to the Rosengarten mountain chain and Latemar, and then on to the Trentino Val di Fassa to the Sella and Marmolada mountains and on to *Cortina d'Ampezzo (www.dolomitisuperski. com)*, the pearl of the Dolomites, in the Veneto region, a chic holiday resort with elegant shops and art galleries. During the cable car ride on the *Freccia del Cielo* to the ✺ *Tofana di Mezzo* (3243m/ 10,610ft), you can enjoy the breathtaking views of Adamello, the Großglockner and the Venice lagoon. After following the Eisack valley to Klausen/Chiusa, the route continues along the *Villnösstal/Val di Funes* valley with its South Tyrolean picture book landscape.

Also popular is the *Pustertal/ Val Pusteria* in the north-east with its little villages such as *Bruneck, Toblach, Innichen* and the beautiful tributary valleys with holiday farms that are ideal for family holidays, e.g. in Gsieser valley *Mudlerhof (4 apartments | Preindl 49 | Teisten | tel. 04 74 97 84 46 | www.mudlerhof.com | Budget)*.

The South Tyrolean wine route starts south of Bolzano and meanders through the vineyards and wine-producing villages of the Etschtal valley past Lago di Caldaro towards Salurn; it is here that you will cross the German-Italian language border that has existed since the 8th century.

To the north-west is *Meran,* an enchanting spa town (pop. 33,000) *(www.therme meran.it)* with parks full of Mediterranean plants, e.g. the *Giardini Trauttmansdorff (April to mid Nov, daily 9am–6pm, in summer Fri to 10pm | www.trauttmansdorff. it)*. To the north of Meran is *Dorf Tirol,* once the family seat of the counts of Tirol, now a popular tourist site and home to the modern South Tyrolean state museum *(mid March–mid Dec, Tue–Sun 10am– 5pm)*.

From Meran it continues into *Vinschgau,* a sunny, dry, fruit-growing valley district which continues right through to Switzerland. The tributary valleys lead south to the Ortler glacier *(Stilfser Joch)*, and in the north to the Oetztal Alps *(Schnalstal* valley) both also summer ski areas. In the Schnalstal, *Castel Juval* rises up before you *(Easter–June and Sept–Nov Thu–Tue 10am– 4pm | www.messner-mountain-museum. it)*, one of the five museums set up by South Tyrol's most famous mountaineer, Reinhold Messner. A cultural highlight, INSIDER TIP▶ *St Prokulus,* a small 7th century church in *Naturns* contains the oldest

---

frescoes in the German-speaking world *(Easter–Oct Tue–Sun 9.30am–noon and 2.30pm–5.30pm, guided tours at 10am and 3pm)*. Castles and monasteries adorn the valley and staying in the little fortress town of **INSIDER TIP** *Glurns* in the stylishly renovated *Grüner Baum (10 rooms | Stadtplatz 7 | tel. 04 73 83 12 06 | www. gasthofgruenerbaum.it | Moderate)* has a special flair.

PADUA (PADOVA)

(180 C4) *(∭ G3)* **This venerable university town (pop. 220, 000) commissioned Italy's top artists in both the late Middle Ages and the Renaissance.**

It was also here that one of the most respected Catholic saints, Anthony of Padua, a disciple of Francis of Assisi, preached and later died. The enormous *Prato della Valle* square is a nice place to relax (an antique market is held here every third Sunday in the month). An excursion tip: a ● boat trip along the Brenta Canal towards Venice past the beautiful noble villas *(www.ilburchiello.it)*.

SIGHTSEEING

BASILICA DI SANT'ANTONIO

Every year, about 4.5 million people make a pilgrimage to the tomb of Saint Anthony in this vast domed church (13th century). Donatello's bronzes in the high altar are particularly stunning. *Daily 7.30am–7.00pm | Piazza del Santo*

CAPPELLA DEGLI SCROVEGNI ★

The rather plain exterior of the 14th century chapel contrasts starkly with the overwhelming, well-preserved interior, painted entirely by Giotto, the trailblazer

between medieval and modern artistic styles. Commissioned by the merchant and money lender Enrico Scrovegni, Giotto – Italy's art superstar in the early 14th century – painted vivid scenes from the life of Jesus and Judgement Day (1302–04). *Daily 9am–7pm | pre-register by phone tel. 04 92 01 00 20 | www. cappelladegliscrovegni.it | Corso Garibaldi*

GATTAMELATA

In 1452, Donatello created a Renaissance masterpiece with the statue of the Venetian military leader Gattamelata: intelligent moderation in place of martial pose. *In front of the Basilica of St Anthony | Piazza del Santo*

MUSEI CIVICI EREMITANI

Interesting archaeological department and priceless art gallery: Bellini, Tiziano, Giorgione, Tiepolo, Giotto and many others. *Tue–Sun 9am–7pm | Piazza Eremitani*

FOOD & DRINK

OSTERIA DAL CAPO

Popular trattoria with delicious local cuisine, always full – so book a table! *Closed Mon noon and Sun | Via degli Obizzi 2 | tel. 0 49 66 31 05 | Budget–Moderate*

LA FINESTRA

Pictures on the wall, framed like windows, reference the name of this pleasant restaurant in the old town which serves imaginative and exquisite southern dishes. *Closed Mon and for lunch apart from Fri, Sat, Sun | Via dei Tradi 15 | tel. 0 49 65 03 13 | www. ristorantefinestra.it | Moderate*

CAFFÈ PEDROCCHI

For generations *the* elegant coffee house in Padua. *Closed Mon in summer | Via VIII Febbraio 15 | tel. 04 98 78 12 31 | www. caffepedrocchi.it | Moderate*

The locals meet for aperitifs at the Palazzo della Ragione on the *Piazza della Frutta* or on the *Piazza delle Erbe;* Padua's nightlife district, the *Ghetto,* adjoins the square to the south.

AL FAGIANO

Eclectically designed and privately run city hotel not far from the Basilica. *40 rooms | Via Locatelli 45 | tel. 04 98 75 00 73 | www. alfagiano.com | Budget*

VILLA MARGHERITA

Live in noble Venetian style in a country villa by the Brenta Canal in Mira. *19 rooms | Mira Porte | Via Nazionale 416– 417 | tel. 04 14 26 58 00 | www.villa-margherita.com | Expensive*

At the station and in *Vicolo Cappellato (behind Caffè Pedrocchi) | tel. 04 98 75 20 77 | www.turismopadova.it.* Ask about the Padova Card, a global ticket valid for sightseeing purposes.

EUGANEAN HILLS (COLLI EUGANEI)
🌿 *(180 C4) (ω G3)*

The volcanic hills that suddenly rise up above the flat Po plain are among the most idyllic places to visit in northern Italy: offering vineyards, forests, the *Benedictine abbey of Praglia* (11th century) and renowned thermal spas such as the ●*Abano Terme* and *Montegrotto Terme* that offer fango treatments, health and fitness programmes *(www.abano montegrottosi.it).* The famous poet Francesco Petrarca died in the mountain village of *Arquà Petrarca.* Further sights include the fortified villages *Castelli Carraresi,* such as *Este* with its castle, park and villas: *Museo Nazionale Atestino* is in Villa Mocenigo with interesting exhibits from prehistoric, ancient and Venetian times *(daily 8.30am–7.30pm).*

TREVISO (181 D3) *(ω G3)*

The clothes brand Benetton comes from this area as does a particularly popular

78 statues line the market square of Prato della Valle

form of red leaf chicory the *radicchio di Treviso*. This tranquil, prosperous town (pop. 88,000) has an idyllic river frontage, medieval *palazzi*, a cathedral of Roman origin with an altarpiece by Titian, the richly decorated Gothic church *San Nicolò*, the *Museo Civico* in the former cloister complex of Santa Caterina *(Tue–Sun 9am–12.30pm and 2.30–6pm)*, with its notable painting collection (Bellini, Lotto, Titian) as well as at the fish market right in the centre on a small island. Also worth a visit is the charming little town of INSIDER TIP *Asolo* 30km/18mi to the north-west.

VICENZA ★ (180 C3) (*M G3*)

Even if the 16th century's most famous architect to the Venetian aristocracy, Andrea Palladio, actually came from Padua, Vicenza is still 'his' town (pop. 112,000). The masterpiece is the *basilica* set within three squares (today an exhibition space), originally Gothic and then surrounded with two-storey stone buttresses by Palladio. Even the exemplary *Teatro Olimpico (Tue–Sun 9am–5pm)* is a design by Palladio, which Vicenzo Scamozzi completed; what is astounding in this particular case is the sense of visual depth achieved with his clever perspective backdrop.

You can obtain information about the visiting times and tours of the numerous splendid villas that once belonged to the Venetian aristocracy in the vicinity of Trevisos and Vicenza: *Piazza Matteotti 12 | tel. 04 44 32 08 54 | also MP3guides | App for Smartphones at www.visitpalladio. com | www.vicenzae.org.* The most well-known is *Villa Rotonda (Tue–Sun 10am–12pm and 3pm–6pm, you can only tour the grounds, mid March to early Nov, Wed and Sat also possible to go inside | www.villarotonda.it)* 4km/2.5mi from Vicenza, Palladio's most exquisite and original work.

TRENTO

(180 B2) (*M F2*) **The fresh mountain air pervades even the narrowest streets of the city (pop. 99,000).**

During the Middle Ages, Trento was an influential episcopal principality (from 1027–1803). It was in *Castello del Buonconsiglio (Tue–Sun 10am–5pm)* that from 1545–1563 the council met to devise strategies to fight the Reformation. The castle grounds include the ★ *Torre Aquila (reserve entrance at the desk | www.buon consiglio.it)* with fascinating frescoes (15th

THE 'OMBRA'

The Venetians have always enjoyed drinking their wines at the market, at festivals and on the piazza. Out in the open, before the age of fridges, people used to look for a place in the shade both for the wine, and for themselves. Thus, the equivalent of 'let's go for a drink' went from *andemo a bever all'ombra* (let's have a drink in the shade) to *andemo a bever un'ombra* (literally 'let's drink the shade'). People still drink *ombra*, the little glass of cold white wine at a bar or – in Venice – in a *bacaro* served with seafood and ham snacks, the *cicchetti*, e.g. in *Cantina del Vino già Schiavi (closed Sun | Fondamenta Nani 992 | Dorsoduro | tel. 04 15 23 00 34 | Budget).*

century) that superbly depict work (done by the farmers) and play (enjoyed by the aristocracy) in the form of a calendar, i. a. **INSIDER TIP** the first snowball fight in art history! On the impressive cathedral aces – some in good condition, others romantic ruins – that provide the stage for annual summer cultural events. Europe's largest castle building towers majestically over the Etschtal valley between Rovereto

An annual calendar depicted in 15th century frescoes: Torre Aqiola in Trento's Castello Buonconsiglio

square with its medieval pillar basilica and beautifully painted old town houses is the town's enticing *Scrigno del Duomo* restaurant *(Piazza del Duomo 29 | tel. 04 61 22 00 30 | www.scrignodelduomo. com | Budget–Expensive)*, part top-class restaurant *(closed noon, Sun, Mon)*, part wine bar *(daily)*. The *MART* museum is a must for aficionados of modern art *(Tue–Thu 10am–6pm, Fri–Sun 10am–9pm | www.mart.trento.it)* in nearby *Rovereto.*

WHERE TO GO

TRENTINO (180 B–C2) *(⍟ F–G2)*
Like South Tyrol, the Tridentine mountain sides, valley entrances, rocky outcrops and old roads, are full of castles and pal-

and Trento – *Castel Beseno*, once the military vanguard of the diocese. Not far from the Comano spa resort is one of the most beautiful Tridentine fortified residences, *Castello di Stenico* much of which has been restored *(guided tours Tue–Sun 9.30am–5pm, end Nov–beginning March only Sat/Sun)*.

In the north-west of Trento, you have a bird's eye view of the mountains from the 2125m/6972ft ⚶ *Paganella*: in the west you can see the Brenta Dolomites and the glaciers Adamello-La Presanella and Cevedale, nestled between which are famous ski resorts such as *Madonna di Campiglio*. There you can find the comfortable 🙂 *Hermitage,* an eco-friendly hotel *(30 rooms | Via Castelletto Inferiore*

*69 | tel. 04 65 44 15 58 | www.biohotel
hermitage.it | Expensive)* with a spa area
and excellent restaurant, which mainly
uses organic ingredients *(Expensive)*.

In the north-east, the Dolomites dominate Trentino, approached by a gradual
progression of valleys: first, the sunny,
vine-growing *Cembratal/Val di Cembra,*
followed by the Fleimstal/Val di Fiemme,
in whose main town, *Cavalese* the *Palazzo
della Magnifica Comunità* (16th century),
bears witness to the fact that in 1110 the
farmers wrested independence from the
Bishop of Trento and set up the first autonomous community in Italy. The alpine
Val di Fassa links up with the *Great Dolomite
Road.* Enjoy the high altitude setting of
the ● *Suoni delle Dolomiti,* summer music concerts held in mountain locations,
e.g. cello solos or klezmer music in the
Fassatal/Val di Fassa at the *Micheluzzi*
mountain lodge or in the Feimstal on the
*Pampeago meadows (Suoni delle Dolomiti |
www.isuonidelledolomiti.it)* – free of
charge. A renowned ski resort is *San
Martino di Castrozza* set against the backdrop of the *Pala Dolomites* with the
formidable *Cimone della Pala* (3186m/
10,450ft).

In addition to the lakes *Lago di Caldonazzo*
and *Lago di Levico,* the north bank of Lake
Garda is very popular with surfers, and is
part of Trentino. *www.visittrentino.it*

TRIESTE

**(181 E3) (*M* H–J3) Streets lined with
houses that once belonged to rich merchants (some of which are now museums) and the impressive 19th century
palazzi on the Piazza dell'Unità d'Italia
by the old harbour all remind visitors
that Trieste (pop. 210,000) was once one
of the most important Adriatic ports of
the Austro-Hungarian Empire.**

Above the old town, the *San Giusto*
hill offers magnificent views of the town
and sea; also here are *San Giusto Basilica*
and the *castle.*

Typical restaurants include the **INSIDER TIP** ▶
*buffets (L'Approdo | closed Sun | Via
Carducci 34 | Budget; Da Pepi | closed Sun |
Via Cassa di Risparmio 3 | Budget)* and the
old **INSIDER TIP** coffee houses (e.g. *Caffè
San Marco | Via Battisti 18; Tergesteo,
Galleria Tergesteo; Tommaseo, Piazza
Tommaseo).* The six tastefully appointed
rooms of the *Residence le 6A* located in
the central pedestrian zone provide the
perfect starting point for a stroll round
the town *(Via S. Caterina 7 | tel. 04 06 72
67 15 | www.residencele6a.it | Budget–
Moderate).* Information: *Piazza dell'Unità
d'Italia 4 | tel. 04 03 47 83 12 | www.turismo
fvg.it*

WHERE TO GO

AQUILEIA ★ (181 E3) (*M* H3)
During the time of the Romans and early
Christianity, Aquileia (45km/28mi to the
north-west) was a powerful town in this
region, as is visible from the *Roman ruins*
and the wonderful Romanesque *basilica
(summer, daily, 8.30am–7pm, winter
8.30am–5pm | www.aquileia.net)* with
its well-preserved mosaic floor.

CIVIDALE DEL FRIULI (181 E2) (*M* H2)
This charming little medieval town (pop.
11,000) in Friuli, picturesquely situated
on the Natisone River, has retained fascinating traces of the ancient Lombards.
They are exhibited in the *Tempietto Longo-
bardo,* the *basilica,* and in the *archaeological* and the *Christian museum.*

TRIESTINE RIVIERA ★
(181 E3) (*M* H3)
The coastal road from Trieste to Duino
between the Adriatic and karst hinterland

is regarded as one of the most scenic routes in Italy. It starts with the sleek neighbourhood of *Barcola*. One destination for a daytrip is to the karst rock formations (where care is needed because much of the ground is hollowed out) to visit the giant caves ● *Grotta Gigante (hourly tours each day)* in ⚘ Villa Opicina, which you can get to from Trieste by tram-cum-cable car. The brightly lit ⚘ *Castello di Miramare (daily 9am–6.30pm)* in the wonderful park high above the sea, built for Archduke Maximilian of Austria in 1860, is one of the main sights, as is the much older ⚘ *Castlel Duino* in its spectacular location on the cliff *(open 2nd half of March, Wed–Mon 9.30am–4.30pm, April–mid Oct Wed–Mon 9.30am–5.30pm, mid Oct–beginning of Nov Wed–Mon 9.30am–4pm)*, which you can also reach via the famous ● *Rilke Path* that starts at the tourist information at the turn-off from the Trieste coastal road to Sistiana Mare and continues to the castle village of Duiono.

UDINE (181 E2) (*ΩΩ H2*)

Udine (pop. 100,000) was the capital of the Friuli Venezia Giulia region until 1956 and still is in the hearts of many in the region. Like the star-shaped fortified town of Palmanova 20km/12.5mi to the south, Udine also bears the seal of Venice because it served as a stronghold against the Huns, Hungary and the Turks for the maritime republic in the 16th and 17th century. There is an interesting collection of paintings in the *castle* and Tiepolo's art in the cathedral worth seeing. There are plenty of beautiful squares such as the *Piazza della Libertà* and *Piazza Matteotti* to wander round.

The remains of the ancient Roman city of Aquileia

VENICE (VENEZIA)

(181 D4) *(✿ G3)* **The city (pop. 60,000) on the water – one of the world's most beautiful and iconic places – draws 14 million visitors a year.**
For a more detailed description refer to the MARCO POLO 'Venice' guide.

SIGHTSEEING

CANAL GRANDE ⭐
The main canal passes through the city like a mirror-inverted letter S, passing exquisite palace façades, whose Gothic, Renaissance and Baroque architecture give Venice its distinctive filigreed Oriental flair. You pass the *Rialto Bridge* from 1592 with its daily market directly after the first loop in the canal. When the boat reaches the *Piazzetta San Marco*, visitors alight on the forecourt of the *Palazzo Ducale (April–Oct daily 8.30am–7pm, Nov–March 8.30am–5.30pm)*, the former residence of the doges, which is full of magnificent artworks.

COLLEZIONE PEGGY GUGGENHEIM
The American collected the works of her friends Picasso, Matisse, Klee, Giacometti and many others. *Wed–Mon 10am–6pm | in Palazzo Venier dei Leoni | Dorsoduro | www.guggenheim-venice.it*

GALLERIA DELL'ACCADEMIA
All of the great Venetian masters (14th–18th century) are represented here: Bellini, Canaletto, Carpaccio, Titian, Veronese and many more. *Tue–Sun 8.15am–3pm, Mon 8.15am–2pm | Campo della Carità Dorsoduron*

Venice's 'main street': the Canal Grande. With traffic to match!

PIAZZA SAN MARCO

The city's magnificent 'drawing room' with the historic municipal buildings of *Procuratie Vecchie* and *Procuratie Nuove,* the beautiful old cafés and of course the sumptuous, oriental style *Basilica di San Marco (Mon–Sat 9.45am–5pm, Sun 2pm– 5pm | Sun admission free)* with its rich cathedral treasury. From the 97m/318ft ⚲ tower *(daily 9am–4pm, July–Sept 9.30am–9pm)* there are stunning views of Venice.

REDENTORE

Andrea Palladio built this magnificent temple-styled basilica on the island of Giudecca opposite Piazza San Marco.

FOOD & DRINK

L'ORTO DEI MORI

Fresh Mediterranean cuisine. In the summer, it is wonderful to sit on the Campo dei Mori; reserve in advance. *Closed Tue | Fondamenta dei Mori 3386 | Cannaregio | tel. 04 15 24 36 77 | www.osteriaortodeimori. com | Moderate*

LA ZUCCA

Wide variety of vegetable dishes; small and popular – arrive early! *Closed Sun | Campo San Giacomo dell'Orio 1762 | Santa Croce | tel. 04 15 24 15 70 | www.lazucca.it | Budget–Moderate*

SHOPPING

Two classic souvenirs from Venice come from the islands in the lagoon: blown glass from Murano and lace from Burano. They are available in many shops or directly from the islands, e.g. in Murano you can buy beautiful vases and glass pearl jewellery from *Ferrevetro (Campo S. Stefano 7)* and in Burano fine lace from *La Merlettaia (Calle San Mauro 298).*

WHERE TO STAY

CA' DOGARESSA

Small stylish guest house in the old Venetian ghetto, good value for money. *9 rooms | Fondamenta di Cannaregio 1018 | Cannaregio | tel. 04 12 75 94 41 | www.cadogaressa.com | Budget–Expensive*

CA' MARIA ADELE

Expensive but very chic, with oriental style roof terrace, near the Guggenheim museum. *12 rooms | Rio Terrà dei Catecumeni 111 | Dorsoduro | tel. 04 15 20 50 78 | www. camariaadele.it | Expensive*

INFORMATION

Piazza San Marco/Calle Ascensione | San Marco | tel. 04 15 29 87 11 | www.turismo venezia.it

WHERE TO GO

LIDO DI VENEZIA

(181 D4) (*Ø G3*)

Anyone wishing to combine a beach holiday with a visit to Venice should choose the Lido, even during the film festival in late summer: either in the glamorous luxury hotels or in the charming *Villa Stella (12 rooms | Via San Gallo 111 | tel. 04 15 26 07 45 | www.villastella.com | Budget– Moderate)* with its beautiful garden.

PO DELTA (DELTA DEL PO)

(181 D4) (*Ø G4*)

The delta landscape of Italy's largest river extends 60km/37mi from the Adige estuary below *Chioggia* (well worth seeing, a mini version of Venice with one of Italy's most important fish markets) down to the picturesque *Comacchio,* where the lagoon landscape of Ferrara begins. Most of the former marshland has been drained, although you will still come across some

Opera in the place where gladiators once fought for their lives: Arena di Verona

protected wetland. The dykes are ideal for cycling and riding, and there are boat trips on the waterways.

VERONA

(180 B3–4) (*𝄞 F3*) Romeo and Juliet, the classic love tragedy, and an evening at the opera in the huge Roman arena (22,000 places) in the town centre are what one normally associates with Verona (pop. 255,000), once an important Roman settlement situated where the Adige flows down from the Alps into the North Italian lowlands.

SIGHTSEEING

ARENA
Towering above Piazza Bra and its many cafés in the town centre is the Roman Empire's largest gladiator arena (1st century), today the summer venue for opera festival. *Tue–Sun 9am–6.30pm, opera season 9am–3.30pm | www.arena.it*

CASA DI GIULIETTA
Pilgrims of love have added a significant shine to the breasts of the bronze Juliet standing in the courtyard of the house she was supposedly born in. *Mon 1.30pm–5.30pm, Tue–Sun 8.30am–7.30pm | Via Cappello 23*

MUSEO D'ARTE CASTELVECCHIO
Exhibits masterpieces such as the 'Madonna of the Quail' by Pisanello or the equestrian statue of Cangrande I from the 13th century, famous for his mysterious smile. *Mon 1.30pm–7.30pm, Tue–Sun 8.30am–7.30pm | Corso Castelvecchio*

PIAZZA ERBE
Towards evening, the in-crowd fills the restaurants under the arcades of this wonderful square lined with Renaissance and Baroque palazzi.

PIAZZA DEI SIGNORI

Palazzo del Comune with its Romanesque courtyard, Gothic staircase and 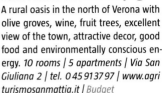 *Torre dei Lamberti (84m/276ft, lift)* as well as the early Renaissance *Loggia del Consiglio* keep the Dante statue company in this square.

SAN ZENO MAGGIORE ⭐

The entrance portal of this wonderful Romanesque basilica is deemed to be one of the most beautiful bronze works of the 12th century. 48 finely sculpted panels vividly portray stories from the Bible. Inside, the altarpiece by Mantegna depicting the Madonna surrounded by saints deserves special attention. The bones of San Zeno, Verona's patron saint, lie in the almost mystical columned crypt, and there is an impressive cloister in the abbey attached to the basilica. *Piazza San Zeno*

FOOD & DRINK

AL CRISTO

Imaginative crossover cuisine and modern styling in old surroundings. *Closed Mon, Tue | Piazzetta Pescheria 6 | tel. 0 45 59 42 87 | www.ristorantealcristo.it | Moderate–Expensive*

SOTTORIVA 23 OSTREGHETERIA

Lively osteria in a popular entertainment area; snacks, cooked meals; meeting place for aperitifs, cultural events. Open until 2am! *Daily | Via Sottoriva 23 | tel. 04 58 00 99 04 | Budget*

WHERE TO STAY

AURORA

Fantastic location near Piazza Erbe, well-kept and welcoming. *19 rooms | Piazzetta XIV Novembre 2 | tel. 0 45 59 47 17 | hotel aurora.biz | Moderate*

AGRITURISMO SAN MATTIA

A rural oasis in the north of Verona with olive groves, wine, fruit trees, excellent view of the town, attractive decor, good food and environmentally conscious energy. *10 rooms | 5 apartments | Via San Giuliana 2 | tel. 0 45 913797 | www.agri turismosanmattia.it | Budget*

IL SOGNO DI GIULIETTA

The gorgeously charming rooms with a view of Julia's balcony invite you to day-dream. *10 rooms | Via Cappello 23 | tel. 04 58 00 99 32 | www.sognodigiulietta.it | Expensive*

INFORMATION

Via degli Alpini 9 (Piazza Bra) | tel. 04 58 06 86 80 | www.tourism.verona.it

LOW BUDGET

▶ In South Tyrol's Eisacktal, you do not have to pay an entrance fee at the large leisure pool, the museums or on public transport if you have a Brixen Card. *www.brixencard.info*

▶ Tips: inexpensive accommodation is available on the mainland, e.g. in Mestre or in Padua (frequent train connections). Look out for tourist travel cards for museums, churches and ferries *(vaporetti)*. In several places you can take a gondola across the Canal Grande for just for 50 cents.

▶ In Verona, it is worth buying a tourist card *(Verona-Card)* for the museums, but also for the churches, because like those in Venice, you have to pay to go inside *(www.veronacard.it)*.

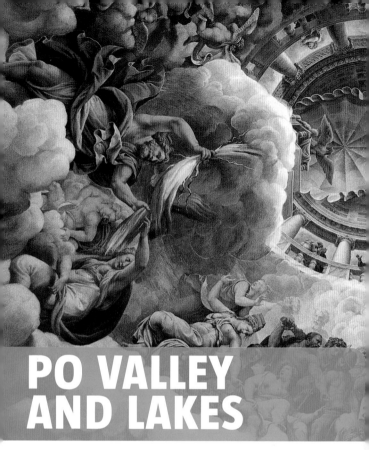

PO VALLEY AND LAKES

The imposing Alps provide a natural border in the north, and their foothills with the beautiful Italian Lakes slope down to Italy's only large plain, the Padania, which stretches from Turin to the Adriatic Sea and is traversed by the Po, Italy's longest and most majestic river.

This fertile plain is also home to most of Italy's industry. In the south, the foothills of the Apennines border the Padania. Where the mountains meet the plains, the excellent road network and abundance of water facilitated the development of vibrant cities – autonomous regions during the Middle Ages and then the courts of ambitious dynasties such as Piacenza, Parma, Reggio Emilia, Modena and Bologna – along the ancient Roman road Via Emilia.

BOLOGNA

(180 C5) *(ΜΠ F4)* **Bologna (population 377,000) boasts 37km/23mi of vault arcades, Europe's oldest university (1088), the famous *tortellini* and *tortelloni* pasta filled with ricotta and spinach or meat, and of course the sprawling and spirited old town with its distinct red-brown façades.**

Photo: Palazzo del Tè in Mantua

In Italy's Lake District, the Po Valley (Padania) and Rimini on the Adriatic coast, holiday-makers are always close to the water

SIGHTSEEING

ARCHIGINNASIO
Built in 1562/63, the Renaissance palace is the seat of the old university. The coats of arms of the students and professors adorn the library's reading rooms and the courtyard. You can also admire the *Teatro Anatomico,* a medical lecture hall from the 17th century. *Mon–Fri 9am–6.45pm, Sat 9am–1.45pm | Via dell'Archiginnasio/ Piazza Galvani*

COMPIANTO DEL CRISTO MORTO
Terracotta was the material of art in the Emilia and the 'Lamentation over the Dead Christ' by Renaissance artist Niccolò dell' Arca, in the church of Santa Maria della Vita is its highlight. *Mon–Sat 10am–6pm, Sun 4.30pm–6pm | Via Clavature 10*

Bologna also has a leaning tower: the almost 100m/328ft Torre degli Asinelli

INSIDER TIP ▶ MUSEO GIORGIO MORANDI

One of the truly great 20th century painters, a famous son of the town; now it is also possible to visit his *studio apartment (registration: tel. 051 6 49 66 11 | Via Fondazza 36)*. *Tue–Fri 11am–6pm, Sat/Sun 11am–8pm | Palazzo Comunale | Piazza Maggiore 6 | www.mambo-bologna.org/ museomorandi.it*

SAN PETRONIO

This enormous Gothic church, which dominates the spacious, almost square Piazza Maggiore, was initially only half finished because the Pope halted construction when he discovered the church was to be larger than St Peter's Basilica. The central portal is a masterpiece by Jacopo della Quercia (15th century). The sun shines into the gloomy interior through a small hole directly onto a meridian line.

The fountain *Fontana del Nettuno* by Giambologna is in the most wonderful Baroque style. Opposite it is the *Sala Borsa,* a magnificent art nouveau hall and popular meeting place with a café, exhibitions as well as the town library. *Piazza Maggiore/Piazza Nettuno*

SANTO STEFANO ★

The triangular shape of the Piazza Santo Stefano points towards this very interesting church complex interlinking several religious edifices. They all date back to the period between the 5th and 14th century. *Daily 7am–12.30pm and 3.30pm–7pm | Piazza Santo Stefano*

TORRI PENDENTI

There is a terrific view from the higher of the two medieval towers – the symbol of Bologna – the Torre degli Asinelli (97.6m/320ft), which has 498 steps to climb. *Daily 9am–6pm, winter to 5pm | Piazza Porta Ravegnana*

FOOD & DRINK

CANTINA BENTIVOGLIO
Wine, beer, pasta as well as cheese, jazz music and lots of people, in short: a real osteria! *Closed noon and Mon | Via Mascarella 4 b | tel. 0 51 26 54 16 | Budget–Moderate*

ROSTERIA LUCIANO
Best traditional Bolognese cuisine in the centre; don't be put off by the sophisticated setting! *Closed Wed | Via Nazario Sauro 19 | tel. 0 51 23 12 49 | Moderate*

SHOPPING

Well-known fashion and shoe shops are located in the streets around Piazza Maggiore and *Galleria Cavour* is particularly elegant. Behind Archiginnasio is the food market district. Here, you will also find INSIDER TIP *Ambasciatori*: bookshop, café and osteria on three floors *(daily 9am–11.30pm | Budget–Moderate)*. Fri and Sat clothing and footwear market at *Parco Montagnola.*

ENTERTAINMENT

Most of the pubs are in the university district around *Via Zamboni,* while the nightlife area is around *Via Mascarella, Via Augusto Righi* and *Via del Pratello.* Friends meet for aperitifs on the *Via Clavature,* e.g. the rustic *Osteria del Sole (Viccolo Ranocchi 2)* and the museum bar *MAMbo (Museo Arte Moderna | Via Don Minzoni 14)* is very popular. In the summer, a comprehensive cultural programme entertains visitors in the squares and parks. Good operas in *Teatro Comunale (Largo Respighi 1 | tel. 0 51 52 99 99 | www.comunalebologna.it).*

MARCO POLO HIGHLIGHTS

⭐ **Santo Stefano**
A complex of religious edifices in Bologna
→ p. 68

⭐ **Ferrara**
Wonderful Renaissance palaces and a Romanesque and Baroque cathedral → p. 71

⭐ **Duomo di Modena**
A must for fans of Romanesque churches
→ p. 71

⭐ **'The Last Supper'**
World famous fresco by Leonardo da Vinci in Milan → p. 73

⭐ **Certosa di Pavia**
Renaissance legacy; charterhouse with monks' cells
→ p. 76

⭐ **Piazza Ducale in Vigevano**
Renaissance arcades line one of Italy's most beautiful squares
→ p. 76

⭐ **Baptistry in Parma**
The Romanesque sculptures of Benedetto Antelami, one of the most important sculptors of his time → p. 79

⭐ **Palazzo Ducale in Mantua**
Wonderful sight: the frescoes of Andrea Mantegna in the bridal chamber
→ p. 81

⭐ **Comacchio**
Unique architecture: the famous abbey of Pomposa and the unique Trepponti bridge → p. 82

⭐ **Ravenna**
Wonderfully preserved Byzantine mosaics in the mausoleum and basilica → p. 83

WHERE TO STAY

You will find numerous appealing B & B places, e.g. two enchanting rooms in an historic palazzo: *Ca'Fosca due Torri* | *www.cafoscaduetorri.com* | *Moderate–Expensive)*; eco-architecture, on the other hand, defines the appearance of the three rooms in 🕐 *A Casa Mia (www.acasamia bologna.it* | *Budget)*.

DEL BORGO

In the north-west of the town, appealing comfort at a good price; guarded parking.

INFORMATION

At the *airport* and *Piazza Maggiore 1* | *tel. 0 5123 96 60* | *www.bolognawelcome.com*, *www.emiliaromagnaturismo.it*

WHERE TO GO

FAENZA (180 C6) *(🗺 G5)*
From Bologna to the beaches on the Adriatic coast, you pass through Faenza (pop. 54,000), a traditional centre for ceramics with ateliers and the *Museo delle Ceramiche (Oct–March Tue–Fri 10am–*

Years to mature: Modena is the home of the real *aceto balsamico*

23 rooms | *Marco Emilio Lepido 195* | *tel. 0 51 40 68 78* | *www.hoteldelborgo.it* | *Budget–Moderate*

METROPOLITAN

In the centre, a pleasant, contemporary city hotel with a superb breakfast. *45 rooms* | *Via dell'Orso 6* | *tel. 0 51 22 93 92* | *www.hotelmetropolitan.com* | *Moderate*

1.30pm, Sat/Sun 10am–5.30pm, April–Sept Tue–Sun 10am–7pm | *Viale Baccarini 19* | *www.micfaenza.org)*. Drink an espresso or a good wine on the central Piazza della Libertà and eat in the *Enoteca Astorre*; in the summer, people sit outside on the square *(closed Sun* | *Piazza della Libertà 16 a* | *tel. 05 46 68 14 07* | *www.enoteca astorre.it* | *Moderate)*.

FERRARA ⭐
(180 C5) (*🗺 G4*)

The family seat of the House of Este during the 14th–16th century and the most stunning Renaissance town in northern Italy (pop. 138,000). Ferrara lies nestled behind green ramparts in the flat landscape of the Po Delta, with its miles of orchards. To the right of the Romanesque Gothic *cathedral* with its gold interior, you will find 15th century shops and artisans' studios, the *Loggia dei Merciai*. To the south-east of the cathedral is the lively, former ghetto district. Also worth a visit is the *Palazzo Schifanoia*, a Renaissance palace that was once the summer residence of the Este, the *Castello Estense* which is surrounded by a moat and the famous *Palazzo dei Diamanti* (1492–1567), nowadays the venue for excellent art exhibitions.

Try the *cappellacci con la zucca* (pasta filled with pumpkin) in the trattoria. Ferrara is characterized by beautiful hotels in old palazzi, e. g. *Duchessa Isabella (32 rooms | Via Palestro 70 | tel. 05 32 20 21 21 | www. duchessaisabella.it | Expensive)* and its charming B & B accommodation, such as *Il Bagattino (6 rooms | Corso Porta Reno 24 | tel. 05 32 24 18 87 | www.ilbagattino. it | Budget–Moderate)*.

MODENA (180 B5) (*🗺 F4*)

The legendary Maserati and Ferrari are produced here and in the expensive Ferrari museum, 17km/10.5mi to the south in *Maranello,* you can view Formula 1 models and *Testa Rossa (Galleria Ferrari | daily 9.30am–6pm, May–Sept to 7pm | Via D. Ferrari 43 | www.ferrari.com)*. Connoisseurs know Modena for its *aceto balsamico tradizionale* and the gourmet *Osteria Francescana (closed Sat noon and Sun | Via Stella 22 | tel. 0 59 21 01 18 | www.osteria francescana.it | Expensive)* in the old town. Art lovers will appreciate the cathedral ⭐ *Il Duomo di Modena*, a masterpiece of Romanesque architecture and sculpture, as well as the impressive cemetery by architect Aldo Rossi in the Madonnina district, a rare **INSIDER TIP** example of contemporary cemetery architecture.

MILAN (MILANO)

(179 D–E3) (*🗺 D–E3*) **City of fashion, design, finance, advertising, business, capital of Lombardy, and despite its mere 1.3 million inhabitants, probably the only Italian city with a cosmopolitan city character.**

For a more detailed description refer to the MARCO POLO 'Milan' guide.

SIGHTSEEING

BASILICA DI SANT'AMBROGIO
St Ambrose rests in this impressive early Christian basilica, the patron saint of Milan.

CITY WHERE TO START?
Piazza del Duomo: The cathedral square, to the north through the Galleria Vittorio Emanuele II to the Scala, to the north-west via Via Dante to the Castello Sforzesco (where you will find the tourist information office). Corso Magenta leads to the 'Last Supper' by Leonardo da Vinci. Metro line M3 *(station: Duomo)*. Car parks: *Autosilo Diaz | Piazza Armando Diaz 6 | south-west of the cathedral square; Parkeon | Via die Missaglie 97 | behind Palazzo Reale, department store La Rinascente | Via Agnello 13 (3 euros/hour).* The city centre is subject to the Ecopass regulations *(see p. 166).*

The famous Renaissance builder Bramante from Fermignano renovated the monastery complex in 1492. *Daily 7am–noon and 2.30pm–7pm | Piazza Sant'Ambrogio*

CATHEDRAL

The Duomo di Milano, the *Santa Maria Nascente* cathedral *(daily 7am–7pm),* with its light marble cladding and innumerable turrets, statues and cornices, towers up like a powerful filigree structure against the backdrop of the large piazza. From the ☀ *roof terrace (daily 9am–4.15pm, longer in summer)* you have a great panoramic view of the Po Valley and the Alps. *Piazza Duomo*

GALLERIA VITTORIO EMANUELE II ●

From the Piazza Duomo you enter the most beautiful domed shopping arcade in Italy. Completed in 1877 it is known as Milan's 'drawing room'. Take time for an aperitif in the traditional bar *Camparino in Galleria. Between the Piazza Duomo and Piazza della Scala*

INSIDER TIP ▶ MUSEO DEL NOVECENTO

There is an impressive collection of 20th century Italian art in the monumental Palazzo dell'Arengario: groups of work by great masters such as de Chirico, Morandi, Lucio Fontana, the Arte Povera of the 1970s, contemporary video art. *Mon 2.30pm–7.30pm, Tue, Wed, Fri, Sun 9.30am–7.30pm, Thu, Sat 9.30am–10.30pm | Piazza Duomo | www.museodelnovecento.org*

NAVIGLI

Of the many canals that used to pass through Milan, just three remain; once

On the roof of the Duomo di Milano: a filigree masterpiece

the workers' and small trade district, now a popular artists' haunt crammed with bars and restaurants – and a wonderful place to wander round on a summer evening. There is an antique and flea market on every last Sunday of the month.

PARCO SEMPIONE

Milan's green lung with jogging paths, museums and cafés as well as the huge castle complex *Castello Sforzesco (Tue–Sun 9am–5.30 pm | Piazza Castello 1 | www.milano castello.it),* home to a valuable collection of paintings, antique art and much more.

PINACOTECA DI BRERA

The richest of the many art collections in Milan exhibits some of Italy's most important works, e.g. the 'Cristo morto' by Andrea Mantegna and Raphael's 'Lo Sposalizio' (The Marriage of the Virgin). *Tue–Sun 8.30am–7.15pm | Via Brera 28 | www.brera.beniculturali.it*

SANTA MARIA DELLE GRAZIE

In the dining room of the Dominican monastery belonging to this beautiful Renaissance church, you will find one of the most valuable art works in the world: ★ *'The Last Supper',* by Leonardo da Vinci 1497 painted on an end wall. The one-point perspective and the emotional presentation of the facial expressions and gestures of the disciples made the fresco a sensation even during the artist's lifetime. *Pre-booking necessary | tel. 02 92 80 03 60 | Tue–Sun 8.15am–7pm | Piazza Santa Maria delle Grazie | www.cenaco lovinciano.net*

TRIENNALE DESIGN MUSEUM

Design collection, exhibitions, café, events in Parco Sempione – a must for every design fan. *Tue–Sun 10.30am–8.30pm | Viale Alemagna 6 | www.triennaledesign museum.it*

FOOD & DRINK

JOIA

Vegetarian cuisine can also serve culinary delights. *Closed Sat noon and Sun | Via Panfilo Castaldi 18 | tel. 02 29 52 21 24 | www.joia.it | Expensive*

BOTTIGLIERA DA PINO

A traditional and very popular trattoria that serves delicious local dishes, near San Babila. *Closed in the evenings and on Sun | Via Cerva 14 | tel. 02 76 00 05 32 | Budget*

TRUSSARDI ALLA SCALA

Fashion-cum-lifestyle brands: Dolce & Gabbana has the VIP restaurant *Gold (Via Carlo Poerio 2 a)*, Armani the sushi restaurant *Nobu* in the Armani Palazzo *(Via Pisoni/Via Manzoni 31)*, and Trussardi now has a restaurant, opposite the Scala – elegant atmosphere and excellent innovative cuisine guaranteed *(closed Sat noon and Sun | Piazza della Scala 5 | tel. 02 80 68 82 01 | www. trussardiallascala. com | Expensive).*

SHOPPING

In *Quadrilatero della Moda*, the sophisticated, outrageously expensive fashion brands are around *Via Monte Napoleone, Via Sant'Andrea, Via Gesù, Via Borgospesso* and *Via della Spiga.* You can buy the same brands a season later at the *stocchisti* at lower prices, e.g. in INSIDER TIP *Il Salvagente (Via Fratelli Bronzetti 16 | www. salvagentemilano.it).* Lifestyle at its best is seen in Milan's first concept store *Dieci Corso Como (Corso Como 10).* You should not miss the window displays in Italy's most gorgeous gourmet shop *Peck* in *Via Spadari 9* either. Two superb department stores: *Excelsior (Galleria del Corso 4)* and *La Rinascente (Via Santa Radegonda 3)* have a ☀ **INSIDER TIP** terrace with a café and restaurant that offers a breathtaking view of the cathedral.

the trendy *Roialto (Via Piero della Francesca 55)* or the *Martini Bar (Corso Venezia 15)* in the Dolce & Gabbana store.

ENTERTAINMENT

THEATRE
Milan's legendary opera house *La Scala (Via Filodrammatici 2 | tel. 02 72 00 37 44 | www.teatroallascala.org)* was recently completely renovated. Modern theatres include *Piccolo Teatro Strehler (Largo Greppi)* and its two branches *Teatro Grassi (Via Rovello 2)* and *Teatro Studio (Via Rivoli 6). Tel. 8 48 80 03 04, tel. from abroad +39 02 42 41 18 89 | www.piccolo teatro.org*

MEETING PLACES & LOUNGE BARS
The nightlife districts are Brera, Corso Sempione and Navigli; in the summer restaurants open in the Lambro and Sempione parks; exclusive aperitif and cocktail meeting places are e.g. at the castle, the *Serendepico (Piazza Castello 1),*

WHERE TO STAY

HOTEL BERNA
Large, appealing and comfortable hotel with an excellent breakfast and central location. *126 rooms | Via Napo Torriani 18 | tel. 02 67 73 11 | www.hotelberna.com | Moderate–Expensive*

BRERA APARTMENTS
Seven well-equipped and stylish apartments of different sizes in the pretty Brera district. *Via San Fermo 1 | tel. 02 36 55 57 08 | www.brerapartments.com | Moderate–Expensive*

RESIDENCE ZUMBINI ROOMS
In the south of the city, convenient, light and modern with garden, cafeteria and parking facilities. *50 rooms | Via Zumbini 6 | tel. 02 36 55 66 04 | www.zumbinirooms. com | Budget*

APERITIF BARS IN MILAN

Meeting with friends at the bar after work to wind down is a way of life in this busy and vibrant town. After all it was here that the legendary Campari was invented in the mid 19th century. The happy hour *aperitivo* continues to be popular in Milan and elsewhere in the north of Italy. It gets going at 7pm, when bars put out refined titbits, exotic salads, pasta, fruit and vegetable snacks. People do not drink heavily: imaginatively decorated, not very alcoholic drinks made of fruit, mint sparkling white wines. Or the Milan

classic *Zucca* made of rhubarb extract, ice cream, soda and slices of orange. It is very trendy to meet in the sophisticated bars of the chic hotels, for example in *hclub* in the *Sheraton Diana Majestic (Viale Piave 42 | www. sheratondianamajestic.it),* near the cathedral in *Straf (Via San Raffaele 3 | www.straf.it),* in the luxurious *Bulgari Hotel (Via Privata Fratelli Gabba 7 b | www.bulgarihotels.com)* or you can try the *Enterprise (Corso Sempione 91 | www.enterprisehotel.com | with a DJ every Thu).*

INFORMATION

Piazza Castello 1 | tel. 02 77 40 43 43 | www. visitamilano.it. You can also obtain the 'Milanomese' here, a monthly magazine (in English) with all the cultural events.

WHERE TO GO

BERGAMO (179 E2) (*E3*)

Enthroned above the busy new town (pop. 129,000), at 370m/1214ft, is the old town 🚡 Città Alta which you can also reach by funicular. Its centre, the *Piazza Vecchia,* presents a superb backdrop: the *Palazzo della Ragione,* the town hall built in 1198, is next to the *cathedral,* begun in the Lombard period, behind which is the Romanesque *Basilica Santa Maria Maggiore.* Adjacent to them is the *Cappella Colleoni* with its magnificent marble façade dating back to the Lombard Early Renaissance and Tiepol's famous dome frescoes, and on the right is the *baptistry.*

Try tasty dishes, delicious cheese and a good glass of wine beneath a high loggia in the old town at *Donizetti (closed Tue | Via Gombito 17 a | tel. 0 35 24 26 61 | www. donizetti.it | Budget–Moderate).* In the surrounding area of the Bergamo Alps is the *Lago d'Iseo,* which in the south adjoins the well-known wine district of Franciacorta and in the north the *Valcamonica (www.invallecamonica.it).* It was in this valley in Capo di Ponte, Nadro and Cemmo that 300,000 INSIDER TIP rock drawings were discovered, the work of an Alpine tribe that lived in the area about 9000 years ago.

BRESCIA (179 E3) (*E3*)

This modern industrial town (pop. 190,000) with the highest number of immigrants in Italy has a surprising elegant old town full of cafés and fine shops. It also has an

The Carthusian monks had a sophisticated sense of beauty: Certosa di Pavia

impressive square with the 'old' cathedral – the medieval *Rotonda (Duomo Vecchio)* – and the 'new' Baroque *cathedral* as well as the *Piazza della Vittoria,* an impressive piece of architecture from around 1930, with the Caffè Impero and the well-preserved art deco Hotel Vittoria. There is also a rich museum complex in the old *Santa Giulia cloister,* dating back to the Lombard period *(Via dei Musei 81/b | Tue–Sun 9.30am–5.30pm).*

PAVIA (179 D–E3) (*D3*)

The *Basilica di San Michele* church has an impressive rustic façade of light sandstone and dates back to the time when Pavia (pop. 87,000) was under the rule of the Lombards (6th–8th century). Another interesting religious building is the Lombard Romanesque church *San Pietro in Ciel d'Oro* with its artistic masonry work. Close by is the impressive *Castello Visconteo*, now a *museum (Feb to Nov Tue–Sun 10am–6pm, July/Aug and Dec/ Jan 9am–1.30pm | www.museicivici.pavia. it)*. The river Ticino (Tessin) is spanned by a covered bridge.

The main attraction in the surrounding area is 10km/6mi to the north, the ★*Certosa di Pavia (Tue–Sun 9am–11.30pm and 2.30pm–5.30pm | www.certosadi pavia.com)*, a remarkable 15th century example of architecture and art produced during the Lombard Renaissance. The Visconti princes lie entombed in the church, and also of interest are the cloisters and cells used by the monks.

VIGEVANO (179 D3) *(ᗰ D3)*

The little town (pop. 66,000) has one of the loveliest squares in Italy, the ★*Piazza Ducale,* designed by Donato Bramante and Leonardo da Vinci: arcades in the early Renaissance style, a 16th century cathedral, a Castello Visconteo and inviting cafés. Retaining its traditional craft, the town still plies the shoe trade. In the castle's old stables, there is a very interesting shoe museum *(Museo della Calzatura | Tue–Sun 10am–1pm and 2pm–5.30pm)*.

ITALY'S LAKE DISTRICT

On the south side of the Alps, lakes cut their way fjord-like through the steep, thickly forested slopes descending down to the plain at the edge of the mountains. The climate is mild, the vegetation abundant and Mediterranean. Magnificent villas on expansive grounds and charming little old towns on the waterside bear witness to the fact that life has always been good here. That is why George Clooney and Russian millionaires reside on Lake Como and why star conductor Claudio Abbado and the Benetton Family like to relax at Lago Maggiore.

LAKE COMO (LAGO DI COMO) ● (179 E2) *(ᗰ D–E2)*

A significant urban centre is the ancient town of *Como* (pop. 83,000) on the farthest south-west tip with its elegant art nouveau architecture and a medieval centre with magnificent churches in the Lombard Romanesque style. Como is also famous for its silk industry.

From the lake, serpentine streets wind up into the mountains and offer magnificent views, e.g. from ☆ *Monte Bisbino* (1325m/4347ft) above Cernobbio. From Sala Comacina or from the neighbouring town of Ossuccio, you come to the picturesque islets in the lake, the *Isola Comacina.* There are ferry connections between the various places, the most beautiful being *Varenna* on the eastern shore and the enchanting *Bellagio* with its winding staircase lanes and paths to the intersection of the Y-shaped lake. Sumptuous villas testify to the long tradition of noble residences on this beautiful lake, a good example being the 15th century *Villa d'Este (www.villadeste.com)* in *Cernobbio,* now one of the most luxurious hotels in Europe, or the Baroque *Villa Carlotta (www.villacarlotta.it)* in *Tremezzo* with its wonderful park. *www.lakecomo.it*

LAKE GARDA (LAGO DI GARDA) (180 B3) *(ᗰ F3)*

Italy's largest lake (140mi², 51km/32mi long and up to 346m/1135ft deep) marks where the south begins for northerners. Here, the Mediterranean climate is ideal for the cultivation of citrus fruit and olives. The 2218m/7277ft ☆ *Monte Baldo* on the eastern shore produces some of the most varied plant life in Europe. A cable railway provides a service up the mountain. The mountain paths along the upper lake offer spectacular views of the landscape *Malcesine,* perched on a rocky outcrop overlooking the lake. A particularly beautiful spot to bathe is the small headland *Punta San Vigilio* with a beach in an olive grove setting. Concealed in a courtyard

The picturesque Limone: tourist stronghold on the north-west shore of Lake Garda

as does the 〰 *Gardesana Occidentale,* the coastal road on the western shore between Gargnano and Limone.

The small and exclusive *Riva del Garda* (pop. 13,000) dominates the north tip of the lake exuding both central European and Mediterranean flair, with the winding streets of the old town and elegant hotels – for example the modern *Feeling Hotel Luise (67 rooms | Viale Rovereto 9 | tel. 04 64 55 08 58 | www.hotelluise.com | Moderate–Expensive)* with a swimming pool and innovative cuisine – as well as the windsurfer paradise *Torbole (www. gardasurf.com).*

On the eastern shore, the castles attest to the rule of the Veronese della Scala family in the 13th and 14th centuries. Of these, the most impressive is 〰 *Castillo*

in *Bardolino* – the namesake of the thriving red wine produced in this area – is the ancient Carolingian church (9th century) *San Zeno (Via San Zeno).*

The Lombardy shore extends along the south-west part of the lake: on an islet off the tip of the *Sirmione* penisula (pop. 4000) is the formidable 〰 *Castillo Scaligero* and the picturesque old centre of Sirmione, the most-visited sights on the lake. In Sirmione, there are well-known thermal springs (the *Centro Benessere Termale Aquaria* is an oasis of wellbeing: *www.termedisirmione.com*), magnificent luxury hotels and first-class restaurants. At the end of the peninsula lie the imposing ruins of a Roman villa, the *Grotto of Catullus (Tue–Sat 8.30am–7pm, Sun 8.30am–1.30pm).* For those that want to party there are the discotheques in Desenzano, Lonato and Bardolino.

The *Vittoriale degli Italiani* on a hilltop north-east of *Gardone Riviera* is well worth a visit *(Oct–March daily 9am–5pm, April–Sept 8.30am–8pm, guided tour of the residence | closed Mon | www.vittoriale. it)*, a beautifully located estate, which was the home of the controversial and eccentric poet Gabriele D'Annunzio from 1921 to 1938. Another quite different poet, André Heller, gave his name to the *botanical gardens (March–Oct daily 9am–7pm | www.hellergarden.com)*. In the little lakeside town of *Salò* nearby, you can stay in pretty and stylish surroundings, and eat well in *Hotel Benaco (19 rooms | Lungolago Zanardelli 44 | tel. 0 36 52 03 08 | www. hotelbenaco.com | Moderate)* on the beautiful, pedestrian promenade. The popular tourist town of *Limone* in the north-west is a reminder of the lemon orchards that once flourished here in the lake's mild climate.

For a more detailed description you can refer to the MARCO POLO 'Lake Garda' guide.

LAGO MAGGIORE (179 D2) (*Ø D2*)

Cannobio, the first little town on the Italian side has a charming old centre overlooking the lake, in which you will find the hotel *Casa Arizzoli (11 rooms | Via Giovanola 92 | tel. 0 32 37 20 01 | www. hotelcasaarizzoli.com | Budget–Moderate)*. The imposing *Mottarone* (1491m/4892ft) rises above Stresa, and you can take the cable car to the ☼ summit to see the lovely *Giardino Botanico*. There are spectacular villas and belle époque style hotels set in gorgeous parks as well as the waterfront promenade *Lungolago* in glamorous *Stresa* (pop. 5000). The promenade looks over to the three enchanting Borromean Islands, the most notable of which is the Baroque *Isola Bella* with its palazzo, re-

fined terraced gardens and waterfront. A lush botanical garden thrives on the *Isola Madre*. The long, narrow *Isola dei Pescatori* is still the preserve of the local fishermen to this day. A wonderful B & B is the ☼ *Villa La Camana (3 rooms | Via per Gignese 10 | tel. 0 32 33 15 53 | www.villalacamana. it | Budget–Moderate)* with a park and magnificent sea view near the village of *Vedasco.*

Palaces, gardens and a beautiful promenade await visitors to *Pallanza,* in the *Verbania* district, which with 30,000 inhabitants is the largest town on the lake. Visitors flock to the *Villa Taranto* to see the beautiful gardens *(April–Oct daily 8.30am–6.30pm | www.villataranto.it)*. You will find the best sandy beaches opposite on the east bank, the *Lido di Monvalle.* Also located on a rocky outcrop on the eastern shore is the ☼ *Rocca Borromeo di Angera (March–Oct daily 9am–5.30pm),* a 13th century fort which still belongs to the Borromeo family. It has a very interesting doll museum *www. lagomaggiore.com*

LAGO D'ORTA (LAKE ORTA) (179 D2) (*Ø D 2–3*)

The small, contemplative Piedmontese Lago d 'Orta is nestled at the base of dark green forested slopes dotted with picturesque little villages. *Orta San Giulio* (pop. 1000), the main town, has some lovely churches, Baroque villas and a Renaissance building with a painted façade. There is a gorgeous view of the little island of San Giulio from the ☼ piazza.

Above the town is the pilgrimage site **INSIDER TIP** *Sacro Monte*, which also has a Baroque puppet theatre. In Omegna on the northern side of the lake, you can buy quality brand kitchen utensils from the *Alessi factory outlet (Mon–Sat 9.30am–6pm | Via Privata Alessi 6 | Crusinallo di Omegna | www.alessi.it)*.

PARMA

(179 F4) (⟨⟨ E4⟩) This affluent town (pop. 180,000) lies along the old Roman road Via Aemilia in the midst of fertile agricultural land. It is the main base of Barilla, Europe's largest pasta manufacturer as well as a musical Mecca: Arturo Toscanini and above all Italy's most famous opera composer Giuseppe Verdi (born in the small farming village of Busseto not far from Parma) have made the place popular with music lovers with fan clubs and a festival.

SIGHTSEEING

CATHEDRAL AND BAPTISTRY

In 1530, Correggio decorated the dome of this Romanesque basilica that has a Gothic campanile (bell tower). Benedetto Antelami, one of the most important sculptors of the Romanesque period, did the sculptures and reliefs in the gracefully structured ★ baptistry. *Daily 9am–12.30pm and 3pm–6.30pm | Piazza del Duomo*

PALAZZO DELLA PILOTTA

The palace is a historic complex of buildings that houses the *Pinacoteca Galleria Nazionale* with works by Bellini and Correggio and the famous *Teatro Farnese* from 1618 which, with 4500 seats, was once the largest theatre in the world. *Tue–Sun 8.30am–1.45pm | Piazza Pilotta*

SAN GIOVANNI EVANGELISTA

Apart from the beautiful cloister, the monastery also contains the old *Storica Farmacia (Tue–Sun 8.30am–1.45pm)*, a pharmacy set up by the Benedictine monks in 1201, *Mon–Wed and Fri, Sat 9am–noon and 3pm–5pm | Piazzale San Giovanni*

About the life of Christ: dome frescoes in the baptistry in Parma

PARMA

FOOD & DRINK

ENOTECA FONTANA
Centrally located, Fontana's popular Parma ham and cheese specialities are served with a nice glass of wine. *Closed Sun/Mon | Via Farini 24 a | tel. 05 21 28 60 37 | Budget*

PARIZZI
Once a butcher, today the town's best state-of-the-art restaurant. Also has 13 elegant suites. *Closed Mon | Via Repubblica 71 | tel. 05 21 28 59 52 | www.ristorante parizzi.it | Moderate–Expensive*

SHOPPING

A delicatessen should be on your list of places to visit: delicate, spicy Parma ham, cured ham *culatello, coppa* (pork neck ham) and fresh, authentic parmesan cheese from Parmigiano-Reggiano.

ENTERTAINMENT

Musical Parma offers a rich programme of operas (naturally a lot of which is Verdi) and concerts: in *Teatro Regio (www.teatroregioparma.org)*, in the concert hall *Auditorium Paganini (www.fondazione toscanini.it)* and in the *Casa della Musica (www.lacasadellamusica.it)*.

WHERE TO STAY

TORINO
Friendly, extremely stylish B & B in the old town, with parking facilities. *39 rooms | Borgo Mazza 7 | tel. 05 21 28 10 46 | www. hotel-torino.it | Moderate*

INFORMATION

Via Melloni 1 a | tel. 05 21 21 88 89 | turismo. comune.parma.it

WHERE TO GO

CREMONA (179 E–F3) (*Ⓜ E3*)
A town (pop. 83,000) that is home to the world's best violin makers, it upholds the legacy of Antonio Stradivari (with workshops, *Stradivari Museum, violin museum*). Cremona's heart is the ● wonderful medieval *Piazza del Comune,* lined with cafés, the *town hall* and the *cathedral*, with its beautiful stonework, Flemish tapestries and frescoes, the octagonal baptistry and the brick *Torrazzo,* Italy's highest bell tower (111m/364ft). Close by in the cosy, Slow Food trattoria *La Sosta (closed Sun evening and Mon | Via Sicardo 9 | tel. 03 72 45 66 56 | Budget–Moderate),* you can order Cremona's typical *mostarda*, fruit preserve spiced with mustard that is served with meat and cheese.

MANTUA (MANTOVA) (179 F3) (*Ⓜ F3*)
Mantua (pop. 62,000), once the ancestral seat of the ambitious dukes of Gonzaga (1328–1708), is partially encircled by the Mincio River. You can explore

the resulting lake landscape and prolific bird life on  INSIDER TIP guided boat trips *(departure from Ponte San Giorgio)*.

Wander through the town's three central squares: the Piazza Mantegna where you will find the *Sant'Andrea* (early Renaissance and Baroque elements), then the Piazza della Erbe, with the Romanesque *Rotonda di San Lorenzo*, and restaurants where in the summer you can eat al fresco in a wonderfully romantic setting. Finally, the

Isabella d'Este 20 | tel. 34 09 62 33 65 | www.casacasari.com | Budget). On the southern outskirts of the town is the summer residence of the Gonzaga, the *Palazzo del Tè (Tue–Sun 9am–6pm, Mon 1pm–6pm)*.

Enjoy specialities such as pike with green sauce or pasta filled with pumpkin in the popular *Osteria da Bice la Gallina Felice (closed Mon | Via Carbonati 4/6 | tel. 03 76 28 83 68 | Budget–Moderate)*.

In Italy's violin industry, Cremona, the home of the Stradivari, calls the tune

Baroque styled cathedral is on Piazza Sordello together with the *bishop's palace* and the imposing ★ *Palazzo Ducale,* behind which is *Castello di San Giorgio*. The castle guards some unique art treasures, including in particular the *Camera degli Sposi,* a bridal chamber with wonderful frescoes by Andrea Mantegna from 1474 *(Tue–Sun 8.15am–7.15pm | pre-register, tel. 04 12 41 18 97)*. It is nice to stay in the centre of the beautiful old town, e.g. in the quiet, spacious B & B *Casa Casari (3 rooms | Via*

Also worth a visit is the little Renaissance town 35km/22mi south-west INSIDER TIP *Sabbioneta (www.sabbioneta.org)* founded by Vespasian Gonzaga. Another excursion tip: the pilgrimage church 8km/5mi west of *Curtatone* INSIDER TIP *Santa Maria delle Grazie* with impressive votive figures and the inviting *Locanda delle Grazie (closed Wed | Via San Pio X 2 | tel. 03 76 34 80 38 | Budget–Moderate)* with Mantuan specialities such as risotto, filled pasta, and roast donkey.

PIACENZA
(179 E3) *(⌀ E4)*

This amiable old provincial town (pop. 109,000) is scenically situated between the Po Valley and the northern foothills of the Apennines. A 16th century fortified wall

A puzzle from the Byzantine era: mosaic in the Galla Placidia mausoleum

running parallel to wide alleys encircles the well-preserved medieval centre with the *Piazza dei Cavalli,* which is adorned with two magnificent Baroque horses. The highlight on the piazza is the imposing *Palazzo Gotico* from 1280. Here, you can enjoy an excellent meal in an impressive palace, the *Antica Osteria del Teatro (closed Sun/Mon | Via Verdi 16 | tel. 05 23 32 37 77 | www.anticaosteriadelteatro.it | Expensive).*

ROMAGNA COAST

(181 D 5–6) *(⌀ G4–5)* Romagna's coastal area fluctuates between two extremes, from Ravenna – a pinnacle of man's artistic creation – to Rimini and the other Adriatic resorts – where summer fun is at its wildest.

In the undulating interior (wonderful hiking areas) there are small picturesque hamlets in which you can often get a far better meal than provided to the masses along the coast.

COMACCHIO ★
(181 D5) *(⌀ G4)*

A little lagoon town (pop. 21,000) with colourful fishermen's houses and palazzi spread across 13 islands in the delta region of the Po and other smaller rivers. The *Trepponti* bridge (17th century) is an ingenious design. The five wide sweeping staircases enable people to cross four canals. Eel fishing and processing are a traditional activity in Comacchio. You can explore the extensive wetland in the south of Comacchio with its old fishing cottages, reed-bed islands and flamingo colonies by boat *(March–Oct several times a day from Stazione di Pesca Foce | www.vallidico macchio.info).* A trip over the Comacchio causeway to Anita d'Argenta demonstrates the efforts undertaken since the time of the Etruscans to reclaim the marshlands of the Po Delta. INSIDER TIP Boat trips through the delta start, e.g. from *Gorino (Freccia del Delta | tel. 33 37 69 10 14)* and from *Porto Garibaldi (Albatros | tel. 05 33 32 50 10). www.parcodeltapo.it*

20km/18kmi north is the grandiose *Abbazia di Pomposa,* a 7th century Benedictine monastery. The basilica (8th/9th century) reflecting Ravenna's style is adorned with wonderful floor mosaic and frescoes from the 14th century.

RAVENNA ★ (181 D5) (*◫ G 4–5*)

Ravenna (pop. 137,000) used to be located by the sea and like Venice was a lagoon city; then the sea receded, today a 10km/6mi long canal keeps the two connected. The town has fantastic examples of early Christian culture *(all sights daily 8.30am–7pm, in the winter 9am–5.30pm | ask for group tickets! | www.turismo.ravenna.it)*. From the 5th century, it was the centre of power following the dissolution of the Roman Empire. Decorated with blue and gold mosaics, the mausoleum *Mausoleo di Galla Placidia* dates from this period as well as the preciously inlaid *Baptistry of Neon,* which dates back to the Ostrogoth King Theoderic (493–526) the stalwart *Mausoleo di Teodorico*, made of stone ashlar without mortar, in the north-east of Ravenna and the breathtaking *Sant' Apollinare Nuovo* (around 500).

The 6th–8th century – the town's period as the capital of Byzantine Italy – saw the building of the octagonal basilica *San Vitale* (consecrated in 547) and the basilica *Sant'Apollinare* (5km/3mi south in *Classe*), both with exquisite interiors decorated with mosaic. The art of laying mosaic has become a tradition at Ravenna, and workshops and schools have been set up for this purpose.

A restaurant in the centre of Ravenna, where both visitors and locals enjoy eating is *La Gardèla (closed Thu | Via Ponte Marino 3 | tel. 05 44 21 71 47 | Budget)*.

RIMINI AND SURROUNDS (181 D5–6) (*◫ G–H5*)

During the summer, 650,000 people live in this beach metropolis with its eclectic choice of sport and entertainment activities – five times its normal population of 130,000. In what was ancient Rome's Ariminum, you can still see the triumphant arch *Arco d'Augusto* from 27 BC; the *Corso Augusto* leads across the well-preserved bridge of Tiberius into the picturesque district of San Giuliano, the former fishing quarter. The palazzi around the Piazza Cavour and the Tempio Malatestiano, renovated in early Renaissance style by Rimini's ruling Malatesta family all date back to the Middle Ages. People meet here at the old fish market for an aperitif, for example in the *Osteria della Piazzetta (closed Sun | Vicolo della Pescheria 5 | tel. 05 41 78 39 86 | Budget)*.

Riccione (pop. 32,000) follows in the south, once a bourgeois resort with villas in beautiful grounds, today a fashion trendsetter with the most sophisticated, outlandish shops, and the wildest discos. *Cattolica* is more suited to families and people with disabilities.

The north of Rimini flows into other beach resorts with endless chains of hotels: for example *Cesenatico,* where a **INSIDER TIP** picturesque fishing harbour with impressive old vessels awaits you. *Cervia* is more traditional with a down-to-earth harbour district and salt works from which even the Etruscans extracted salt (today a nature reserve). By contrast, *Milano Marittima* is probably the most refined seaside resort with villas surrounded by pines, well-run hotels and very trendy cocktail bars. Popular destinations in the hills inland are hamlets such as Sant'Arcangelo di Romagna, Montegridolfo and the castle villages of San Leo and Verucchio, all with nice trattorias. *www.adriacoast.com*

SAN MARINO (181 D6) (*◫ G–H5*)

Europe's oldest republic (pop. 25,000) was founded in the 9th century and covers only 23.5mi². The medieval capital, surrounded by walls and castles, is perched on ☀ Monte Titano (749m/2457ft), a popular destination for coin and stamp collectors.

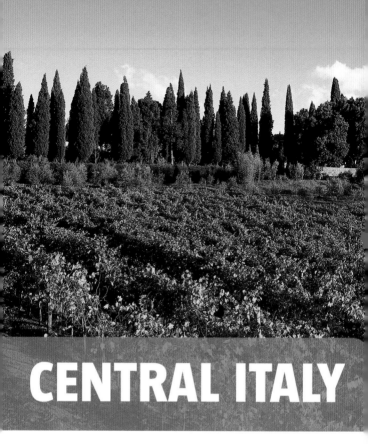

CENTRAL ITALY

They are also called the three sisters. They straddle the central Apennine region between the Ligurian-Tyrrhenian coast in the west and the Adriatic in the east, right across Italy's 'boot leg'.

Together, they exude a feeling of harmonious proportion. They have beautiful towns with distinctly medieval and Renaissance features, such as Florence, Siena, Pisa and Lucca in Tuscany, and Perugia, Gubbio, Assisi, Orvieto, and Todi in Umbria, as well as Urbino and Ascoli Piceno in the Marche. There are a variety of landscapes: the Apuan Alps, which separate Tuscany from Liguria and the Po Valley and provide the white marble from Carrara; then there is the Tyrrhenian coast lined with pine woods, the ash-grey clay hills of *Crete* to the south of Siena and the darkly forested volcanic Monte Amiata on the border to Lazio; away from the coast, the undulating landscape of Umbria with its dense forests is called the green heart of Italy and is increasingly popular with the Tuscany fraction; finally the Marche whose fertile slopes of wine terraces, wheat, maize and flax fields, sunflowers and bright green alfalfa gently descend to the Adriatic coast with its flat sand and pebble beaches. In the cosy trattorias, you can savour the full-bodied wines with an excellent meal. There is a general sense of quality of life, which not

Photo: Vineyard near Greve in Chianti

Tuscany, Umbria and the Marche: the three regions of central Italy known for their gently rolling hills and opulent towns

only the tourists enjoy, but which the locals also take full advantage of.

FLORENCE (FIRENZE)

(182 B1) (🗺 F5) It is Europe's richest art centre, full of incomparably exquisite
architecture, monuments, sculptures and paintings.

From the 14th century, the powerful Medici family steered the city's political and cultural destiny, which reached its zenith during the Renaissance. It was here in 1256 that Dante was born, the writer whose poetical language was to provide the basis for the Italian language. A good 370,000 people live in the capital of Tuscany and

Brunelleschi's distinctive dome and Florence's landmark is visible from the motorway

they have to put up with the onslaught of millions of visitors each year. From the raised square, ⚘ *Piazzale Michelangelo*, on the left bank of the Arno, there is a fantastic view of the whole town, including the river banks, the palaces, the towering cathedral dome. MARCO POLO covers this city in detail in its 'Florence' guide.

SIGHTSEEING

CATHEDRAL AND BAPTISTRY ★
Artistic highlights of the octagonal-shaped baptistry (consecrated in 1059) present themselves as you walk in; the south portal is by Andrea Pisano, the north and east portal by Lorenzo Ghiberti. Construction of the cathedral, the fourth largest Christian church, began in 1296; the powerful 25,000t ⚘ dome did not follow until 1420–1434. It was built by Filippo Brunelleschi, who art historians regard as a pioneer of the Renaissance style. And no less than Giotto designed the ⚘ steeple.

Baptistry: Mon–Sat noon–7pm, Sun 8.30am–2pm; dome Mon–Wed and Fri 10am–5pm, Thu 10am–3.30pm, Sat 10am–4.45pm, Sun 1.30pm–4.45pm; dome Mon–Fri 8.30am–7pm, Sat 8.30am–5.40pm; campanile daily 8.30am–7.30pm; Museo dell'Opera del Duomo Mon–Sat 9am–7.30pm, Sun 9am–1.40pm | Piazza Duomo 9 | www.operaduomo.firenze.it

GALLERIA DEGLI UFFIZI
This vast building complex houses one of the most important art collections in the world, with masterpieces by 13th to 16th century European artists – a must for all art lovers. Since 2006, the museum complex has been extending and rearranging the museum complex, called the Nuovi Uffizi. *Tue–Sun 8.15am–6.50pm, advance reservation advisable in high season, online under www.b-ticket.com or at the visitor centre in Loggiato degli Uffizi in the Piazza della Signoria | www.polo museale.firenze.it*

GUCCI MUSEO

Following the Ferragamo Museum with its impressive shoe fashion *(Via dei Tornabuoni 2)*, the world famous fashion brand Gucci, which opened its doors in Florence 90 years ago, has now also opened its style museum, right on the Piazza della Signoria in the Palazzo della Mercanzia. The adjoining Gucci Café serves good and relatively inexpensive meals *(daily to 11pm | Budget–Moderate). Daily 10am–8pm*

MUSEO NAZIONALE DEL BARGELLO

Renaissance sculptures of the finest quality, with works by Donatello, Michelangelo, Giambologna and many others. *Daily 8.15am–1.50pm; closed 1st, 3rd, 5th Sun and 2nd and 4th Mon in the month | Via del Proconsolo 4*

PALAZZO PITTI/GIARDINO DI BOBOLI

The enormous palace which belonged to the Pitti merchant family (15th century) and later to the Grand Dukes of Tuscany on the left bank of the Arno now accommodates a number of museums. You can relax afterwards in the Baroque park *Giardino di Boboli (daily 8.15am–dusk; closed first and last Mon of the month | entrance fee 7 euros)*. The ticket also includes the park museums as well as the wonderful INSIDER TIP *Giardino Bardini* close by *(entrance Via dei Bardi and Costa San Giorgio)*. Enjoy the view of the town from the loggia of the park café!

PIAZZA DELLA SIGNORIA

This square has been the urban centre for over 700 years – the municipal authorities still meet in the Gothic *Palazzo Vecchio*. World famous sculptures adorn the square, such as Michelangelo's David (a copy; the original is in the *Galleria dell' Accademia* museum | *Tue–Sun 8.15am–6.50pm)*, the group of sculptures (also copies) by Giambologna and Cellini under the *Loggia dei Lanzi*, the *Fontana del*

Nettuno by Bartolomeo Ammanati (1576), and cafés to relax afterwards.

PONTE VECCHIO ⚜

Italy's most famous bridge with numerous goldsmiths' ateliers (since the 16th century) provides a connection between the royal residences of Palazzo Vecchio and Palazzo Pitti.

SAN LORENZO

The private church of the powerful Medici clan contains the family tombs, *Cappelle Medicee,* by Michelangelo in the Sacrestia Nuova. *April–Oct daily 8.15am–4.50pm, Nov–March 8.15am–1.50pm, closed 2nd and 4th Sun as well as 1st, 3rd and 5th Mon in the month. Entrance Piazza Madonna degli Aldobrandini*

SAN MARCO

At the beginning of the 15th century, a monk resided in the Dominican monastery who was also a fantastic artist: Fra Angelico. His cell frescoes and panels draw thousands of visitors. *Mon–Fri 8.15am–1.50pm, Sat/Sun 8.15am–4.50pm; closed 1st, 3rd, 5th Sun, 2nd, 4th Mon in the month, Piazza San Marco 3*

FOOD & DRINK

IL CIBREO

A real emporium of Tuscan cuisine: in the top-class restaurant *(Cibreo, Expensive),* in the rustic trattoria *(Cibreino, Budget–Moderate),* in the *Caffè. Closed Mon | Via del Verrocchio/Via dei Macci 118/122 | tel. 05 52 34 11 00 | www.edizioniteatrodelsalecibreofirenze.it*

OSTERIA PEPÒ

Comfortable trattoria near the well-stocked market hall Mercato Generale with delicious home cooking, vegetable soups and good meat. *Daily | Via Rosina 4/6 r | tel. 0 55 28 32 59 | www.pepo.it | Budget*

INSIDER TIP SANTINO ☺

A small bistro bar with an excellent delicatessen and organic wines, ideal place for a snack and attached to the popular *Il Santo Bevitore* restaurant next door, located on the left bank of the Arno. *Closed Sun | Via Santo Spirito 60 r | tel. 05 52 30 28 20 | Budget*

SHOPPING

The big fashion names are located in *Via Tornabuoni, Via della Vigna Nuova* and in *Borgo Ognissanti.* The clothes and leatherware market *Mercato San Lorenzo* is cheaper *(Mon–Sat 8am–7pm; closed Jan/Feb on Mon)* around its namesake basilica. A gift tip: you can obtain rose water, violet powder etc. in the historical INSIDER TIP *Officina Profumo-Farmaceutica (Via della Scala 16)* at the Santa Maria Novella church. The leading *La Rinascente* department store is on the Piazza della Repubblica: a highlight is the ⚜ terrace café on the roof with a bird's eye view of the cathedral dome. Traditional handcraftsmanship can be found in the *Oltrarno* district on the left side of the Arno.

ENTERTAINMENT

The *Piazza Santo Spirito,* the 'Rive Gauche' of Florence is popular with the bohemian crowd while the bars in the *San Niccolò* district are more fashionable. On the right bank of the Arno is the *Santa Croce* district populated by students and young tourists. More glamour can be found in the bars of the elegant hotels, e.g. the *Fusion Bar* in *Gallery Art Hotel (Vicolo dell'Oro 5).* The monthly magazine *Firenze Spettacolo (www.firenzespettacolo.it)* provides information about what is going on.

HOTEL AZZI – LOCANDA DEGLI ARTISTI
Small hotel with flair, near the station. *16 rooms | Via Faenza 56–58 r | tel. 0 55 21 38 06 | www.hotelazzi.com | Budget–Moderate*

HOTEL BURCHIANTI
Beautifully decorated rooms in an old palazzo, nice service and central location. *11 rooms | Via del Giglio 8 | tel. 0 55 21 27 96 | www.hotelburchianti.it | Moderate–Expensive*

Available from the station forecourt and Via Cavour 1 r | tel. 0 55 29 08 32 | www.firenzeturismo.it

AREZZO (182 C1) (*ᗰ G6*)
Of Etruscan origin (pop. 95,000, 75km/47mi south-east of Florence), Arezzo was under Roman rule from the 3rd century BC, later becoming a medieval city republic. Today, visitors flock to see the frescoes by Piero della Francesca in the main chancel of the impressive *Basilica San Francesco (tel. appointment for reservations, at the till or tel. 05 75 35 27 27 | Mon–Fri 9am–6.30pm, Sat 9am–5.30pm, Sun 1pm–5.30pm or see www.pierodellafrancesca-ticketoffice.it),* the Romanesque *Pieve di Santa Maria* on the central Corso Italia and the renowned *antiques market* on the first weekend in the month on the Piazza Grande with loggias designed by Giorgio Vasari. For an overnight stay, try the elegantly appointed *Hotel Vogue (26 rooms | Via Guido Monaco 54 | tel. 0 57 52 43 61 | www.voguehotel.it | Moderate–Expensive)* in the centre.

CASENTINO (182 C1) (*ᗰ G5*)
In the north of Arezzo, hidden away in the mountain world of Casentino are some lovely monasteries, such as the one belonging to the Camaldolese in *Camaldoli,* still inhabited by monks today and the

La Verna was founded by Francis of Assisi in the 13th century

13th century *La Verna* or the *Benedictine abbey Vallombrosa*. In the east of Arezzo, you come to the Tiber Valley: for example to the village of *Monterchi* with the famous fresco 'Madonna del Parto' by Piero della Francesca. The trail of this great Renaissance artist leads on to Sansepolcro (with pinacotheca).

VAL DI CHIANA
(182 C2) (*Ø G6*)

The Chiana Valley runs across the south of Arezzo, the breeding grounds of the white Chianina cattle used for Italy's *bistecca alla fiorentina*. Medieval fortress towns sit perched on the edge of the hills overlooking this plain, a prime example being picturesque  *Cortona,* once an important Etruscan settlement. In *Chiusi*, the *Museo Archeologico* is well worth a visit *(daily 9am–7.30pm)*. The proprietor of *La Zaira (closed Mon | Via Arunte 12 | tel. 0 57 82 02 60 | Moderate)* is also happy to show guests round the wine cellar in the ancient Etruscan vaults.

CHIANTI (182 B1–2) (*Ø F5–6*)

South of Florence, this – for connoisseurs – legendary highland area rich in forests and vineyards extends down to Siena, encompassing pretty villages such as *Greve* with its arcade-lined piazza (farmer's market on Saturday ☺ with lots of organic products). From the garden of the B & B ☘ *Ancora del Chianti* in an enchanting farmhouse, *(7 rooms | Via Collegalla 12 | Greve in Chianti | tel. 0 55 85 40 44 | www. ancoradelchianti.it | Budget)*, you have a wonderful view of the landscape. Castle-like vineyards dominate the hilltops, in which the vintners press the red Chianti. Many of the vineyards also offer accommodation, e.g. in *Castello di San Polo (9 apartments | tel. 05 77 74 60 45 | www.san-polo.de | Moderate)* in Gaiole in Chianti.

LUCCA ★ (182 A1) (*Ø E5*)

Lucca (pop. 91,000) deserves its epithet 'Italy's largest open air museum'. Its 16th century fortified walls encircle the old town, which is brimming with treasures,

Unusual setting for a square: Lucca's oval Piazza del Mercato was once a Roman amphitheatre

such as the *San Martino* cathedral (6th/13th century) containing the marble tomb of Ilaria del Carretto by Jacopo della Quercia (1408), or the oval *Piazza del Mercato* with the medieval houses lining a Roman amphitheatre. Standing in the shade of the trees on *Torre Guinigi*, you can look across to *Garfagnana*, a beautiful place for day trips and walks in the north of Lucca. One highlight: the INSIDER TIP camellia blossoms in spring in the gardens of the old villas.

MEDICI VILLAS (180 B1) (*F5*)

There are some magnificent Medici villas between Florence and Pistoia, including the *Villa Medicea La Ferdinanda* in Artimino in Carmignano and the *Villa Medicea Ambra* in Poggio a Caiano. *Visiting times vary; enquire with the tourist office in Florence*

PISTOIA (180 B6) (*F5*)

Stop off in Pistoia on the way to Lucca (35km/22mi, pop. 90,000). In the bustling

old town, you can visit the *cathedral* and the *Chiesa Sant'Andrea,* two of Tuscany's most impressive Romanesque Gothic buildings. Inviting restaurants and shops line the *Piazze degli Ortaggi* and *della Scala*. A further highlight is the *Marino Marini museum* in the *monastery (Corso Silvano Fedi 30 | Mon–Sat 10am–5pm)*. A native Pistoian, Marini was a leading 20th century sculptor and the museum exhibits both his modern work and pieces inspired by antiquity.

THE MARCHE

Many popular seaside resorts cluster along this predominantly flat coast, which has been heavily developd by the beach tourism industry.

Further inland, many of the ancient towns, villages and abbeys – with their more tranquil and simple way of life – offer excellent panoramic views of the hill landscape down to the sea.

ADRIATIC RESORTS (183 D–E 1–2) (*H5–6*)

The lively *Gabicce Mare* is one of the most popular resorts in the Marche (boasting the largest number of discos and a curious festival of love in July), *Senigallia* with the most beds and most impressive marketplace as well as the highly acclaimed seafood restaurant or down in the south *San Benedetto del Tronto* with marina and palm-fringed promenade. Many places have two distinct sections: a little medieval town on the hilltop and a modern beach district, e.g. *Civitanova Marche, Cupra Marittima* and *Grottammare.*

A venerable little harbour town directly by the sea is *Fano,* which has a picturesque old town, Roman architecture, a fortress and palazzi. From here, the route continues to *Cartoceto,* 18km/11mi inland, famous for its excellent olive oil and for one of the best restaurants in Italy (with four guest rooms): *Symposium | closed Mon/Tue and, except for Sat/Sun, for lunch | Via Cartoceto 38 | tel. 0721898320 | www.symposium4stagioni.it | Expensive*

ANCONA (183 E1) (*∅ H6*)

The most important seaport (pop. 106,000) in the centre of the Adriatic is the capital of the Marche and an important port for the ferries travelling to Greece. The harbour (which still has an impressive Napoleonic military hospital from 1789) and the centre of the town offer some beautiful squares with churches and palazzi (14th/15th century) and the shopping mile *Corso Mazzini*. In AD 115 the *Arco di Traiano* was built at the farthest point of the harbour in honour of Emperor Trajan. Rising in the background is ☆ *Monte Guasco,* with the town's landmark, the magnificent Romanesque Gothic *San Ciriaco* cathedral.

ASCOLI PICENO ★
(183 E2–3) (*∅ H6*)

This picturesque little town (pop. 56,000), encircled by two rivers, is set against the mighty mountain backdrop of Monti Sibillini, today a national park and popular hiking destination south of the Marche. Spanning one of the rivers is the beautifully preserved Roman *Ponte di Solestà*. Sit in the venerable *Caffè Meletti* on the ● *Piazza del Popolo* – with its mirror-smooth travertine flagstones, surrounded by Renaissance façades – and admire the lovely Gothic *San Francesco* church. The *Palazzo Comunale (Oct–mid March Tue–Fri 10am–5pm, Sat/Sun 10am–7pm, mid March–Sept 10am–7pm)* has an art gallery that is well worth a visit.

CINGOLI AND FABRIANO
(183 D2) (*∅ H6*)

Owing to its epithet 'Balcony of the Marche', the ancient little town of *Cingoli* (pop. 10,000) deserves a mention. Indeed, it is true that the loveliest view of the undulating landscape is from the ☆ *Belvedere* behind the San Francesco church. The charming *Fabriano* (pop. 30,000) is famous for the production of high-quality paper; you can admire it (and also make it yourself if you wish) in the *Museo della Carta (Tue–Sun 10am–1pm and 2.30pm–7.30pm | Largo Spacca | www.museodellacarta.com),* and buy it in *Bartolini (Via Largo Bartolo di Sasso-*

BORGHI BELLI – BEAUTIFUL VILLAGES

The *Borghi più belli d'Italia (www.borghitalia.it/?lang=en)* is an association that has set itself the task of identifying the most picturesque villages in Italy, and its search has been particularly successful in central Italy. The list includes, for example, *Barga,* the little old town in the Garfagnana woods, the peaceful spa village of *San Casciano dei Bagni* in the south; in the Marche the intact castle village of ☆ *Gradara* with its wonderful panorama and *Offida* with its magical torchlight procession during the carnival; in Umbria *Vallo di Nera,* where you can try fresh trout from the Nera River, and on the other side of the Tiber Valley *Lugnano* in Teverina nestled amongst the olive groves. And many, many more … everywhere in Italy.

ferrato 7) in the Palazzo Podestà. Stylish accommodation is available in the manor house of an estate in the nearby village *Moscano: Le Gocce di Camarzano (6 rooms | tel. 3 36 64 90 28 | www.goccedicamarzano. com | Budget)*.

FERMO (183 E2) (*ϖ H6*)

Only 7km/4mi away from the coast, the town (pop. 35,000) offers a spacious piazza, stately palazzi, an impressive cathedral, prized churches, and above all the INSIDER TIP *piscine romane*, Roman pools built built between 41 and 60 BC to conserve and purify the town's water. After wandering around the 30 subterranean basins, you can enjoy a good glass of wine with a selection of excellent pecorino cheeses from the Marche on the central *Piazza del Popolo* in the *Enoteca Bar a Vino (closed Mon and Wed | tel. 07 34 22 80 67 | Budget–Moderate)*. In short: the ideal daytrip from the nearby beaches along the coast.

JESI (183 D1) (*ϖ H6*)

This is where the Verdicchio grape grows, the dry, slightly bitter white wine from the Marche, the ideal accompaniment to *brodetto,* the local fish soup. The sightseeing programme offers the Renaissance palace *Palazzo della Signoria* and the pictures of the leading Marche painter Lorenzo Lotto (16th century) in *Palazzo Pinetti*. The fantastic ⚡ dripstone caves *Grotte di Frasassi* further inland are absolutely spectacular.

LORETO (183 E1) (*ϖ H6*)

The imposing Gothic church *Santuario della Santa Casa* in this fortified medieval hill town (pop. 11,000) is one of Italy's most important pilgrimage sites, as is clear from the rich collection of votive pictures and objects. It was here in 1295 that angels are said to have carried the

house of Mary of Nazareth. That is why the Madonna di Loreto is the patron saint of pilots. Over the years, leading artists have contributed to the church and its interior.

Pilgrimage destination for pilots: Loreto's Santuario della Santa Casa church

MACERATA (183 E2) (*ϖ H6*)

Every year, fans of melodrama flock to this town (pop. 44,000) with its southern flair and impressive and largely intact Renaissance centre for the Macerata opera festival *(mid July–mid Aug, www.sferisterio. it)*. It takes place in a Neoclassical *pallone (ball game) arena* built in 1829. To the north of Macerata are the ruins of a massive *amphitheatre,* the remains of the old

Roman settlement *Helvetica Ricina*. In the countryside towards the south, you can visit the impressive Romanesque church *San Claudio al Chienti* as well as the Cistercian abbey *Chiaravalle di Fiastra*.

Impressive Adriatic: Monte Conero's steep cliffs in Sirolo

PESARO
(183 D1) (*Ɱ H5*)
Second largest centre of the Marche (pop. 90,000) offering both urban and beach life. Pesaro is the birth place of the opera composer Gioacchino Rossini with a museum in the house he was born in and a renowned Rossini summer festival *(www.rossinioperafestival.it)*.

INSIDER TIP ▶ RIVIERA DEL CONERO
(183 E1) (*Ɱ H6*)
To the south of Ancona, the Apennines push out into the sea; the 572m/1877ft, green, maquis-covered *Monte Conero* crowns the headland with its steep cliffs and wonderful bays, some only accessible by boat. Exclusive hotels, charming little country resorts, a golf course, sailing, surfing and scuba diving facilities, good restaurants and ecological awareness combine to create a first-rate coastal region *(www.conero.it)*. The European eco label has been awarded to the 🌿 *Country House Acanto* in Sirolo *(7 rooms | Via Ancarano 18 | tel. 0719331195 | www.acantocountryhouse.com/en.html | Budget–Moderate)*.

URBINO ★ 🌤
(183 D1) (*Ɱ G5*)
The most beautiful view of the exceptional urban masterpiece, Urbino (pop. 16,000), is from the west, from the garden of *Fortezza Albornoz* fortress. During the rule of the Renaissance Duke Federigo da Montefeltro, artists of the calibre of Raphael ('The Mute') and Piero della Francesca ('The Flagellation of Christ) worked here – and you can admire their oeuvre in the *Galleria Nazionale delle Marche* in *Palazzo Ducale (Mon 8.30am–2pm, Tue–Sun 8.30am–7pm)*. The ducal palace also has a study completely decorated with precious inlay work. Urbino is now a lively student town.

PERUGIA

(182 C2) (*G6*) **Umbria's capital (pop. 164,000) the green heart of Italy has managed to protect its urban medieval and Renaissance layout, yet still remain vibrant.**

Perugia was one of the first towns in Italy to pedestrianise the centre in order to stop the escalating volume of traffic. Escalators and lifts provide a connection to the car parks below the town. There is a great deal of activity around the squares, narrow alleys leading to palazzi, churches and businesses, all bustling with students. The prestigious university for foreigners, Università per gli Stranieri, offers regional and cultural studies as well as Italian courses.

SIGHTSEEING

CORSO VANNUCCI

The main artery through the centre, a car-free boulevard, strings together some of the town's highlights: the imposing Gothic church of *San Lorenzo* with its beautiful choir stalls and staircase, in front of which is the famous *Fontana*

BOOKS & FILMS

▶ **Detective stories** – A whole series of Italian detective novelists open up trails for you in Italy. Valerio Varesi and cult author Carlo Lucarelli investigate in the northern region of Emilia-Romagna. With the crime novels by Marco Vichi and Michele Giuttari, you learn about Tuscany and Florence, while Roberto Costantini and Carlo Emilio Gadda take you through the back streets of Rome, and with Giannico Carofiglio you chase round Bari and Apulia, and then cross the sea to Sicily with Andrea Camilleri and Leonardo Sciascia. All of these authors (and a lot more besides) are available in English.

▶ **Gomorrah** – This explosive documentary about the mafia uncovers just how brutal and cynical life can be behind Italy's postcard surface. Directed by Roberto Saviano, this film is well worth watching despite the fact that it is currently only available with English subtitles.

▶ **Under the Tuscan Sun** – An enchanting memoir by Frances Mayes (1996) that recounts the adventures of buying and restoring an abandoned villa in the Tuscan countryside. It has all the elements of a great Italian travel story and was also made into a romantic comedy drama (2003) starring Diane Lane and directed by Audrey Wells.

▶ **Two Greedy Italians** – Antonio Carluccio and Gennaro Contaldo left Italy to live in Britain over 30 years ago, where they became leading authorities on Italian cuisine. In this fascinating book, they return to their native land 'to reveal Italian food, as cooked by real Italians'.

▶ **A Room with a View** – The beautiful screen adaptation of E.M. Forster's novel with Helena Bonham Carter, Denholm Elliott and Maggie Smith is a classic and a must-see for romantic couples on their way to Florence.

Maggiore fountain by the master craftsmen Giovanni and Nicola Pisano (13th century), and finally the formidable *Palazzo dei Priori,* a magnificent palace from the Italian Gothic period, adorned with Renaissance frescoes from Perugino (Pietro Vannucci), Raphael's teacher. It houses a fabulous collection of paintings *Galleria Nazionale dell'Umbria (Tue–Sun 8.30am–7.30pm).*

IPOGEO DEI VOLUMNI

Underground burial chambers belonging to the rich Etruscan family from the second half of the 2nd century BC with tomb statues and urns. *Daily 9am–1pm and 3.30pm–6.30pm | Ponte San Giovanni | SS 75*

SAN PIETRO

In the southern part of the town, through the beautiful Renaissance town gate of San Pietro, is the monastery complex from the 9th–10th century with an abbey, cloister and appealing kitchen. *Borgo XX Giugno*

SANT'ANGELO

In the north of the old town, this early 5th century Christian temple stands aloft on a green field. Inside, 16 Roman columns dominate the space. *Porta Sant'Angelo*

FOOD & DRINK

LA LUMERA

On the northern edge of the old town, Umbrian Slow Food cuisine with a lot of vegetables and good meat. *Closed Mon | Corso Bersaglieri 22 | tel. 07 55 72 61 81 | Budget–Moderate*

LA BOTTEGA DEL VINO

Good atmosphere and good wine, tasty little dishes and jazz evenings; a great place to meet for an aperitif. *Closed Sun | Via del Sole 1 | tel. 07 55 71 61 81 | Budget*

WHERE TO STAY

INSIDER TIP ▶ ETRUSCAN CHOCOHOTEL

A unique chocolate-themed hotel, modern and friendly with a fantastic chocolate shop. *94 rooms | Via Campo di Marte 134 | tel. 07 55 83 73 14 | www.chocohotel.it | Moderate*

B & B LE NAIADI

In the old town, a fresh cheerful atmosphere; well-kept and friendly. *3 rooms | Via Bonazzi 17i | tel. 33 37 41 74 08 | www.beblenaiadi.it | Budget*

INFORMATION

Piazza Matteotti 18 | Loggia dei Lanari | tel. 07 55 73 64 58 | turismo.comune.perugia.it

WHERE TO GO

ASSISI

(183 D2) (∅ G6)

In 1226, two years after the death of the charismatic founder of the order St Francis of Assisi, work started on the large twin church ★ ● *Basilica di San Francesco,* which is absolutely bursting with magnificent frescoes by some of the best artists: by Simone Martini, Cimabue and his students, especially Giotto, who painted the life story of St Francis on the lower walls of the *Chiesa Superiore.* No less richly decorated is the *Chiesa Inferiore* with the crypt *(lower church daily 6.30am–6pm, upper church 8.30am–6pm).* Assisi (pop. 27,000) with its churches and cloisters has long been a must for art connoisseurs and the disciples of St Francis. On your visit, do the one hour walk up to the *Eremo delle Carceri* on Monte Subasio. In this scenic location 10km/6mi to the east, nestled in green hills behind ancient walls is the beautiful country hotel *Le Silve (19*

The Sala dei Notari in Perugias Palazzo dei Priori is embellished with frescoes

rooms | Armenzano | tel. 07 58 01 90 00 | www.lesilve.it | Moderate–Expensive) with swimming pool and restaurant.

Santa Maria degli Angeli (daily 7am–7pm) in the west of Assisi is a richly decorated, 16th century basilica; it includes the *Porziuncola* chapel in which Francis of Assisi founded the order, as well as the *Cappella del Transito,* in which the saint later died.

Further opportunities to view impressive frescoes in Umbria can be found on the way from Assisi to Spoleto in the little town of *Spello* with work by Pinturicchio in the Romanesque church *Santa Maria Maggiore* as well as in the lofty ☀ *Montefalco* with the frescoes by Benozzo Gozzoli in the *Museo Civico Chiesa di San Francesco (Tue–Sun 10.30am–1pm and 2.30pm–6pm, later in the summer),* which like those of Giotto in Assisi, also focus on the life of St Francis.

INSIDER TIP ▶ **CITTÀ DI CASTELLO**
(182 C1) *(𝄂 G6)*

In the town on the Tiber (pop. 15 000), it is also possible to get to know the work of one of the most important contemporary artists in Italy: Alberto Burri's material pictures, paintings and sculptures in two permanent exhibitions in *Palazzo Albizzini* in the centre *(Tue–Sat 9am–12.30pm and 2.30pm–6pm, Sun 10.30am–12.30pm and 3pm–6pm)* and on the edge of the town in the former drying plant *Ex Seccatoio Tabacchi (same times, in winter by prior appointment: tel. 07 58 55 98 48 | www.fondazioneburri.org).* The *Pinacoteca* is also worth a visit *(Tue–Sun 10am–1pm and 3pm–6pm)* in *Palazzo Vitelli* as well as the beautiful woven fabrics in the *Tela Umbra (Tue–Sun 9am–1pm and 3.30pm–7.30pm | Via Sant'Antonio 3).*

In *Montone,* 20km/12.5mi out in the middle of the countryside, the dream retreat

Torre di Moravola (7 suites | tel. 07 59 46 09 65 | www.moravola.com | Expensive) in a renovated medieval watchtower is a very successful example of how old and new can be brought together in design.

DERUTA
(182 C2) *(ⓜ G6)*

Ceramics, ceramics and more ceramics, and that since 1290: there is one workshop, one factory after another! A *ceramic museum (daily in the winter Wed–Mon 10am–1pm and 3–6pm)* with a splendid majolica collection is in the *Palazzo Comunale.*

GUBBIO ✤
(183 D2) *(ⓜ G6)*

This enchanting town (pop. 32,000) ascends in broad storeys up the slope of Monte Ingino and overlooks a fertile plain. Founded by ancient Umbrian people in pre-Roman times and called Iguvium, it was rebuilt during the Middle Ages in hard limestone, thus explaining its excellent condition. In the *Palazzo dei Consoli,* built by the citizens of Gubio in 1337, the museum houses the Eugubinian tablets, seven bronze plates with Latin and Etruscan texts recording the ancient Umbrian language. There is also an imposing ducal palace (with renowned exhibitions of contemporary art), churches, palazzi, a Roman theatre and a large loggia complex: all good reasons to stay overnight, for example in the well-established *Grotta dell' Angelo (18 rooms | Via Gioia 47 | tel. 07 59 27 34 38 | www.grottadellangelo.it | Budget)* with a pleasant restaurant.

NORCIA
(183 D3) *(ⓜ H7)*

St Benedict came from this picturesque little town (pop. 5000), founder of the Benedictine fraternity. The beautiful Piazza San Benedetto and the Gothic church were both named after him. The Norcini are famous for their skill in breeding pigs and for producing ham and salami. In the autumn they supplement their cuisine with black truffles, which they serve with the famous Castelluccio lentils from the nearby Monti Sibillillini. They are tastefully prepared in the *Locanda de' Senari (5 rooms | Via della Bufera | Castelluccio | tel. 07 43 82 12 05 | www. agriturismosenari.it | Budget),* one of the many local *agriturismo* establishments.

ORVIETO (182 C3) *(ⓜ G7)*

Set on a plateau of a tuff rock rising up from the Praglia Valley, this old town (pop. 24,000) is clearly visible from a distance. The Etruscans established a rich centre here 2500 years ago. In the rock cliffs below the town an intricate labyrinth of tunnels open up forming an exciting **INSIDER TIP** underworld *(guided descent daily at 11am | meeting point Piazza Duomo 23 | www.orvietounderground.it).* Owing to a lack of space on the hilltop, Orvieto has continued its growth in the valley. This has enabled the beauty of the old town to be preserved, in particular the 14th century ★ *Duomo Santa Maria* cathedral with a façade that is an elegant mixture of French and Italian Gothic that is second to none in Italy; the interior has radiant frescoes by Luca Signorelli.

SOLOMEO
(182 C2) *(∅ G6)*
Many bon vivants live in Umbria's valleys. One of them is Brunello Cucinelli *(www. brunellocucinelli.it),* who manufactures elegant cashmere clothing, a shrewd businessman and, at the same time, a humanist idealist. He started his factory in the deserted medieval village of Solomeo halfway between Perugia and Lago Trasimeno: in the wonderfully restored rooms, some of which are adorned with frescoes. You can buy the soft cashmere pullovers with a 40 per cent discount in the *Cucinelli Outlet* on the Piazza Alberto Dalla Chiesa 6.

SPOLETO
(183 D3) *(∅ G7)*
The town was a Roman settlement, seat of the Lombards and later of the papal governors. The most important sight is the *cathedral* (12th century) with Romanesque and Renaissance elements as well as frescoes. Spoleto (pop. 38,000) is famous for its renowned theatre and music festival *dei Due Mondi* in July *(www.festival dispoleto.com).* Pretty accommodation

is available in the atmospheric old town in the *Hotel Aurora (23 rooms | Via Apollinare 3 | tel. 07 43 22 03 15 | www. hotelauroraspoleto.it | Budget)* with a good restaurant. It is well worth making a trip to ☀ *Monteluco* for the breathtaking panoramic view of Umbria.

The Gothic façade of Orvieto's cathedral is very elegant

TODI
(182 C3) *(∅ G7)*
This medieval town (pop. 17,000) overlooks the wonderfully winding Tiber. A broad, much photographed staircase leads to the piazza – widely regarded as one of Italy's particularly stunning squares.

VALNERINA (183 D3) *(⑂ G7)*

Experience nature at its best in the wild, secluded Nera Valley, where you will discover the solitary old abbey *San Pietro in Valle,* now a small charming hotel *(www.sanpietroinvalle.com),* and *Ferentillo* with its castle ruins and celebrated Santo Stefano church with its crypt of mummies as well as the spectacular waterfalls *Cascate delle Marmore* south of Terni. The water from Velino, dammed further up the valley in order to produce energy, is released several times a day for the waterfall (only on Sundays in the winter).

SIENA

(182 B2) *(⑂ F6)* **This town (pop. 67,000) is a medieval jewel, its golden age lasted until the 16th century, clearly evident from the palazzi, churches and art collections.**

An unswervingly confident focus on conservation has since been an integral part of Siena's lifestyle, thus ensuring that the town has remained intact. For a more detailed description refer to the MARCO POLO 'Tuscany' guide.

You seldom see Siena's shell-shaped Piazza del Campo as empty as this

SIGHTSEEING

DUOMO SANTA MARIA DELL'ASSUNTA

This magnificent example of Italian Gothic architecture was started in the mid 12th century and displays skilful marble black-and-white inlay work, graffito technique on the floor, as well as many masterpieces by painters and sculptors. Pinturicchio painted the frescoes in the famous, early Renaissance cathedral library *Libreria Piccolomini (Duomo and Libreria March–Oct Mon–Sat 10.30am–7.30pm, Sun 1.30pm–7.30pm, Nov–Feb Mon–Sat 10.30am–5.30pm, Sun 1.30pm–5.30pm | www.operaduomo.siena.it).*
The Gothic baptistry *San Giovanni* has a hexagonal-shaped baptismal font with bas-reliefs by Donatello, Ghiberti and Jacopo della Quercia (1427–1430).
Next to the cathedral is the *Spital Santa Maria della Scala* with its vividly painted scenes in the pilgrim hall *(daily 10.30am–6.30pm | www.santamariadellascala.com),* the old prayer chapel and the new and interesting Etruscan collection. *Piazza del Duomo*

MUSEO CIVICO

Highlights of the exhibition in Museo Civico, Siena's city museum, include the Sala del Mappamondo with frescoes by Simone Martini as well as Sala della Pace with frescoes by Ambrogio Lorenzetti depicting the 'Effects of Good Government on Town and Country'. *Daily 10am–7pm, in winter to 6pm | Palazzo Pubblico | Piazza del Campo*

MUSEO DELL'OPERA METROPOLITANA

Exhibits include masterpieces by Pisano, Lorenzetti and Jacopo della Quercia; the main attraction is the altarpiece panel 'Maestà' by Duccio di Buoninsegna. *Same opening times as the cathedral | Piazza del Duomo*

PIAZZA DEL CAMPO ★

Many people regard the shell-shaped Piazza del Campo as one of the most beautiful squares in the world. Its brick paving slopes down three sides, from which a sea of ochre-coloured houses fans out. The town hall, *Palazzo Pubblico,* from the 13th/14th century is on the straight side of the square. The ⚝ *Torre del Mangia* affords a magnificent view over the town *(April–Oct daily 10am–7pm, Nov–March 10am–4pm).* On 2 July and 16 August, the Piazza del Campo provides the stages for the famous Palio, a hair-raising horse race between Siena's different districts.

PINACOTECA NAZIONALE

One of Tuscany's most important galleries is in the Gothic Palazzo Buonsignori. *Mon, Sun 9am–1pm, Tue–Sat 8.15am–7.15pm | Via San Pietro 29*

FOOD & DRINK

COMPAGNIA DEI VINATTIERI

Fantastic wine cellar, which also serves hungry guests fine Tuscan specialities, occasional live jazz, and a good atmosphere. *Daily | Via delle Terme 79 | tel. 05 77 23 65 68 | www.vinattieri.net | Moderate*

WHERE TO STAY

BERNINI

A simple and affordable hotel, very centrally located in the old town. With ⚝ terrace. *10 rooms | Via della Sapienza 15 | tel. 05 77 28 90 47 | www.albergo bernini.com | Budget*

PALAZZO FANI MIGNANELLI

In the old town, pretty rooms of various sizes in an old palazzo. *11 rooms | Via Banchi di Sopra 15 | tel. 05 77 28 35 66 | www.residenzadepoca.it | Budget–Expensive*

SIENA

INFORMATION

Piazza del Campo 56 | tel. 05 77 28 05 51 | www.terresiena.it

WHERE TO GO

LE CRETE AND THE SOUTH
(182 B2) (*∅ F–G6*)

Ash-grey hills of clay soil, slopes suddenly torn by deep ravines, ridges dramatically furrowed by erosion – it is with this landscape, called the *Crete,* that the region south-east of Siena begins its journey to the Benedictine abbey *Monte Oliveto Maggiore.*

Further south, on a hill, is the medieval *Montalcino,* home of the excellent wine Brunello di Montalcino. You can choose from a selection of this wine at the lovely *Caffè Fiaschetteria Italiana* on the *Piazza del Popolo.* 10km/6mi to the south, the monks still sing Gregorian masses in the atmospheric surroundings of the *Sant' Antimo* abbey dating from the Carolingian period.

Travelling east, the route takes you to the enchanting little Renaissance town of *Pienza,* which is also full of atmosphere in the evening. The eight stylish rooms of the hotel *Arca di Pienza (Via San Gregorio 19 | tel. 05 78 74 94 26 | www.arcadipienza. it | Budget)* offer a hospitable welcome. Nearby, on a solitary clay mountain, is the fortified ⚒ *Monticchiello,* the annual stage for INSIDER TIP▶ one of Italy's most interesting theatre events: at the end of July, the villagers enact a play they write themselves *(www.teatropovero.it).*

Montepulciano (pop. 14,000), place of origin of the Vino Nobile di Montepulciano and the venue of interesting cultural events, presents a wonderful setting with its steep, narrow streets and a beautifully arranged square with medieval palaces. Resplendent at the foot of the hill is the 16th century pilgrimage church *Madonna di San Biagio.* With so many good trattorias, it is difficult to decide where to go. One tip is the cosy and popular *Osteria Acquacheta (closed Tue | Via del Teatro 2 | tel. 05 78 71 70 86 | Budget–Moderate)* with tasty soups, succulent meat and, naturally, excellent wine.

MASSA MARITTIMA (182 B2) (*∅ F6*)

The town (pop. 10,000) on a hill belonging to the metalliferous Colline Metallifere is famous for its beautiful Romanesque Gothic *Cattedrale di San Cerbone.* Mining for ore, silver and copper has been the basis of the town's livelihood since the

ART GARDENS IN TUSCANY

Tuscany's glorious landscape inspires the aesthetic senses of artists and art connoisseurs. The artist Niki de Saint Phalle is a case in point with her sculpture garden *Giardino dei Tarocchi (see p. 105)* in Maremma. This also applies to the Swiss artist Daniel Spoerri and many of his colleagues for whom the South Tuscan countryside provides the ideal setting for their works, which can be viewed in *Giardino di Daniel Spoerri* in Seggiano *(Easter–Oct Tue–Sun 11am–8pm | www.danielspoerri.org).* How well contemporary art fits in this arcadia is also visible in *Parco delle Sculture del Chianti in Pievasciata,* Castellina in Chianti *(Easter–Oct daily 10am–sunset | www.chiantisculpturepark.it).*

The pilgrimage church Madonna di San Biagio in the hills of Montepulciano

Middle Ages. The *Museo della Miniera (guided tours April–Sept Tue–Sun 10am, 11am, noon, 12.45pm, 3.30pm, 4.30pm, 5pm and 5.45pm, Oct–March 10am, 11am, noon, 3pm, 4pm and 4.30pm,)* in a former mine provides information on this subject.

MONTE AMIATA (182 B2) (𝄞 F6)
The crests of the densely forested volcano, which is 1738m/5702ft high, dominate the landscape in the south of Tuscany and are a popular hiking area. Old villages and castles such as Arcidosso, Santa Fiora, Castell'Azzara, Piancastagnaio and Abbadia San Salvatore are dotted around the summit.

SAN GALGANO (182 B1) (𝄞 F6)
The romantic *ruins* of this 13th century Cistercian abbey, one of the first examples of Gothic sacral architecture in Tuscany,

provide the spectacular stage for concerts during the summer. A small Romanesque church, with beautiful interior masonry and frescoes by Ambrogio Lorenzetti, forms part of the complex.

SAN GIMIGNANO ★ (182 B1) (𝄞 F6)
Today, just 13 of the once 72 towers remain and keep lookout over the little medieval town (pop. 8000) – and you can climb up two of the towers. Apart from enjoying the atmosphere in the pretty squares and alleys, you should also visit the *cathedral* and the *Sant'Agostino* church with frescoes by the famous Benozzo Gozzoli (15th century). It is best to find a place to stay in the gorgeous surrounding countryside, e.g. about 8km/5mi to north-west in *Cellole* in the *Casale del Cotone* country house *(12 rooms | tel. 05 77 94 32 36 | www.casaledelcotone. com | Moderate).*

VOLTERRA (182 B1–2) (*♬ F6*)

The town (pop. 15,000) preserves rich traces of the great cultural eras of the past 3000 years – seen for instance in the remains of the city walls and the *Arco Etrusco* – and has one, one of the best museums in Italy about Etruscan culture, *Museo Guarnacci (Nov–mid March daily 9am–1.30pm, mid March–Oct 9am–7pm)*. The archaeological sites also include an ancient Roman theatre. Medieval streets and buildings still lend the town a distinctive character. Turning and polishing alabaster is a traditional craft in Volterra, and there are plenty of shops and ateliers for you to browse round.

THE TUSCAN COAST

ETRUSCAN RIVIERA
(182 A1–2) (*♬ E5–6*)

The Etruscan Riviera begins in the south of Livorno, taking its name from the many former settlements found there. A highlight is ⚜ *Populonia*, which has an Etruscan necropolis overlooking the INSIDERTIP *Golfo di Baratti*. Camping sites are dotted along the coast in the shade of the pines. In between you will discover coastal towns, such as the elegant *Castiglioncello*. Towards Vada, the cliff beaches of Catiglioncello join up with the light sandy beaches INSIDERTIP *spiagge bianche* of *Rosignano Solvay*, which are open to the public.

LIVORNO (182 A1) (*♬ E5*)

If you wish to get away from the tourist hotspots and hustle and bustle of harbour life, you should visit Livorno (pop. 160,000) and enjoy the typical Livornese fish soup *cacciucco*, for example in the rustic *Osteria La Barrocciaia (closed Sun/Mon | Piazza Cavallotti 13 | tel. 05 86 88 26 37 | Budget)* in the market square or in the small seafood restaurant *Osteria del Mare (closed Thu | Borgo dei Cappuccini 5 | tel. 05 86 88 10 20 | Moderate)* near the harbour.

MAREMMA
(182 B3) (*♬ F6–7*)

Apart from the hilly hinterland of Grosseto, Maremma also boasts some lovely, transformed coastal areas, formerly malaria-infested swamps and grazing land for wild horses and cattle. The *Parco Regionale della Maremma*, a nature reserve south of Grosseto with the estuary area around the river Ombrone, the mountain range Monti dell'Uccellina and its coast, sometimes rocky, sometimes with long unspoilt sandy beaches (only accessible on foot), retains its primordial nature. Excursions are available from *Alberese* in the centre of the park.

Punta Ala has become an expensive tourist resort. Looming up from the sea on the southern horizon is *Monte Argentario* (635m/2083ft), with pretty harbour towns such as *Porto Santo Stefano,* the fine *Port'Ercole* and the little lagoon town of *Orbetello.*

To the east of the largely modern provincial capital of *Grosseto,* you reach the tuff stone mountains of south Tuscany with their ruggedly romantic little towns built high up on rock plateaus such as ⚜ *Pitigliano, Sorano* or *Sovana* with interesting Etruscan rock tombs. The spa resort of *Saturnia* is here. You can enjoy its hot sulphurous water in either one of the exclusive spa hotels *(Terme di Saturnia | 140 rooms | tel. 05 64 60 01 11 | www.termedisaturnia.it | Expensive)* or ● free of charge under the INSIDERTIP hot waterfalls, the *Cascata del Molino* (3km/ 1.8mi towards Montemerano).

Near *Capalbio*, where Italy's smart set likes to meet, is the dream INSIDERTIP

Giardino dei Tarocchi (April–mid Oct daily 2.30pm–7.30pm, Nov–March 1st Sat in the month 9am–1pm | www.nikidesaint.com) with Niki de Saint Phalle's colourful and exuberant sculptures inspired by the tarot symbols.

PISA (182 A1) (*[M] E5*)

Hardly any other monument in Pisa (pop. 88,000) is as famous as the *Leaning Tower*. Its tilt started quite soon after its construction in 1173 on the shifting sands of a former estuary. After lengthy stabilisation measures, it is now possible to climb it again – for 15 euros! – *(April, May, Sept daily 8.30am–8pm, June–Aug 8.30am–10.30pm, Oct 9am–7pm, Nov–March 10am–5pm; no children under 8 | registration only possible via internet: www.opapisa.it)*. It stands, or rather leans on the ★ ☆ *Campo dei Miracoli* (Field of Miracles), as does the magnificent Romanesque *cathedral*, the *baptistry* and the *Camposanto,* a cemetery full of precious sculptures and frescoes from the town's golden age. Good food and a lively atmosphere are available in the *Osteria dei Cavalieri (closed Sat lunch and Sunday | Via San Frediano 16 | tel. 0 50 58 08 58 | www.osteriacavalieri.pisa.it | Budget–Moderate)*.

VERSILIA (180 A6) (*[M] E5*)

Versilia denotes the fashionable upper region of the Tuscan coast from Liguria to Viareggio: 25km/15.5mi of fine sandy beaches, shady pines, holiday resorts, villas and hotels, and in the background the steep ★ ☆ *Apuan Alps*. For hundreds of years, people have been quarrying enormous blocks of marble from the mountain. You can visit the marble quarries *(cave)* and workshops of *Carrara* and also visit the especially pretty *Pietrasanta*. Elegant bathing resorts on the Versilia coast are *Forte dei Marmi* and *Viareggio*.

The angels are not too sure either. Is the tower going to topple over or not?

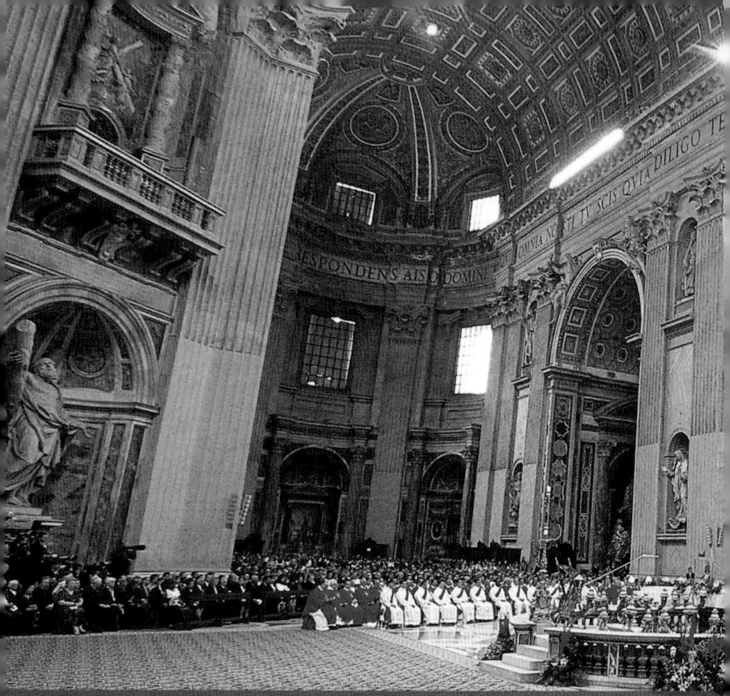

ROME AND THE APENNINES

Since the completion of the motorway to L'Aquila, the inhabitants of Rome have discovered new destinations: they now visit the large Abruzzo National Park and its wildlife, the rugged mountains full of attractive villages, or they go skiing on the Gran Sasso, which at 2912m/9554ft is the highest summit of the Apennines. Located further south, Molise nonetheless belongs to this part of Italy, both geographically and culturally. It shares the Adriatic coast's wide beaches and coastal towns with Abruzzo. The centre includes Rome, the city swathed in history and myths, and the green melancholic Lazio: together with Rome the ancient heartland of the Roman Empire, which embraces the historic towns of Tarchna (today Tarquinia) and Caisra (today Cerveteri) home of the Etruscans, the mysterious, highly advanced civilisation that inhabited central Italy before the Romans.

L'AQUILA

(183 E3) (*H7*) **The route to this pretty medieval university town (pop. 65,000), which leads from Rome or the Adriatic coast via Teramo, passes through a surprisingly impressive mountain pano-**

Photo: St Peter's Basilica in the Vatican

Bears and wolves in Abruzzo, the Adriatic and Apennines, the vibrant capital and the ancient civilisation of the Etruscans

rama; the imposing Gran Sasso massif looks down on L'Aquila, the capital of Abruzzo.

In 1240, Count Conrad IV of Hohenstaufen set up an outpost here against Papal Rome. In the ensuing period, the town nonetheless came under the influence of the Papal State, and this is still visible today in the many churches. The ruins of the Roman theatre in *Amiternum* 9km/ 5.5mi to the north-west and the *Santa Maria ad Cryptas* church in Fossa, 10km/ 6mi to the south-east – whose precious medieval frescoes were damaged during the severe earthquake on 6 April 2009 – bear witness to the earlier settlements here and their cultural creativity.

During the earthquake, 308 people were killed and 30,000 lost their homes. The beautiful old town of L'Aquila is still secured by barriers and supports. Many of the houses are vacant and have not been repaired. That does not mean that you should avoid the town, however. On the contrary, the Aquilans regard interested visitors as heralds of the new beginning; thankfully the ornate façades of their churches were largely spared from

MUSEO NAZIONALE D'ABRUZZO

Located in a park, the *Castello* is a powerful fortress built in the Spanish style of the 16th century. Until the severe damage it suffered during the earthquake, it housed an extensive art collection with works by Abruzzo artists spanning from the Middle Ages to the present. The ad-

Harvesting saffron in L'Aquila is hard physical work

damage. Colourful new buildings have been constructed on the outskirts of the town. Some of the construction projects have tried to implement innovative eco-architectural criteria, one example being: ☺ *www.pescomaggiore.org*

SIGHTSEEING

FONTANA DELLE 99 CANNELLE

The 'Fountain of 99 Spouts', constructed in 1272, is a huge fountain with 99 stone masks that spout water. They recount the story of L'Aquila's foundation, according to which the town originally consisted of 99 castles, each one of which had a church, a square and a fountain. *Via Jacopo*

ministrators are currently putting together a provisional museum location in a former abattoir.

SAN BERNARDINO DI SIENA

The highlight of this richly decorated church is the beautiful Renaissance façade by Cola d'Amatrice; owing to the earthquake, it is not possible to enter the church at the moment. *Via di San Bernardino*

SANTA MARIA DI COLLEMAGGIO ★

This sacral building is regarded as one of the most splendid examples of Romanesque architecture in Abruzzo, due to its grandiose façade and three Romanesque Gothic rosette windows and three Romanesque portals. Whilst the façade can already be admired in its full splendour again, the interior with scaffolding and the windows still bear traces of the earthquake. *Piazza di Collemaggio*

FOOD & DRINK

LA CONCA ALLA VECCHIA POSTA
Not far from Santa Maria di Collemaggio, you can savour Abruzzese delicacies, such as homemade pasta with saffron and lamb. *Closed Sun evening and Mon | Via Caldora 12 | tel. 08 62 40 52 11 | Budget–Moderate*

SHOPPING

An ideal souvenir is the famous soft *torrone* made of nougat and honey from *Fratelli Nurzia – Fabbrica del Torrone dal 1835(Piazza Duomo 74)*. You can also buy the highly acclaimed L'Aquila saffron called *zafferano di Navelli* from the local grocery stores.

WHERE TO STAY

LA COMPAGNIA DEL VIAGGIATORE
Well-managed modern guesthouse with good restaurant and small pool located out in the countryside 6km/3.5mi to the north-west. *33 rooms | Canzasassa district | SS80 | tel. 08 62 31 36 27 | www.compagniadelviaggiatore.it | Budget*

INFORMATION

Container kiosk at the car park of the rugby stadium Acquasanta in the east of the town | tel. 08 62 41 08 08 | www.abruzzoturismo.it

WHERE TO GO

ATRI (183 E3) (*J7*)
The small medieval town (pop. 11,000) on the ridge of a hill 12km/7.5mi from the Adriatic has a very interesting Romanesque Gothic cathedral *Santa Maria Assunta* (13th century) with prized frescoes. It is

MARCO POLO HIGHLIGHTS

★ **Santa Maria di Collemaggio in L'Aquila**
Abruzzo's most beautiful Romanesque building with an impressive façade → p. 108

★ **Parco Nazionale d'Abruzzo, Lazio e Molise**
Wolves and walks → p. 111

★ **San Clemente Abbey in Casauria**
Masterful Romanesque stonework → p. 112

★ **Forum Romanum**
The ancient world empire was governed from here → p. 114

★ **Vatican museums**
The largest museum complex in the world → p. 116

★ **Tivoli**
Roman villas of the Emperor Hadrian, theatre, temple, spas and the most beautiful park in Italy before the gates of Rome → p. 120

★ **Tarquinia**
Etruscan site with necropolis and museum → p. 121

★ **Sistine Chapel in the Vatican**
The famous depiction of the Book of Genesis by Michelangelo → p. 116

Mountain villages nestled in the lush green slopes of the Gran Sasso

also popular for its liquorice specialities and the impressive eroded rock formations on the way to Teramo, called *calanchi, balze* or *bolge*.

BOMINACO (183 E4) (*Ø H7*)
The sleepy hilltop village about 25km/15.5mi south-east of L'Aquila has two art highlights: firstly, the Biblical scenes from the 13th/14th century still in good condition displayed in the frescoes that richly adorn the *San Pellegrino* church and, secondly, the *Santa Maria Assunta* built in the most beautiful Romanesque style.

CHIETI ✂ (183 F3) (*Ø J7*)
Built on the summit of a hill, the provincial town (pop. 55,000) merits a visit in particular for its historic centre and the view it affords of the Maiella massif and the sea. There is a vibrant town centre with shops and cafés on and around the *Corso Marrucino,* as well as the remains of three Roman temples, an amphitheatre,

spa, a Gothic Baroque *cathedral* and Abruzzo's leading *archaeological museum (Tue–Sun 9am–8pm | Villa Frigerj | Via Villa Comunale 2)* with prehistoric and Roman exhibits, such as the famous 'Warrior of Capestrano'.

In the nearby *Guardiagrele,* one of the *borghi* 'beautiful villages in Italy' *(www.borghitalia.it),* a well-stocked handicraft market sells wrought-iron work, copper items and jewellery *(Mostra dell'Artigianato Artistico Abruzzese | www.artigianatoabruzzese.it). Villa Maiella* is a good place to stay, and its first-rate Abruzzo cuisine is especially recommendable, *(14 rooms | closed Sun evening and Mon | Via Sette Dolori 30 | tel. 08 71 80 93 62 | www.villamaiella.it | Moderate).*

GRAN SASSO D'ITALIA
(183 E3) (*Ø H–J7*)
The 'great rock of Italy' includes the highest peak of the Apennines, the *Monte Corno* (2912m/9554ft), tunnelled through by

the 10km/6mi long motorway from L'Aquila to Teramo. Those who want to enjoy some wonderful landscapes should opt for the ❄ scenic route (SS 80) on the north-west side of the massif, past the ancient Sabine town of Amiternum towards Montorio al Vomano. From here, the road runs along the coast and goes past the commanding Romanesque abbeys of *San Clemente al Vomano* and *Santa Maria di Propezzano*.

Extending on the south side of the Gran Sasso is the impressive landscape of the *Campo Imperatore* plateau. In *Assergi*, you will find the *Park Office (Via del Convento 1 | tel. 0 86 26 05 22 47 | www. gransassolagapark.it)*, which provides information about walking and skiing, flora and fauna. In the picturesque mountain village of INSIDER TIP *Santo Stefano di Sessanio*, some 27 guest rooms are available throughout the village, organised by *Sextantio (tel. 08 62 89 91 12 | www. sextantio.it | Moderate–Expensive)*, a so-called *albergo diffuso,* a new method for revitalising the old mountain villages, in rustic style, but very elegantly done – which is reflected in the prices. The six nice holiday flats in the centre of the village offer a more inexpensive alternative, *Residenza la Torre (tel. 0 86 28 94 48 | www.residenza-latorre.it | Budget)*.

The Navelli plain in the south, famous for cultivating saffron extends betweens the stupendous mountains of Abruzzo – providing a magnificent backdrop for the picturesque village of *Navelli*. You can stay in the hospitable *Abruzzo Segreto* B & B *(4 rooms | Via San Girolamo 3 | tel. 08 62 95 94 47 | www.abruzzo-segreto.it | Budget)*.

MOLISE (183 F5) *(𝕄 J8)*

Off the beaten track, a visit to the Molise, the second smallest region in Italy, takes you through pastoral landscapes, with

traces of prehistoric and ancient settlements. The region's capital *Campobasso* (pop. 20,000) has an old town full of little alleyways, an imposing castle, and an INSIDER TIP enchanting procession with the local children on Corpus Christi, as well as a number of very good restaurants, e.g. *Miseria e Nobiltà (closed Sun | Via Sant'Agostino Abate 16 | tel. 0 87 49 42 68 | Budget–Moderate)*.

Isernia (pop. 18,000) is world famous among palaeontologists. It was here that they found the oldest traces of early human life; the remains of hunting trophies and fireplaces are at least 730,000 years old *(Museo Paleolitico Nazionale | daily 8.30am–7pm, closed 1st and 3rd Mon in the month | Corso Marcelli)*.

PARCO NAZIONALE D'ABRUZZO, LAZIO E MOLISE ★

(183 E4) *(𝕄 H–J 7–8)*

This approximately 232mi² nature park is one of the most famous in Italy – thanks to its wild, unspoilt landscape and its unique wildlife, which includes wolves and small brown bears from Abruzzo. There are 150 trails on which visitors can explore this austere landscape; four visitor centres with exhibitions and wildlife.

The focal point in the park is *Pescasseroli,* which is also a winter ski resort. In addition to the campsites and mountain chalets, you will also find hotels in Pescasseroli, e.g. in *Il Bucaneve (15 rooms | Viale Colli dell'Oro | tel. 08 63 91 00 98 | www.hotel bucaneve.net | Budget–Moderate),* ideal for the summer and winter season. Information: *Via Principe di Napoli | tel. 08 63 91 04 61 | www.pescasseroli.net, www.parcoabruzzo.it*

PESCARA (183 F3) *(𝕄 J7)*

This large urban centre (pop. 130,000) on Abruzzo's flat Adriatic coast offers a contrast to the mountains: there is no old town worth mentioning, but instead shopping, beaches, innumerable hotels, beautiful beach promenades and seafood restaurants. Pescara's dried cod specialities *(baccalà)* are particularly good in *Taverna 58 (closed Sat lunch and Sun | Corso Manthone 58 | tel. 0 85 69 07 24 | www.taverna58.it | Budget–Moderate);* if there is a table, an excellent gourmet address directly on the sea is: *Café les Paillotes (closed Sun, Mon | Piazza Le Laudi 2 | Lungomare Cristoforo Colomco | tel. 08 56 18 09 | Moderate–Expensive).* Outside the town, the best beaches in the north are *Silvi Marina,* in the south *Lido Riccio* and *Lido dei Saraceni.*

SULMONA (183 E4) (*⌕ J7*)

The impressive Maiella mountain range rises above this delightful little town (pop. 24,000), popular for its tradition of *confetti,* glazed almonds. In addition to the many churches, picturesque streets and squares, it is the elegant Gothic and Renaissance 15th century palace and church complex *Santa Maria Annunziata* that deserves special attention.

You can eat extraordinarily well in the traditional family restaurant INSIDER TIP *Taverna de Li Caldora (closed Sun evening, Mon lunch and Tue | Piazza Umberto I | tel. 0 86 44 11 39 | Moderate)* in the pretty village of ⠶ *Pacentro* 8km/5mi to the east. A scenically impressive trip leads through the ⠶ *Gola del Sagittario* gorge to the very charming mountain village of *Scanno.* For those wishing to spend a bit longer in this magnificent setting, a good choice of accommodation is the organic farm ☺ *Le Prata (5 rooms | Le Prata | tel. 08 64 57 83 03 | www.agriturismoleprata.it | Budget).* On the way from Sulmona to the coast, you will see in a garden the splendid Romanesque abbey ★ *San Clemente in Casauria (Mon–Sat 8am–2pm | www.sanclementeacasauria.beniculturali.it).*

TERMOLI (184 B2) (*⌕ K8*)

The picturesque medieval town of Termoli (pop. 21,000) juts out into the sea on a narrow spur just above the ankle of Italy's 'boot'. There is always a lot of activity in the fishing harbour. It is from here that the ferries depart for *Isole Tremiti,* a popular group of islands just off Apulia's Gargano promontory. The coast up towards Pescara between Vasto and Ortona is called INSIDER TIP *Costa dei Trabucchi,* taking its name from the wooden fishing structures suspended above the water, which are a ubiquitous sight here.

ROME (ROMA)

▨▨ **MAP INSIDE BACK COVER**
▨▨ (182 C4) (*⌕ G8*) **Rome's appeal is in its unique mix of ancient past, dynamic present and a mild climate that allows much of life to be al fresco.**

> **CITY** **WHERE TO START?**
> Piazza del Popolo (127 D2) (*⌕ X5*): From here, it is possible to explore the centre on foot (Metro A, Flaminio). You can work your way south along the Via del Corso (Spanish Steps, Trevi Fountain, Forum Romanum, and Colosseum). If you decide to take the car to Rome, you look for a car park near your hotel accommodation *www.my parking.eu/parcheggio_rome.php (3 euros/hr).* From the main station, Stazione Termini, there are connections with the underground Metro A and Metro B as well as numerous city buses *(ticket 1 euro, single day ticket 4 euros).*

In the centre of this metropolis (pop. 2,800,000) awe-inspiring ruins bear testimony to the city's time as the pulsating heart of the Roman Empire, while magnificent churches and palazzi from the medieval, Renaissance and Baroque periods provide equally clear evidence of its role as a centre of Christianity. Enthroned above it all is the ostentatiously monumental ⚡ *Vittoriano* 'altar of the fatherland', offering a breathtaking panorama from the roof café – after all, Rome is also Italy's capital.

A fresh wind is blowing through the city: new museums for contemporary art have been inaugurated (*MACRO* and *MAXXI*), first-class concerts, exhibitions and film festivals are now regular features in the lively cultural scene, and besides well-established, traditional trattorias and local bars, there are sophisticated restaurants and trendy lounge bars, and in addition to the classically elegant boutiques, there are also stores of a younger style. Walk through the fashionable areas such as the serene Trastevere and vibrant Testaccio

or to the elegant Piazza del Popolo. It is not that surprising to see crowds at Rome's magnificent Baroque fountain Fontana di Trevi. It is believed that anyone who throws a coin in here will return to Rome again one day. MARCO POLO's 'Rome' guide provides a more detailed description of the city.

SIGHTSEEING

ARA PACIS AUGUSTAE (U C2) (𝄐 d3)
Ancient meets modern: In 2006, the American architect Richard Meier designed a modern cover building over this magnificent piece of sculptural art, the carved altar to peace in honour of Augustus (9 BC), also the venue for art exhibitions. *Tue–Sun 9am–7pm | Lungotevere in Augusta | www.arapacis.it*

BOAT TRIPS
Cruises through Rome on the Tiber run from April–Oct, leaving several times a day from the Sant'Angelo bridge and on the Tiber island *(www.battellidiroma.it)*.

Mix of old and new: Rome's residents carry on with life between its the ancient buildings

Capitoline museums: home to the famous Roman she-wolf

FORUM ROMANUM ★
(U E4–5) (*ØØ f–g 6–8*)

The Roman Empire was once governed from here. Today, it is an impressive park of ruins: the remains of once magnificent residences on the Palatine, of temples, markets and triumphal arches. Each emperor built his own forum. *Daily 8.30am–1 hour before sunset | entrances Via San Gregorio and Largo della Salaria Vecchia | archeoroma.beniculturali.it*

CAPITOLINE MUSEUMS
(MUSEI CAPITOLINI) (U D4) (*ØØ f6*)

In addition to the Roman copies of Greek and Hellenic statues, the palaces on the wonderful Campidoglio Square also exhibit the legendary Capitoline she-wolf from 6 BC. Offering a fascinating contrast is the exhibition of ancient sculptures from the Capitoline museums INSIDER TIP in the dramatic setting of a disused power station (*Centrale Montemartini | Tue–Sun 9am–7pm* (O) *| Via Ostiense 106 | www. centralemontemartini.org). Tue–Sun 9am–8pm | Piazza del Campidoglio | www.musei capitolini.org*

CHURCHES ●

Among the many outstanding churches that are to be found in Rome, the capital of Christianity, are also the four patriarchal basilicas: *San Giovanni in Laterano* ((O) *(ØØ j8) | Piazza San Giovanni),* the oldest early Christian papal cathedral (consecrated AD 324) and Catholic mother church, richly decorated with marble, gold and statues, then of course the largest Christian church there is: *St Peter's Basilica* ((U A3) *(ØØ A4–5) | Piazza San Pietro)* built over the grave of St Peter; the third is *San Paolo fuori le Mura* ((O) *| Via Ostiense)* built over the burial place of St Paul; its splendid interior is subdivided into five naves and also includes a particularly beautiful cloister; the fourth is dedicated to the Virgin Mary *Santa Maria Maggiore* ((U F4) (*m h5*) | *Piazza Santa Maria Maggiore),* is also of early Christian origin, and is famous for its fantastic apse mosaic.

COLOSSEUM (COLOSSEO)
(U E–F5) (*m g7*)

This gigantic amphitheatre could hold about 70,000 people. At its inauguration in AD 80, Emperor Titus ordered 100 days of non-stop, bloodthirsty games. Five million people visit the amphitheatre every year and continue to enter during the restoration work, which will finish in 2015; the restoration work is being financed by the shoe company Tod's. *Daily 8.30am– 1 hour before sunset, end of March–Aug to 7.15pm | Piazza del Colosseo*

MAXXI (O)

The audacious and stylishly dynamic building by star architect Zaha Hadid for collections of modern art, architecture and photography in the midst of tenement buildings in the north of the Flaminio residential area has been representing 21st century Rome since 2010. *Tue–Fri and Sun 10am–7pm, Sat 11am–10pm | Via Guido Reni 4/A | www.fondazionemaxxi.it*

MUSEO NAZIONALE ROMANO

The most comprehensive collection of art from Roman antiquity distributed between four different exhibition sites: *Palazzo Massimo* ((U F3) (*m j5*) | *Largo di Villa Peretti 1),Palazzo Altemps((U C3) (*m d5*) | Piazza Sant'Apollinare 44),Crypta Balbi* ((U D4) (*m e6*) | *Via delle Botteghe Oscure 31),Terme di Diocleziano((U F2–3)* (*m h4*) | *Viale De Nicola 79);* the collection includes the excavations of the grandiose imperial villa *Domus Aurea* ((U F5) (*m h7*) | *phone booking, tel. 06 39 96 7700)* in the Colosseum. *Every Tue–Sun 9am–7.45pm | archeoroma.beniculturali.it*

PANTHEON
(U D3) (*m e5*)

This temple to the gods dating back to AD 27 is the only ancient domed structure still in existence; many Italian kings and the artist Raphael are interred within the impressive interior. In the evening, the square is a popular meeting place. *Mon– Sat 8.30am–7.30pm, Sun 9am–6pm | Piazza della Rotonda*

ST PETER'S BASILICA
(SAN PIETRO) (U A3) (*m a4–5*)

You enter the most important sanctuary of Catholicism via the harmonious square, created by Rome's master of the Baroque style, Gianlorenzo Bernini, 1667. Bramante, Carlo Maderna and Michelangelo worked on the gigantic cathedral, the *Basilica di San Pietro,* which can hold 60,000 people. From its ✹ dome (entrance), you have a splendid view. Inside are the relics of St Peter and St Paul and among the many artworks Michelangelo's 'Pietà'. *Daily 7am–7pm | Piazza San Pietro*

SQUARES

The *Campo de' Fiori* (U C4) (*m d6*), 'field of flowers' – during the Middle Ages it was a cattle pasture and a place of execution – today it is one of the most beautiful Roman fruit, vegetable and flower markets; if you want a quick snack, go to number 22 and try the delicious *pizza bianca* from the *Forno Campo de Fiori* bakery. The elongated *Piazza Navona* (U C3) (*m d5*) boasts the magnificent Baroque *Fontana dei quattro fiumi* (fountain of the four rivers) by Bernini and flower-laden balconies, street artists and street cafés. A broad, stage-like staircase the *Scalinata Trinità dei Monti,* the (Spanish Steps) at the ✹ *Piazza di Spagna* (U D2) (*m e–f 3–4*) provides a popular place to sit for tired tourists and young people.

TRASTEVERE (U B–C 5–6) (_ c8)
Once known mainly for its narrow, winding streets and traditional-folksy character, Trastevere has now become the in-place to live for members of the cultural scene and well-to-do foreigners, and its creative shops, bars, cafés and trattorias make it a popular nightlife area.

VATICAN MUSEUMS ★ (U A2) (_ a4)
With 14 museums, the Vatican City has the largest museum complex in the world; an immeasurable abundance of masterpieces from antiquity and leading artists such as Giotto, da Vinci, Caravaggio, Raphael and many others. The highlight has to be the ★ _Sistine Chapel (Cappella Sistina)_ with Michelangelo's paintings based on the Book of Genesis (1508–1512) on the ceiling of the large chapel, still used by Catholic popes today. **INSIDER TIP** A tip when visiting the chapel: arrive early in the morning when it opens. That will give you half an hour to wander through the museum almost on your own – soon afterwards it will be teeming with people. It is generally worth reserving a ticket (_biglietteriamusei.vatican.va_),
in order to avoid having to queue. _Mon–Sat 9am–6pm, in spring and autumn Fri also 7pm–11pm, entrance only possible via online reservation, 15 euros entrance plus 4 euros reservation fee, entrance free on the last Sun of the month | main entrance Viale del Vaticano | mv.vatican.va_

VIA APPIA ANTICA AND CATACOMBS (0) ●
In the lovely archaeological park on the south-east border of Rome, you can easily imagine how the most important road towards the south of the Roman Empire must have looked (on Sundays car-free pedestrian paradise); the site encompasses the subterranean burial chambers, the _Calixtus (closed Wed)_, _Sebastian (closed Sun)_ and the large _Domitilla catacombs (closed Tue)_. _All 9am–noon and 2pm–5pm | www.parcoappiaantica.it_

VILLA BORGHESE (U E–F1) (_ f–g 1–2)
While wandering through this popular public park, you will come to the _Galleria Nazionale dell'Arte Moderna_, which is well worth seeing and has an **INSIDER TIP** inviting terrace café, the Etruscan museum _Villa Giulia_, the cinema centre _Casa del Cinema_ and the _Museo di Galleria Borghese (phone, visit only by appointment, tel. 0 63 28 10 | bzw.www.ticketeria.it | Mon 1pm–7pm, Tue–Sun 9am–7pm | www.galleriaborghese.it)_ with the famous marble sculptures by Bernini. A highlight in all senses is the ⟳ _Belvedere Pincio_ overlooking the Piazza del Popolo.

FOOD & DRINK

CAFÉS
Historic figures such as Byron, Goethe, Keats and Wagner have had coffee in the _Antico Caffè Greco_ on the elegant _Via Condotti 86_ (U D2) (_ f4); Rome's most famous ice cream parlour is the _Gelateria_

Giolitti (U D3) *(⊞ e5)* in the *Via Uffici del Vicario 40;* a classic favourite is the art nouveau *Caffè della Pace* (U C3) *(⊞ d5)* in the *Via della Pace 3.*

CASA COPPELLE (U C3) *(⊞ d–e5)*

A cheerfully elegant trattoria not far from the Piazza Navona with local homemade pasta dishes and excellent meat. *Daily | Piazza delle Coppelle 49 | tel. 06 68 89 17 07 | www.casacoppelle.it | Moderate*

IL MARGUTTA RISTO-ARTE
(U D2) *(⊞ e3)*

Vegetarian lunch buffet, imaginative vegetable dishes, Wi-Fi bar and art events in the tranquil artists' street not far from the hubbub of Via del Corso. *Daily | Via Margutta 118 | tel. 06 32 65 05 77 | www.ilmarguttavegetariano.it | Budget– Moderate*

NECCI DEL 1924 (O)

Café, trattoria with modern inspired Roman cuisine, meeting place for aperitifs in the popular Pigneto district behind the station. *Daily | Via Fanfulla da Lodi 68 | tel. 06 97 60 15 52 | www.necci1924.com | Moderate*

OLIVER GLOWIG (O) *(⊞ f1)*

Two Germans hold top ranking in the Roman gourmet scene with their modern interpretation of Mediterranean cuisine. Heinz Beck in the Hilton and Glowig in Aldrovandi Villa Borghese are both very highly regarded. *Closed Sun, Mon | Via Ulisse Aldrovandi 15 | tel. 06 3 21 61 26 | Expensive*

SHOPPING

The best fashion designers have their top-quality shops on and around the *Via Condotti* (U D2) *(⊞ e–f4);* *Via del Corso* (U D2–3) *(⊞ e–f 3–5)* offers more variety. There is a flea market at the *Porta Portese* (U C6) *(⊞ d8)* in Trastevere on Sundays.

A permanent guest in Caffè della Pace

ENTERTAINMENT

Superb aperitifs and cocktails are served in the garden bar *Stravinskij* in the luxury hotel *De Russie* ((U D1) *(⊞ e3)* | *Via del Babuino 9).* An ever-popular choice among the hip places to meet for drinks is the Trastevere: *Freni e Frizioni* ((U C5) *(⊞ d7)* | *Via del Politeama 4–6);* alternative bar crowd in *Monte Testaccio* (O). Good range of music venues in the *Auditorium (www. auditorium.com).* A highlight for jazz musicians and jazz lovers: *Casa del Jazz (Viale di Porta Ardeatina 55 | www.casajazz.it).* Rich cultural programme during the summer *(estate romana | www.estateromana. comune.roma.it).*

ROME (ROMA)

For B & B rooms, see *www.bedandbreak-fastroma.com,* apartments *www.trianon borgopio.it* and *www.palazzo-olivia.it*

ANDREINA (U F3) (*ⅲ j5*)
Simple, tastefully conceived hotel on the fourth floor of an ancient building; friendly staff and good position. *20 rooms | Via Giovanni Amendola 77 | tel. 0 6 48 18 6 57 | www.hotelandreina.com | Budget–Moderate*

FONTANA DI TREVI
(U D3) (*ⅲ f4–5*)
Charming hotel opposite the Trevi fountain. *27 rooms | Piazza di Trevi 96 | tel. 0 66 79 10 56 | www.hotelfontana-trevi. com | Expensive*

IQ HOTEL ROMA ⅿ
(U F3) (*ⅲ h5*)
Centrally located, modern, comfortable city hotel with a full breakfast buffet and roof terrace. *88 rooms | Via Firenze 8 | tel. 0 64 88 04 65 | www.iqhotelroma.it | Moderate–Expensive*

MEDITERRANEO (U F3) (*ⅲ h5*)
Not far from the main station a comfortable hotel in 1930s style with original art deco furniture and a beautiful ⅿ roof terrace. *251 rooms | Via Cavour 15 | tel. 0 64 81 47 98 | www.romehotelmediterraneo. it | Moderate–Expensive*

Numerous information points in the town (first and foremost the new *Visitor Centre* in Via Fori Imperiali), at the airports and at the station Stazione Termini. *Tel. 06 06 08 | www.turismoroma.it, www. roma-antiqua.de, www.romaculta.it, www. romaepiu.it*

ABBEY OF MONTECASSINO
(183 E5) (*ⅲ H8*)
Founded by St Benedict of Norcia in AD 529, this abbey in Cassino is the oldest Benedictine monastery complex; it was bombed in 1944 but has since been beautifully restored.

INSIDER TIP BRACCIANO AND CERVETERI (182 C4) (*ⅲ G7*)
A beautiful ⅿ panoramic route leads around the crater lake, Lago di Bracciano, north-west of Rome, through picturesque villages to the little town of *Bracciano* (pop. 11,000) and its Renaissance castle *Castello Orsini-Odescalchi.* One of the most interesting Etruscan necropolises, the *Necropoli della Banditaccia (Tue–Sun 8.30am–1 hour before sunset),* is in nearby *Cerveteri:* the 400 opened burial tombs (including burial chambers you can walk into) with stone decorations (and many more unopened in the ground), are a Unesco World Heritage Site and an absolute sensation; you can admire some of the artistic burial objects in the *museum* in *Rocca Ruspoli (Tue–Sun 8.30am–7.30pm).*

CASTELLI ROMANI (183 D4) (*ⅲ G8*)
When the Romans drive south-east of the city for a day's ⅿ outing here in the summer, they cool down in the *taverne* with a pleasant white wine, such as Colli Albani, Marino or Frascati, or during their walk by the cool, dark crater lake *Lago di Albano* and *Lago di Nemi.* In *Ariccia* the piazza designed by Bernini is well worth seeing. Every year in the summer, the Pope comes to *Castel Gandolfo* for a summer break. Bernini was also responsible for the very fine work on the church *San Tommaso da Villanova* (1661).
Frascati was particularly popular with the cardinals and patricians, as is obvious

The ancient theatre of Ostia, still used as a venue to this day

from the magnificent Renaissance and Baroque villas, of which only the parks of *Aldobrandini* and *Belvedere* are open to the public. Pretty villa hotels in the country entice you to stay overnight, for instance at the Grottaferrata Park Hotel ⚜ *Villa Grazioli (58 rooms | Via Umberto Pavoni 19 | tel. 06 94 54 00 | www.villa grazioli.com | Moderate–Expensive)* with park and a wonderful view of Rome in the distance. Of the numerous restaurants and osterias in Frascati, the traditional Slow Food restaurant *Zarazà* is highly recommended *(closed Mon | Via Regina Margherita 21 | tel. 0 69 42 20 53 | Moderate)* with ⚜ a panoramic terrace. The ruins of the ancient town of *Tuscolo* (5km/3mi from Frascati) also offers a spectacular view of Rome.

CIOCIARIA (183 D4) (ᗰ H8)

Popular excursion area south-east of Rome with beautiful little towns in the mountains of Monti Ernici, such as *Anagni* (frescoes in the cathedral crypt as well as the Palace of the Popes), *Alatri, Ferentino* or the spa

Fiuggi with a magnificent hotel, the *Grand Hotel Palazzo della Fonte (153 rooms | Via dei Villini 7 | tel. 07 75 50 81 | www.palazzo dellafonte.it | Expensive)*, and in *Acuto* the excellent restaurant *Le Colline Ciociare (closed Sun evening, Tue lunch and Mon | Via Prenestina 27 | tel. 0 77 55 60 49 | www. salvatoretassa.it | Expensive)*.

OSTIA ANTICA (182 C4) (ᗰ G8) ●

A well preserved ancient Roman port city, once a trading port, at the mouth of the Tiber (building began 4 BC). The huge *Roman Theatre* has space for 2700 spectators and excellent acoustics; in the summer, performances still take place there. Ostia Antica is easy to reach from Rome on the Roma–Lido train (26 min), which runs from the town station Stazione Ostiense and takes you directly to Ostia.

PALESTRINA ⚜ (183 D4) (ᗰ H8)

From the ancient Etruscan Praeneste, there is a fantastic view across to the Alban Mountains and Monti Lepini in the south. The archaeological museum,

Museo Nazionale Archeologico Prenestino is very interesting *(daily 9am–7.30pm | Piazza della Cortina).*

PARCO NAZIONALE DEL CIRCEO
(183 D5) *(ⁿ H8)*

This national park and wildlife reserve is a vast area of woods and lakes, which starts just below Latina and stretches to the promontory of ☆ Monte Circeo (541m/ 1775ft). *San Felice Circeo* harbours the ruins of a Roman *Acropolis,* at the tip of the promontory is the *Grotta della Maga Circe* named for the sorceress Circe and along the coast there are large lakes with an abundance of fish and birdlife. Long unspoilt beaches roll up to *Sabaudia* (interesting architecture built in the modernist style of the 1920s); from San Felice Circeo in the south towards Terracina, they have been extensively developed for tourists.

SPERLONGA (183 E5) *(ⁿ H8)*

The old part of this town, between Terracina and Gaeta, perches picturesquely in typical white Mediterranean style on a hilltop overlooking the sea. Below it are particularly beautiful and exclusive beaches as well as a museum with precious finds from ancient Roman villas and caves.

TIVOLI ★ (183 D4) *(ⁿ G8)*

The huge complex of ruins of *Villa Adriana (daily 9am–1.5 hour before sunset)* 30km/ 18.5mi east of Rome was once the splendid country residence of Emperor Hadrian (AD 117–138) and includes palaces, temples, spas, libraries and theatre. Also in Tivoli is the *Villa d'Este,* a Renaissance palace *(Tue–Sun 8.30am–1 hour before sunset | www.tibursuperbum.it)* with the most stunning grounds.

VITERBO

(182 C3) *(ⁿ G7)* **The town (pop. 61,000) steeped in Etruscan history has an enclosed medieval centre with palaces churches and squares.**

Three squares, the *Piazza del Plebiscito*, the *Palazzo dei Priori* (15th century with an attractive courtyard, fountain and frescoes) and the *Palazzo del Podestà* (13th century with 15th century tower)

TERRAZZE ROMANE

Terrazza romana, the Roman roof terrace is the epitome of Roman joie de vivre: celebrating on roof terraces in a mild climate and against the backdrop of the hills, church domes and parks is all part of this lifestyle, something shown in Woody Allen's film 'To Rome with Love' (2012). Visitors to Rome can also experience it in the roof top restaurants and bars of many elegant hotels, such as the *St George* (**(U B4)** *(ⁿ c5)* | *Via Giulia 62),* the *Capo d'Africa* (**(U F5)** *(ⁿ h7)* | *Via Capo d'Africa 54),* the *Exedra* (**(U F3)** *(ⁿ h4)* | *Piazza della Repubblica 47),* the *Locarno* (**(U C1)** *(ⁿ d3)* | *Via Penna 22).* There is a wonderful choice of terrace cafés as well: the wine bar *Il Palazzetto* at the top of the Spanish Steps, the *Caffè Capitolino* in the Capitoline museums on Piazza del Campidoglio, the *caffetteria* on the fourth floor of the Castel Sant' Angelo and the *Caffetteria Italia* at the Altare della Patria Vittorio Emanuele (**(U D4)** *(ⁿ f6)).*

form the heart of the town. Even more impressive is the *Piazza San Lorenzo* with the *San Lorenzo* cathedral and the *Palazzo Papale* with its wonderful pillared loggia. The *Museo Archeologico* exhibits Etruscan treasures *(Tue–Sun 8.30am–7.30pm | Piazza della Rocca)* in *Rocca Albornoz* fortress.

You can dine on home-made pasta with pumpkin flower and stuffed pigeon in the rustic *Al Vecchio Orologio (closed Sun, Mon | Via Orologio Vecchio 25 | tel. 0761 30 57 43 | Budget–Moderate)* in the old town. You can also enjoy thermal and spa treatments in the elegant thermal hotel *Niccolò V Terme dei Papi (23 rooms | Strada Bagni 12 | tel. 0761 35 01 | www. termedeipapi.it | Expensive)*.

In nearby *Bagnaia*, the Baroque park and gardens of *Villa Lante* exude enchantment *(Tue 9am–2 hours before sunset)*.

In Tarquinia's museum: tomb frescoes from the Etruscan necropolis

WHERE TO GO

LAGO DI BOLSENA (LAKE BOLSENA)
(182 C3) (*ω* G7)
Take a trip (20km/12.5mi) to the crater lake Lago di Bolsena: a serene summer resort on crystal-clear water. It is from the medieval *Montefiascone* with its interesting twin church of Romanesque origin *San Flaviano* as well as a lovely castle park where the wine Est! Est! Est! comes. Further on towards Orvieto is the hamlet ☆ *Civita di Bagnoregio* dizzily perched on a steep tuff cliff, and at risk of landslides – a tourist attraction with cafés, trattorias and wine bars.

The main lakeside town, *Bolsena,* has a charming medieval town centre and is where you will find the *Santa Cristina* church (with its interesting catacombs). *Da Picchietto* serves deliciously prepared fresh fish from the lake *(closed Mon | Via Porta Fiorentina 15 | tel. 0761 79 91 58 | Moderate)*.

TARQUINIA ★ (182 C4) (*ω* G7)
Towers dominate the skyline of this little medieval town and on the main square is the splendid Gothic Palazzo Vitelleschi. Inside the palace is the *Museo Nazionale Tarquiniese (Tue–Sun 8.30am–7.30pm)*, which like the *necropolis* (4km/2.5mi to the east) is a must for anyone wishing to learn more about the Etruscans and their ancient town of Tarxna, also called Turchuna. In 2004, the necropolises of Tarquinia and Cerveteri were added to the Unesco World Heritage List.

TUSCANIA (182 C3) (*ω* G7)
Even the Etruscans made use of the strategic location on this tuff stone hill. The *Museo Nazionale Etrusco (Tue–Sun 8.30am–7.30pm)* exhibits numerous terracotta tombs from the Etruscan site of Tusena, which belonged to the city-state of Tarxna (Tarquinia).

SOUTHERN ITALY

The light is blinding, there is a fragrant mix of sea, pines and salt in the air and the midday calm of the weathered little town highlights the beauty of its stage-like squares – a fitting backdrop for an evening stroll.

We have arrived in the south. Travellers have always been drawn to the south – on a honeymoon to the Gulf of Naples, to the *Costa Divina* 'divine coast' of Amalfi and Positano and to Mount Versuvius. Travellers on the grand tour followed the trail of the ancient civilizations to the ruins of the Greek temples and the Greek towns of the Magna Graecia, which once thrived along the southern Italian coast,

and on to Roman Pompeii. And in Apulia they looked for the medieval cathedrals and castles that revealed the creative combination of the Nordic culture of the Normans and Hohenstaufens and the Byzantine influence of the Orient. These days, Apulia is admired for its splendid cliffs and sandy coast, fertile landscape and rustic *trulli* houses and the white *masserie* – old manor houses that have been transformed into attractive country hotels – and for its neat, almost Oriental little towns, the good fresh food, in short: Apulia is a kind of Tuscany of the south.

The neighbouring region of Basilicata presents a highlight in the form of its

Photo: Coastline at Foggia, Gargano

Greek temples and cave towns, Oriental flair and secluded beaches: southern Italy is a region of cultural intersection

spectacular cave town of Matera. Together with rugged Calabria, it shares the secluded mountain region of Pollino, now a nature reserve and and an ideal wilderness area for hikes.

On the partly developed Calabrian coast with its lovely clean sea, stylish resorts have been set up that are now advertised in the catalogues of exclusive travel agents. The most beautiful strip of coast

is the Gulf of Maratea. It joins up with the Cilento in the north, an area of physical beauty and scenic diversity with wonderful beaches, crystal-clear water, grottoes, and mountains – unspoilt nature at its best – and naturally the fascinating, vibrant Naples.

The MARCO POLO 'Naples and the Amalfi Coast' guide offers a more detailed description of the region.

Santa's house? The bones of St Nicolas rest in the crypt of San Nicola

BARI

(185 D4) (_Ø L9_) Apulia's capital (pop. 323,000) is also called the 'Milan of the South': for centuries it has been a trade window to the Orient, and each year in September, it hosts the largest trade fair in the Mediterranean, the _Fiera del Levante._

Bari's white old town with the beautiful old church exudes the air of a Kasbah. Until a few years ago, it was still a bit grim and by no means completely safe, but in recent years a lot has been restored, and the two attractive squares _Piazza Ferrarese_ and _Piazza Mercantile_ have become a centre of the _baresi_ nightlife thanks to the new cafés, bars and nice restaurants.

The elegant hotels as well as vibrant shopping avenues full of people browsing are in the chessboard-styled new town of Bari, which is on the other side of the busy Corso Vittorio Emanuele. You should however, avoid the proliferating, neglected outskirts at all costs.

SIGHTSEEING

BASILICA SAN NICOLA

This stately Apulian Romanesque church (11th/12th century) is very impressive. Inside, look out for the ancient episcopal throne, made of marble and borne by tiny, groaning figures. Below the silver altar is a crypt supported by 26 columns holding the reliquary of St Nicholas, Bishop of Myra, patron saint of Bari and highly respected in the Orthodox Church – which is why there are a lot of Russian pilgrims. _Piazza Elia_

CATTEDRALE SAN SABINO

Bari's cathedral, like the Basilica San Nicola, is one of the best examples of Romanesque architecture in Apulia. In the church's archive, there is a precious

Exsultet Roll (scroll bearing the Catholic Easter liturgy) from the 11th century. *Piazza Odegitria*

HOHENSTAUFEN CASTLE

This massive castle overlooking the sea was reconstructed by Emperor Frederick II of Hohenstaufen on an earlier Byzantine Norman bastion. Inside, a collection of plaster casts show how artistic the decoration on Apulian church façades can be. *Thu–Tue 8.30am–7.30pm*

FOOD & DRINK

LA CANTINA DI CIANNACIANNE

Popular restaurant in the old town near the Lungomare. Try the small meat balls *bombette!* Good seafood dishes. *Daily | Via Corsioli 3 | tel. 08 05 28 93 82 | www. ciannacianne.com | Moderate*

LOCANDA DI FEDERICO

Orecchiette, Apulian 'ear-shaped' pasta, fresh fish on the piazza. *Closed Mon | Piazza Mercantile 63/64 | tel. 08 05 22 77 05 | www.locandadifederico.com | Moderate*

WHERE TO STAY

HOTEL ADRIA

Renovated, friendly, functional and centrally located, with restaurant. *38 rooms | Via Zuppetta 10 | tel. 08 05 24 66 99 | www. adriahotelbari.com | Moderate*

HOTEL ORIENTE

This stylish palazzo hotel, not far from the equally stylish Teatro Petruzelli, is an appropriate choice for Bari. *79 rooms | Via Cavour 3 | tel. 08 05 25 51 00 | www.hotel orientebari.it | Expensive*

⭐ **Castel del Monte**
Strict geometric design on Apulian limestone mountains
→ p. 127

⭐ **Cathedral in Trani**
Unusual seafront cathedral that is the town's landmark → p. 129

⭐ **Sassi di Matera**
Former cave dwellings in the tuff stone cliffs of the town → p. 131

⭐ **Bronzi di Riace in Reggio**
Two 2500 year old Greek bronze statues
→ p. 134

⭐ **Cattolica in Stilo**
The 10th century Byzantine church has five impressive domes
→ p. 136

⭐ **Mosaic artworks in Otranto**
Incredible mosaic floor made up of 10 million little stones turns the cathedral into a work of art
→ p. 137

⭐ **Santa Chiara in Naples**
The majolica arbour in the magnificent cloister → p. 141

⭐ **Paestum**
The Greek temple complex for Hera and Ceres is well preserved
→ p. 144

⭐ **Museo e Gallerie Nazionali di Capodimonte in Naples**
Enthroned high above the city, the Bourbon palace houses a fantastic art collection → p. 140

⭐ **Pompeii**
Wrested from the lava stone of Mount Versuvius: a complete Roman city
→ p. 145

MARCO POLO HIGHLIGHTS

BARI

INFORMATION

Piazza Aldo Moro 32 a (station forecourt) | tel. 08 09 90 93 41 | www.infopointbari. com, www.viaggiareinpuglia.it

WHERE TO GO

ALBEROBELLO (185 E4) (*ω M9*)

Home of a unique vernacular architecture: the *trulli*, little circular white drystone houses with dark conical roofs. You can see them dotted around in the triangle between Bari, Taranto and Brindisi, scattered among the olive groves, almond orchards, vegetable fields and grapevines of the garden-like Valle d'Itria. In Alberobello (pop. 10,000), they form a town, even the Sant'Antonio church is built in *trulli* style, which has turned Alberobello into a tourist magnate. Inhabited until about 20 years ago, some of the buildings have now been transformed into hotels, holiday homes, souvenir shops and pizzerias. The somewhat rustic INSIDER TIP holiday accommodation offered in the *trulli*, which was initially rather damp and spartan, has nonetheless improved tremendously, for instance *Trulli e Puglia B & B (Via Monte San Michele 58/60 | tel. 08 04 32 43 76 | www.trullipuglia.com | Budget–Moderate)* and *Trulli Holiday Residence (Contrada Gabellota | tel. 08 04 32 59 70 | www.trulliholidayresidence.eu | Budget–Moderate)*. A beautiful hotel with a swimming pool and good food (20km/12mi to the east in Fasano) is the *Masseria Marzalossa (12 rooms | Pezze Vicine 65 | tel. 08 04 13 78 0 | www.marzalossa.com | Expensive)*, a fine example of how elegantly and charmingly Apulia's beautiful manor houses, once at risk of all falling into disrepair, are now being used.

As curious as its name: *trulli,* the circular structures in and around Alberobello

CASTEL DEL MONTE AND
CANOSA DI PUGLIA (184 C4) (*M L9*)

From afar, one sees the 'crown of Apulia' on the hill, the octagonal ★ ⊿⊾ *Castel del Monte* (built 1240–50) with eight towers, eight interior rooms and an octagonal courtyard. It was one of the architectural projects of Emperor Frederick II of Hohenstaufen, and displays an almost esoteric touch. Once this austere castle *(April–Sept daily 10am–7.45pm, Oct–March 9am–6.30pm | www.casteldelmonte. beniculturali.it)* was richly adorned with marble and Byzantine mosaics. Plan a culinary treat in the nearby village of *Montegrosso d'Andria* and enjoy the meticulous Apulian Slow Food cuisine in *Trattoria Antichi Sapori (closed Sat evening and Sun | Piazza Sant'Isidoro 9 | tel. 08 83 56 95 29 | Budget–Moderate).*

You can drive to the castle inland via *Canosa di Puglia*, a fine example of Apulia's cultural diversity: the Romanesque *cathedral* ruins of the Byzantine *Basilica San Leucio* and in the Via Cadorna the Roman *Ipogei Lagrasta,* burial caves dug into the tuff stone and dating back to 4 BC.

GARGANO
(184 C2–3) (*M K–L8*)

In the centre of Gargano, the ancient *Foresta Umbra*, a protected forest of shady deciduous trees, spreads out over 42mi² on the massive 1000m/3281ft high promontory, the spur of the Italian boot (and national park: *www.parks.it/parco.nazio nale.gargano).* The coast in the southeast is steep and rocky with little sandy coves and bizarre rock formations, such as at Pugnochiuso. Picturesque fishing towns such as *Rodi Garganico, Vieste* and *Peschici* turn into teeming holiday spots in the summer. In the north there are sandy beaches and two lagoon lakes. Holiday resorts, hotels and campsites offer accommodation.

In Manfredonia in the south, there are two sanctuaries that are reminders of the ancient town of Sipontum: the Romanesque Oriental church of *Santa Maria di Siponto,* a square construction with a crypt, and 7km/4mi further on *San Leonardo di Siponto* with beautiful sculptures on the portals and capitals. In *Manfredonia* itself, the *Museo Archeologico Nazionale del Gargano (daily 8.30am–7.30pm, closed 1st and last Mon in the month)* in the Hohenstaufen Angevin fortress complex is worth seeing as it contains the mysterious stone stelae of the Daunians, who settled around the Tavoliere – the Apulian plain around Foggia and the Gargano – about 2500 years ago.

Above Manfredonia there is a magnificent ⊿⊾ panoramic drive up to *Monte Sant'Angelo* with the cave sanctuary of St Michael (note the wonderful bronze door from 1076!) and the unusual terrace house architecture in the medieval district of *Junno.* 25km/15.5mi northwest in *San Giovanni Rotondo* more than six million pilgrims come to pay homage to a contemporary saint, the faith healer Padre Pio.

Bizarre rocks rise up from the beach of the hotel *Baia delle Zagare (150 rooms | tel. 08 84 55 01 55 | www.hotelbaiadelle zagare.it | Expensive),* which has a stunning location on terraces between olive trees on the coastal road 17km/10mi north-east of Mattinata.

From *Vieste* – which has a picturesque old town and a Hohenstaufen castle on a steep cliff surrounded by sandy beaches on the east tip of Gargano – boat trips set off to the spectacular *grottoes* such as *Smeralda* and *Campana,* which can only be reached by sea. Soaring up from the edge of the beach is the Gargano landmark, the *Pizzomunno*, a towering chalk monolith, the 'top of the world'. Following

Italy's most beautiful dripstone caves: chamber in the Grotte di Castellana

a scenic coastal route, the boat arrives at *Peschici* high up the farthest side of the promontory, with a pleasing old town and a small harbour, a particularly popular holiday hamlet in Gargano. Other typical landmarks are the *trabucchi,* the fishing structures which stretch right out into the sea, some of which are now used as restaurants.

GROTTE DI CASTELLANA
(185 D4) *(ඛ M9)*
In Castellana on the road to Putignano, visitors can stop off in Italy's amazing *dripstone caves* (see 'Travel with Kids'), a labyrinth of passages and caves. A highlight is the *Caverna Bianca,* a cavern of alabaster. *Daily, hourly tours, a short (500m) and a long (3km/1.8mi), tour temperature inside 15 degrees*

MARTINA FRANCA
(185 E4–5) *(ඛ M9)*
The elegant little Baroque town (pop. 45,000) in the centre of the Murgia, at an elevation of 430m/141ft, used to be the family seat of an aristocratic family whose enterprising work triggered a building boom among the middle classes. Whole roads of Baroque façades were the result, e.g. the Via Cavour, with its richly embellished stonework. The blacksmith's trade is still pursued to this day. Every June/July, the famous **INSIDER TIP** music festival *(www.festivaldellavalleditria.it)* takes place. Rather original accommodation is available in renovated apartments right in the centre: **INSIDER TIP** *Villaggio In (48 apartments | Via Arco Grassi 8 | tel. 0 80 70 59 11 | www.villaggioin.it | Budget– Moderate).*
This is a good base for tours to the ceramic centre of Grottaglie, to Taranto, to see the many *trulli,* to the grotto churches between Massafra, Mottola and Matera, and to the pretty, whitewashed little towns

with their Oriental flair such as Cisternino, the popular Ostuni or Ceglie Messapica, which all have a whole range of good restaurants, including the *Al Fornello da Ricci (closed Mon evening and Tue | Contrada Montevicoli | tel. 08 31 37 71 04 | Moderate–Expensive)*. ❄️ *Polignano a Mare* has a fantastic position on the cliffs overlooking the sea.

RUVO DI PUGLIA
(185 D4) (*Ⓜ L9*)

This friendly little country town 35km/ 22mi to the north-west is worth a visit to see the wonderful Romanesque *cathedral* and the *Museo Nazionale Jatta (Sun–Thu 8.30am–1.30pm, Fri, Sat 8.30am–730pm | Piazza Bovio 35)*, for the beautiful antique vases and the *rython*, INSIDER TIP drinking vessel in the shape of animal heads.

TARANTO
(185 E5) (*Ⓜ M9*)

Don't let be deterred by the steel foundries of the industrial and harbour town of Taranto (pop. 202,000). If you are looking for traces of Tarras's past, which was one of the richest and most developed trading towns two and a half thousand years ago, visit the *Marta-Museo Archeologico Nazionale (daily 8.30am–7.15pm|*

Via Cavour 10 | www.museotaranto.org). After years of restoration, it is now possible to go up to the first floor again to see the gold collection.

The topographical location of the town is interesting. It extends over two headlands that form a sort of inland sea, the *Mare Piccolo,* with a little island, on which the old town extends, with a castle (1480) and a cathedral of Romanesque origin with a Baroque façade.

TRANI
(185 D3–4) (*Ⓜ L8–9*)

This pleasant town (pop. 45,000) has carved out a special reputation among the little coastal towns between Bari and the Gargano spur thanks to its Norman Romanesque ⭐ ❄️ *cathedral* and its unusual architecture, precious stone embellishments and the bronze portal (currently being restored) as well as its unique position on the coast – once a point of orientation for seafarers. It also has some of the most beautiful churches in Apulia. Directly on the coast is the *Hohenstaufen castle.* The old town on the *lungomare,* the sea promenade, turns into a vibrant nightlife area each evening, with bars, pubs and restaurants. *www.traniweb.it, www.pugliaimperiale.com*

PASTA ANTIMAFIA

Do you want to support the fight against the mafia on your trip to Italy? You can do so by buying *Libera Terra* pasta in cooperative supermarkets, 🕙 organic food chain NaturaSi and Alce Nera, and in 🕙 fair trade shops, which can now be found in all of the main towns. Hundreds of acres of land on Sicily have been confiscated from the convicted

Mafia bosses and given to dedicated organic farmers who cultivate wheat, tomatoes, olives, and grapes on the land, and turn them into pasta, tinned tomatoes, oil and wine. The Sicilian example is catching on, so that now new legal farming enterprises are being set up on former mafia land in Campania, Calabria and Apulia. *www.liberaterra.it*

ISOLE TREMITI (TREMITI ISLANDS)
(184 B2) (*Ⓜ K7*)

People refer to them as Italy's most beautiful 'tropical islands': first the large flat mountain ridge of *Isola San Domino* covered in pine woods and with a coast full of grottoes, a diver's paradise *(www.merlintremiti.it | www.tremitidivingcenter.com)*, then the uninhabited cliff splinter *Isola Cretaccio,* finally the *Isola San Nicola* with a fortified *Benedictine abbey* from the 9th century that acquired a Gothic character under the Cistercians. 300 peo-

BASILICATA

APPENNINO LUCANO
(184–185 C–D5) (*Ⓜ L9–10*)

From the coast of Metapontos eroded river valleys lead up into the mountain world of Basilicata, through the Valle del Basento to the Lucanian Dolomites. They are named after their bizarre cliff formations. The district also encompasses beautiful woods and two very picturesque mountain towns *Pietrapertosa* and *Castelmezzano.* Nice ac-

Pine woods and fishing villages, diving sites and swimming bays: the Isole Tremiti

ple inhabit the group of islands in the little fishing villages that are now tailored to the tourist industry. On some days in the summer, ships from Manfredonia, Vieste, Rodi Garganico, Ortona, Vasto and especially Termoli in Molise bring over 10,000 day trippers to the islands.

commodation is available in the old restored mill. It also offers tasty meals as well: *Il Molino della Contessa (4 rooms | Camastra-Castelmezzano | tel. 09 71 98 60 99 | www.molinodellacontessa.com | Budget).* Near the coastal town of Policoro, you enter the *Val d'Agri* (with Europe's largest onshore oil field) at the beginning of which is the impressive medieval church complex *Santa Maria d'Anglona,* which is well worth a visit. Continuing along the valley, the surrounding mountains rise to an elevation of 1800m/5906ft. In 2006, the *Parco Nazionale dell'Appennino Lucano (www.parcoappenninolucano.it)* was set up here.

INSIDERTIP MARATEA
(184 C6) *(Μ K10)*

The 26km/16mi long Costa di Maratea on the Golfo di Policastro is one of the most beautiful stretches of coast in southern Italy. The mountains back on to the sea, the sand and pebble bays are great for bathing, and the clean water is a paradise for divers. Pretty coastal and seaside resorts such as *Acqua-fredda, Cersuta, Fiumicello San Venere, Castrocucco* provide a contrast to the more elevated old towns such as *Maratea Borgo* and *Maratea Superiore.* The enchanting hotel *Villa Cheta Elite* overlooks the beautiful beach of Acquafredda *(23 rooms | tel. 09 73 87 81 34 | www.villa cheta.it | Moderate–Expensive).*

MATERA (185 D5) *(Μ L9)*

A Romanesque Norman cathedral (13th century), a *feudal fortress* from 1515, the restored *Chiesa del Purgatorio* with macabre scenes of purgatory, and naturally the main sight, the ★ ● *sassi:* a subterranean cave town cut into the rock beneath the new Matera (pop. 52,000). Over 20,000 people lived here well into the 1950s, but their living conditions in the dark, unhealthy cave homes were regarded as a national disgrace. New buildings and resettlements were the results; there is now a resurgence of interest (using public funds) because, ironically, the *sassi* are now on Unesco's World Heritage List. Luxurious hotels with an atmosphere all of their own are now in the cave dwellings, such as the ☆ INSIDERTIP *Hotel Sant'Angelo (23 rooms | Rione Pianelle | Piazza San Pietro Caveoso | tel. 08 35 31 40 10 | www.hotelsantangelo sassi.it | Expensive),* but also comfortable B & B accommodation *(www.sassiweb.it, www.bbresidenzasassi.it | Budget).*

MELFI (184 C4) *(Μ K9)*

An important northern stronghold in the Basilicata is Melfi (pop. 15,000) on the northern face of Monte Vulture (1327m/ 4354ft). Its thick woods are a reminder of the region's original name: Lucania (from *lucus* = wood). A popular destination thanks to the *Monticchio crater lakes* with two 12th century *Benedictine monasteries,* one of which is a ruin, the other rebuilt in the 18th century. Melfi itself was the first stronghold of the Normans in southern Italy. Today the castle, which was later remodelled by Friedrick II, houses the *Museo Nazionale Archeologico (Mon 2pm–8pm, Tue–Sun 9am–8pm)* with interesting exhibits about the early history of the Lucanians, the original settlers and the sarcophagus of a Roman woman with wonderful stone reliefs dating back to 165–170 BC. On the outskirts of Melfi, you will find the *rupestrian churches Madonna della Spinelle, Santa Lucia* and *Santa Margherita* with Byzantine inspired wall paintings from the 13th century. Ask about tours in the tourist centre *Pro Loco (Piazza Umberto I/11 | tel. 09 72 23 97 51).*

Melfi produces a famous southern Italian red wine, the full-bodied Aglianico – traditionally stored in rock cellars to mature – in villages such as Barile, Rapolla, Rionera in Vulture. It is served along with delicious regional cuisine in the country inn *Cantuccio del Vulture (7 rooms | closed Sun evening, Mon, Tue | Piano delle Nocelle-Rionero | tel. 09 72 73 13 14 | www. cantucciodelvulture.it | Budget)* with seven simple rooms.

20km/12mi to the east of Melfi, you reach *Venosa* with its stately *castle* and *cathedral* from the 15th century including the *birthplace* of the Roman poet Horace (born here in 65 BC). Highlights on the north-east outskirts of the town are the archaeological excavations of the Roman *Venusium* the impressive early Christian abbey *Santissima Trinità* as well as the wildly romantic unfinished ruin church *Incompiuta.* A short distance further on you reach the early Christian *catacombs,* which have been accessible for some years now.

METAPONTO (185 D5) (*L9–10*)

Today ● Metaponto is a modern town on the Ionian coast, which earns its living from the summer tourists and vegetable cultivation. It was once the famous Greek town of Metapontum in which Pythagoras lived and died (AD 497). The *Tavole Palatine,* the temple dedicated to the Greek goddess Hera, with its remaining 15 Doric columns that loom into view near the main road 106. Among the Greek remains is also the *Parco Archeologico* as well as the *Antiquarium (with the archaeological museum | Tue–Sun 9am–8pm)* with a rich collection of archaeological finds, vases and jewellery. A second important Greek town was *Heraclea,* 20km/12mi to the south of Metaponto. The *Museo Nazionale della Siritide (Wed–Mon 9am–8pm, Tue 2pm–8pm)* in *Policoro* contains the finds from this site and from *Siris,* a third Greek town, as well as from the *Parco Archeologico di Herakleia.*

In Italy there is history in nearly every stone – columns, pedestals, sculptures in Metaponto

CALABRIA

ASPROMONTE (186 C5) *(Ⓜ K–L12)*

The toe of the boot, the most southern point of the Apennine peninsula between the Tyrrhenian and the Ionian Sea, is surrounded by more than 300km/186mi of coastline. High mountain ranges traverse the area, in the south of the Aspromonte, rugged, impassable end of the Apennines: crags and labyrinthine folds covered in thick vegetations. ✀ INSIDER TIP Traversing the Aspromonte, for example from Bagnara Calabra by the Tyrrhenian Sea to Melito di Porto Salvo on the Ionian Sea offers fantastic views of the landscape. It is here at the top that pilgrims visit the *Santuario Madonna di Polsi,* which has a special feast day at the end of Aug/beginning of Sept. Stretching off towards the north-east is the *Costa dei Gelsomini* with numerous seaside resorts and beaches.

CROTONE AND DI CAPO RIZZUTO (187 D4) *(Ⓜ M11)*

The craggy peninsula (a nature reserve since 1991) offers a beautiful spectacle: cliffs and rock plateaus roughened by wind and erosion, little streets running down to the beaches and bays, the cape *Capo Rizzuto* jutting out into the crystal-clear sea. Equally spectacular is the fortress on the coast ✀ *Le Castella* in the south and the Greek ruins at *Capo Colonna* in the north. And even the industrial town of *Crotone* (pop. 60,000), founded 2500 years ago as the Greek Kroton, still has a nice old town.

LOCRI (186 C5) *(Ⓜ L12)*

On the Ionian coast with its beaches and resorts, near the modern town of Locri (pop. 13,000) towards Bovalino, is the archaeological site of the Greek *Locri Epizephyrii.* It contains remains of an Ionic and Doric temple, a Greco-Roman theatre as well as the holy shrine of Persephone. The *museum (Tue–Sun 9am–8pm)* exhibits Persephone votive plaques made of terracotta. You can savour a delicious Slow Food meal in *Zio Salvatore (closed Tue | Piazza San Nicola | tel. 09 64 38 53 28 | Budget)* in *Siderno Superiore,* the historic old town 5km/3mi further to the north. Above Locri is *Gerace* (11km/7km), a medieval hamlet spread out over three terraces, which boasts a wonderful Romanesque *cathedral;* the columns in the interior and the crypt are remains from ancient Locri. Continuing up into the mountains along the pass, you will reach the other side of the coast on the Tyrrhenian Sea at Gioia Tauro. The ✀ *Passo del Mercante* (952m/ 3117ft) offers a view of both seas.

INSIDER TIP ▶ MONTE POLLINO
(186 C2) (*ØØ L10*)

Castrovillari, a small modern town (pop. 17,000) situated in a fertile basin – a picturesque centre, Aragonese *castle* and the Renaissance church *San Giuliano* – that is one of the starting points for excursions to the Pollino massif, southern Italy's highest mountain range (up to 2248m/ 7375ft). There are river valleys full of verdant vegetation and rough, bare, chalky heights, a national park since 1992, which northern Calabria shares with the southern Basilicata. The symbol of this wild mountain world is the *pino loricato,* a rare pine unique to the area. Tours leave from i.a. *Rotonda* (the park administration: *Via delle Frecce Tricolori 6 | tel. 09 73 66 93 11 | www.parcopollino.it*) and *San Severino Lucano* with nice restaurants. The centre in the north-east of the park is *Terranova del Pollino;* an ideal base for hiking tours is the farm ☺ *La Garavina (Contrada Corte del Conte | tel. 0 97 39 33 95 | www.laga-ravina.it | Budget)* with six simple rooms and delicious regional cuisine using its own organic ingredients. Hiking enthusiasts regard the ☆ route from coast to coast through the Pollino mountains as a highlight.

Information regarding the park and the trekking trips can be found on the following websites: *www.guidaparcopollino.it, www.parcopollino.it, www.aptbasilicata.it* and *www.bikebasilicata.it.* First-class local cuisine is available in *Castrovillari* in *La Locanda di Alia (14 rooms | closed Sun | Via Jetticelle 69 | tel. 0 98 14 63 70 | www.alia.it | Moderate).*

Morano Calabro is a mountain village worth special mention, with picturesque old houses clustered around the ruined castle. The Baroque *Collegiate of Maddalena* church with its colourfully shingled dome roof stands out among the churches.

REGGIO DI CALABRIA
(186 C5) (*ØØ K12*)

This ancient Greek town (pop. 186,000) tends to be better known for its ugly urban sprawl and *mafioso* connections, but it has a surprisingly elegant palm-lined waterfront promenade ● *Lungomare Falcomatà.* Named after the late mayor who was responsible for reviving the quality of life in the troubled town: you can sit here and enjoy the sunset and the views of Sicily, which seems almost close enough to touch. A further reason to come here are the two magnificent bronze figures, the ★ *Bronzi di Riace* (5 BC), found in the sea in 1972. Both date back to 5 BC or from the time of the Magna Graecia. Normally kept in the *Museo Nazionale (Piazza De*

LOW BUDGET

▶ The inexpensive local trains allow you to undertake scenic countryside tours: e.g. with the *Trenino del Gargano* from San Severo right across Gargano to Peschici or with the *Ferrovie Appulo-Lucane* from Bari to Matera and Potenza in the Basilicata.

▶ Stock up in the local supermarkets with sun-dried tomatoes, southern Italian biscuits *(taralli),* pickled vegetables, local pastas, organic lemons, wine and olive oil – the same quality costs twice as much in the shops at home.

▶ *Metro dell'Arte* in Naples: you can admire major contemporary art free of charge in the Metro stations Dante, Museo, Materdei and Salvator Rosa.

The five domes of the Cattolica di Stilo church have stood for more than 1000 years

Nava 26 | www.museonazionalerc.it), which is currently closed for renovation, the bronzes can be admired in the headquarters of the regional government, the *Palazzo Campanella (Via Cardinale Portanova | daily 9am–7.30pm)*.

ROSSANO
(187 D3) (∅ L10–11)

Located on the eastern slopes of the Sila Greca, once the centre of Byzantine culture, this town (pop. 36,000) guards a very special treasure in the *Museo Diocesano di Arte Sacra (in winter Tue–Sat 9.30am–12.30pm and 4pm–7pm, Sun 10am–noon and 4.30pm–6.30pm, in summer daily 9am–1pm and 4.30pm–8 pm)*. Here, pages of the 'Codex Purpureus Rossanensis' are on display, a gospel written and painted by Greek monks on purple-dyed parchment in AD 6. Rossano is also famous for its liquorice manufacture, e.g. in the little tins from *Amarelli (museum and shop Contrada Amarelli on the main road SS 106)*.

SAN DEMETRIO CORONE
(187 D3) (∅ L10)

One of two dozen Albanian villages in Calabria. At the end of the 15th century, Albanians fleeing from the Turks ended up in Italy. They settled in southern Italy and Sicily, mostly in Calabria, east and west of the Sila Greca. Every year in May, a large colourful Albanian festival takes place in the nearby *Santa Sofia d'Epiro*.

SCILLA ☀ (186 C5) (∅ K12)

A highlight on the coast of Calabria is this mythical ('Skylla and Charybdis') fishing village (pop. 5000) picturesquely situated on the coast overlooking the Strait of Messina to Sicily and the Aeolian Islands, also known for its swordfish fleet. The winding streets of the fishing district of Chianalea are among the most beautiful villages in Italy.

STILO (187 D5) (∅ L12)

In this hamlet (pop. 3500), perched at 400m/1312ft on a rocky hillside overlooking the Ionian Sea, you will see one of the most important sights in Calabria: the ★ *Cattolica,* a small Byzantine brick church from AD 10 with five domes and a partially preserved mosaic floor.

TROPEA ✹ (186 C4) (𝄞 K12)

Tropea (pop. 7500), with an important *cathedral* in a superb location on a steep cliff above the beach, is one of the most attractive and expensive coastal towns in Calabria. Bizarre rock forms rise from the sea and a fine sandy beach leads into the still clean water, for example at ✹ *Capo Vaticano* at the southernmost point.

Not far from the vibrant centre of Tropea, you can stay in the charming Mediterranean *Villa Antica (20 rooms | Via Pietro Ruffo di Calabria 37 | tel. 09 73 60 71 76 | www.villa anticatropea.it | Moderate).*

LECCE AND SALENTO

(185 F5) (𝄞 N9–10) Lecce (pop. 91,000) offers unique scenes of Baroque magnificence from the 16th, 17th and 18th century, a result of the Spanish influence. Lecce is the urban centre of INSIDER TIP Salento *(www.salentonline.it, www.salento dolcevita.com, vacanze.salento.com).* The flat, island-shaped boot heel, with its ancient olive groves and enchanting seaside towns with *masserie* – farmhouses converted into holiday accommodation – and lively music scene, which culminates in the *Pizzica Taranta* festival in the summer on numerous village squares, deserves consideration on any holiday itinerary. Yellow tuff stone ornaments adorn Lecce's palazzi, churches and especially the spectacular cathedral complex. In the centre, there is a Roman *amphitheatre* and a *castle* built by Charles V (large market daily).

In recent years, a whole range of INSIDER TIP pretty B & B accommodation has become available in Lecce *(www.bb planet.com, www.abitalecce.it | Budget)* also in the atmospheric old town, e.g. *L'Orangerie d'Époque (3 rooms | Viale Lo Re 24 | tel. 08 32 24 41 31 | www.lorangerie depoque.com | Budget).* Try *Taralli, Burrata, pomodori secchi* and *lampascioni* at the bistro *Mamma Elvira (closed Sun | Via Umberto I 19 | tel. 08 32 169 20 11 | www. mammaelvira.com | Budget).* Beach life takes place along the Adriatic. In *San Cataldo* and from there down to pretty *Torre dell'Orso* and further south in the direction of Otranto, you will reach the popular sandy beaches of *Alimini* as well as *Baia dei Turchi.*

WHERE TO GO

GALLIPOLI (185 F6) (𝄞 M10)

One of the most beautiful towns (pop. 20,000) in southern Italy (certainly the old town) on an ✹ island off the coast in the Ionian Sea, full of narrow, winding alleys, whitewashed buildings and Baroque palaces. The church *Santa Maria della Purità* is decorated with lovely majolica. The fresh, beautifully prepared fish served at the traditional *Grotta Marina* restaurant in the heart of the old town comes from Gallipoli's famous fish market *(restaurant open daily in summer | Via Battisti 13 | tel. 08 33 26 40 30 | Moderate– Expensive).* There are numerous terrace restaurants on the ✹ promenade around the old town, ideal in the summer to sit and relax. Especially lovely sandy beaches – in summer the youth meet here – stretch south towards Pescoluse and Torre San Giovanni.

GREEK VILLAGES (185 F5–6) (𝄞 N10)

There are still villages in Salento where an ancient form of Greek is spoken: Calimera

Harmonic ensemble in yellow tuff stone: Lecce cathedral square in the evening light

Sternatia, Soleto, Martignano, Martano, Castrignano de'Greci and Corigliano d'Otranto. It is called *Griko* and more recently cultural associations have been trying to save it from extinction. Every year at the end of August, thousands of young people gather in *Melpignano* for the INSIDER TIP *Notte della Taranta (www. lanottedellataranta.it),* to dance the traditional rhythmic folk dance of the Salento.

OTRANTO (185 F5) (⌖ N10)

Italy's easternmost town on the peninsula where the Ionian Sea meets the Adriatic is one of country's most attractive holiday resorts. Otranto (pop. 5000) has a picturesque, whitewashed lively old town, clean sea and a variety of places to stay, from simple B & Bs, to holidays on the farm (in the stately, pale grey *masserie)* and luxurious resorts. It also has one of the most important ★ mosaic artworks in the world: on the *floor of the cathedral* a 1596m²/17,200ft² area displaying images of mythological figures, enigmatic symbolism and Biblical stories. It is a unique example of the mystical union between Christian and Eastern culture that the monk Pantaleone created from 1163–66, using around 10 million mosaics. One of the most beautiful coastlines in Italy is the a rocky coast south from Otranto down to *Santa Maria di Leuca*, with attractive places, such as the elegant spa town *Santa Cesarea Terme* or the meandering *Castro.* There is a marvellous view of the coast and sea from the ⬩ terrace of the country hotel *Masseria Panareo (16 rooms | Litoranea Otranto | tel. 08 36 81 29 99 | www.masseriapanareo.com | Moderate),* which has a very good restaurant and is 12km/7.5 mi south of Otranto in Santa Cesarea Terme.

On the ⬩ forecourt of the pilgrimage church *Finis Terrae* in *Santa Maria di Leuca* – on the extreme tip the boot's heel – you really do feel as if you have reached the 'end of the world'.

NAPLES (NAPOLI)

CITY WHERE TO START?
Via Benedetto Croce–Via San Biagio dei Librai–Via Vicaria Vecchia: the 3km/1.8mi main street cuts through the old town, which is why it is called *Spaccanapoli* ('Naples splitter'). The other axis **(Via Toledo)** connects the main Piazza del Plebiscito with the archaeological museum. Parking garages are available in the centre and at the port terminals Molo Beverello and Molo Mergellina *(Italpark | Via Giulio Cesare 50; Parking Ferraris | Via Brun Stefano 20 | www.myparking.it | 3 euros/hr | from here take Bus R3 to the old town).*

(183 F6) *(∅ J9)* **Seen from the sea, in the distance, Naples – one of the most densely populated cities in Europe (pop. 1 million) – appears wonderfully promising. Dominating the south is the broad cone of Mount Vesuvius, Italy's second largest active volcano after Mount Etna, which has been passive for the last 50 years.**

The city has existed for the last 3000 years, initially merged together from three Greek settlements, later becoming Roman and Byzantine; from 1159 it became part of the Kingdom of Sicily and

The sleeping giant: Vesuvius always dominates the view of Naples and its Gulf

seat of the French, Spanish, Habsburg and Bourbon kings of Naples.

In the city's interwoven fabric, you will find legacies of this royal past – elegant public squares, palazzi and gardens – right next to labyrinthine districts of chaotic proportions. Building speculation, rubbish disposal problems and Camorra intrigues fill the local headlines in Naples, yet none of these can really detract from the beauty and vibrancy of the city. Contemporary art centres such as *PAN* (Palazzo delle Arti di Napoli, actions and ateliers) and the exacting exhibition halls of *MADRE* (Museo d'Arte Contemporanea Donna Regina / *www.museomadre.it)* are proof of that. The rubbish problem may not have been solved, but the centre of the town has been cleaned up.

For a more detailed description of the city, refer to the MARCO POLO 'Naples and the Amalfi Coast' guide.

SIGHTSEEING

CAPPELLA SANSEVERO
The small rococo church contains some exceptional sculptures, especially the 'Veiled Christ' by Giuseppe Sammartino (1753). *Mon and Wed–Sat 10am–5.40pm, Sun 10am–1.10pm | Via de Sanctis 19 | www.museosansevero.it*

CASTEL NUOVO
Also called the Maschio Angioino, this castle was the residence of Neapolitan kings from the 13th century; the wonderful Renaissance arch was added in the 15th century. Today, it hosts exhibitions. *Mon–Sat 9am–7pm | Piazza Municipio*

CASTEL DELL'OVO 🌿
Standing on a small rocky outcrop, this formidable Norman castle has become a symbol of the indestructibility of Naples: Virgil is said to have placed an egg in the wall, prophesying that Naples would continue to exist for as long as the egg remained intact. Access to the castle – today a lavishly restored congress centre – is via a small causeway. The castle overlooks the busy fishing harbours of *Porto Santa Lucia* and *Borgo Marinaro* and the many trattorias and cafés.

CASTEL SANT'ELMO AND CERTOSA SAN MARTINO
The 1329 weir rises above the eastern rim of the Vomero plateau; in front of it is the Baroque Carthusian cloister of *Certosa San Martino (Thu–Tue 8.30am–7.30pm)* home to the museum of city history with a beautiful *collection of nativity scenes.* There are magnificent views of the gulf from the 🌿 park.

NAPLES (NAPOLI)

CATACOMBE DI SAN GENNARO
An impressive subterranean cemetery with early Christian graffiti (2nd century). *Mon–Sat 10am–5pm, Sun 10am–1pm | Tondo di Capodimonte 13 | www.catacombedinapoli.it | Entrance in the Basilica della Madre del Buon Consiglio*

DUOMO SAN GENNARO
In the repeatedly redesigned French Gothic cathedral of the patron saint of Naples is the San Gennaro (St Januarius)

to go and see the collection of artistic and unambiguous erotica from ancient pleasure houses, exhibited in *Gabinetto Segreto. Wed–Mon 9am–7.30pm | Piazza Museo*

MUSEO E GALLERIE NAZIONALI DI CAPODIMONTE ★
The magnificent royal palace of Capodimonte, set in a beautiful 🌿 park high above the city, houses the art collections handed down over the years by the dif-

Napoli Sotterranea: Naples underworld – this time the literal one

chapel with reliquaries, also a vial of what is thought to be his blood, which liquefies twice a year in September and May when it is brought out during a special religious ceremony. *Via Duomo*

MUSEO ARCHEOLOGICO NAZIONALE
The museum contains one of the largest and most famous archaeological collections in the world, i.a. with murals from Pompeii and Herculaneum. Don't forget

ferent rulers of Naples and includes works by Simone Martini, Masaccio, Caravaggio, Bellini, Correggio, Titian, Breughel and many others. The residential chambers include a salon made entirely of porcelain, a work by the famous porcelain manufactory of Capodimonte. You can also go and see the exhibitions of contemporary art. *Thu–Tue 8.30am–7.30 pm | Via di Capodimonte | museodicapodimonte. campaniabeniculturali.it*

INSIDER TIP NAPOLI SOTTERRANEA
(NAPLES UNDERGROUND) ●

The town lies on tuff stone, into which caves, cisterns and catacombs have been dug. On the *Piazzetta San Gaetano 68,* you can walk down into Naples's underworld, a labyrinth of tunnels, cisterns, storage cellars, and caves, cut into the soft volcanic lava by the Greeks and Romans Two hour tours. *10am–6pm | www.napoli sotterranea.org*

PALAZZO REALE

This impressive royal palace (17th century) was the seat of the government from 1734 to 1860. You can visit the lovely staircase and the magnificently decorated rooms *(Thu–Tue 9am–8pm).* The palazzo is on the broad restored *Piazza del Plebiscito,* which is framed by the neoclassical church of San Francesco di Paola. Classicist modelled on the Roman Pantheon.

SAN LORENZO MAGGIORE

One of the most stunning medieval churches in Naples. Interesting Greek and Roman remains have been found under the Franciscan monastery. *Mon–Sat 9.30am–5.30pm, Sun 9.30am–1.30pm | Piazza San Gaetano*

SANTA CHIARA ★

The *Convento dei Minori* belongs to the French-Gothic church, which is famous for its *Chiostro delle Clarisse,* a garden with majolica tiled benches and beautiful porticos. *Mon–Sat 9.30am–5.30pm, Sun 10am–2.30pm | Via Benedetto Croce | www.monasterodisantachiara.com*

TEATRO SAN CARLO

World-famous temple of melodrama, originally decked out in the Baroque and then restored in neoclassical style after a fire in 1816. One of the most beautiful opera houses in Italy, open to the public. *Via San Carlo 93 | tel. 08 17 97 24 12 (season Nov–June) | www.teatrosancarlo.it*

RACK RAILWAY (FUNICOLARI) ☃

This will take you up to the Vomero, once the appropriately higher ground for the upper classes: Funicolare Centrale *Via Toledo–Piazza Fuga,* Funicolare di Chiaia *Via Parco Margherita–Via Cimarosa,* Funicolare di Montesanto *Piazza Montesanto–Via Morghen,* lovely views during the ride with the Funicolare di Mergellina *(Via Mergellina–Via Manzoni).*

FOOD & DRINK

LA CHITARRA

Down-to-earth little trattoria serving typically Neapolitan cuisine, exactly the right thing after a walk through the old town. *Closed Sat lunch, Mon evening and Sun | Rampe San Giovanni Maggiore 1 b | tel. 08 15 52 91 03 | Budget*

DA MICHELE

The restaurant is always full because, as the Neapolitans say themselves, you can eat the best pizzas here, in a convivial atmosphere sitting on wooden benches at marble tables. *Closed Sun | Via Cesare Sersale 1/3 | tel. 08 15 53 92 04 | Budget*

PALAZZO PETRUCCI

Chic modern atmosphere and light Mediterranean creative cuisine in the residence of the court secretary to the former king of Naples. *Closed Sun evening and Mon lunch | Piazza San Domenico Maggiore 4 | tel. 08 15 52 40 68 | palazzo petrucci.it | Moderate–Expensive*

SHOPPING

The streets *Via Chiaia, Via dei Mille, Via Roma* are full of exclusive boutiques. The

NAPLES (NAPOLI)

Spaccanapoli and their side streets are full of businesses and tradesmen. From 8 Dec, there is INSIDER **TIP** *nativity market* on *Via San Gregorio Armeno*.

ENTERTAINMENT

Besides national, puppet and avant-garde theatre as well as opera, Naples has a lively music scene. A popular meeting point is the snug *Piazza Bellini* with its tree-shaded cafés, such as the *Intra Moenia*. Event programmes and tickets: *Box Office | Galleria Umberto I 16 | tel. 08 15 51 91 88*

WHERE TO STAY

NAPOLIDAY RESIDENCE

In the elegant Chiaia district guests stay in pretty B & B rooms or self-catering studio apartments. *15 rooms | Via Cappella Vecchia 11 | tel. 08 12 48 11 06 | www.napilday.it | Budget–Moderate*

HOTEL PIAZZA BELLINI

Successful contrasts: ultramodern interior, superb comfort and perfect location in the middle of the old town. *50 rooms | Via Santa Maria di Costantinopoli 101 | tel. 0 81 45 17 32 | www.hotelpiazzabellini.com | Budget–Moderate*

INFORMATION

Main Station, Via San Carlo 9 and *Piazza Gesù Nuovo | tel. 08 15 52 33 28 | incampania.com, www.inaples.it*. Naples and the surroundings also offer a visitor's pass that provides discounts and is valid for three or seven days: *Campania Artecard (www.artecard.it)*.

WHERE TO GO

AMALFI AND THE SORRENTO PENINSULA (183 F6) (*ØJ9*)

South of Naples, the rocky ⭐ peninsula of Sorrento juts far out into the sea towards the island of Capri, a powerful partition between the Gulf of Naples and the Gulf of Salerno. On the south side is the 'divine' ⭐ *Costa Amalfitana* with the famous Oriental towns of Positano, Amalfi, Ravello: probably Italy's most beautiful coast with rugged cliffs, precipitous cliffs, gorges and bays, to the gentler slopes and terraces of lemon groves, vineyards, almonds and olive trees and everywhere climbing flowers, wild roses, and bougainvillea.

PIZZA NAPOLETANA

It appeared for the first time in the 18th century as a fast and cheap snack on the streets of Naples: a simple, malleable dough made of flour, yeast, water and salt, seasoned with olive oil, oregano and basil. Tomatoes and anchovies came later. At the beginning of the 19th century, Naples was already full of pizzerias, but nobody had heard about them in the rest of Italy. They only caught up in the 20th century and then via America. There pizza had spread like wildfire thanks to the Italian immigrants and it was from there that it began its triumphal march through Europe. Although you can now get it everywhere, the taste of a real *pizza napoletana* (with tomatoes, mozzarella and anchovies) in Naples remains a special experience.

The picturesque little town of Positano clings to the cliffs

Situated on a rocky plateau, high above the coast, *Sorrento* (pop. 17,000) – a lively tourist centre with many traditional luxury hotels – specialises in the craft of wood carving/inlay. In this wonderful part of the world there are masses of superb, star-studded (and expensive) gourmet addresses: in *Vico Equense* the *L' Accanto* (www.laccanto.it), the highly acclaimed *Torre del Saracino* (www.torredelsaracino. it) and quite a few more, in *Nerano-Massa Lubrense* the *Quattro Passi* (www.ristorante quattropassi.com) and the *Taverna del Capitano* (www.tavernadelcapitano.it).

On the south side of the Sorrento Peninsula is the enchanting *Positano* (pop. 4000): bright and red-tinted houses with arcade loggias cling to the cliffs, including the *Santa Maria Assunta* church with majolica dome.

From a historical point of view, *Amalfi* (pop. 6000), once an influential maritime republic is more important. The superb architecture seems to cling to the cliffs, such as the *cathedral* with its magnificent steps, colourful mosaic façade and Arabic Norman *campanile*.

It earns the epithet 'divine coast' because of its position, fame and enchanting luxury hotels, but also for its charming and reasonably affordable accommodation, e.g. in Positano ⚓ *Palazzo Talamo* (11 rooms | Viale Pasitea 117 | tel. 0 89 87 55 62 | www.palazzotalamo.it | *Moderate–Expensive*) or a mile outside of Amalfi *Locanda Costa d'Amalfi* (6 rooms, 3 apartments | Via G. Augustoriccio 50 | tel. 08 9 83 19 50 | www.locandacostadamalfi.it | *Budget–Moderate*). A shopping tip is Amalfi's handmade paper: you can buy

One of the 1200 rooms in Caserta's Baroque Palazzo Reale

is a breathtaking view of the gulf. *www. amalficoast.com*

CASERTA AND CAPUA
(183 F6) *(㎿ J9)*

Visit the impressive gardens in Caserta, a Unesco site, and site of the enormous Baroque castle *Reggia di Caserta (Wed–Mon 8.30am–7.30pm, park 9pm–2 hours before sunset)* with 1200 rooms, 1790 windows and 94 steps (construction period of the facade 1752–74): the ambitious 'Versailles' of Bourbon King Charles III of Naples. In *Capua* in the *Museo Campano (Tue–Sat 9am–1.30pm, Sun 9am–1pm, Tue, Thu also 3pm–7pm)*, the INSIDERTIP quite unique votive statues (AD 7–1) of Mater Matuta, goddess of fertility and maternity, are well worth seeing. The stone mother figures hold swaddled babies in their arms. Equally fascinating is the Roman *amphitheatre* in *Santa Maria Capua Vetere* – the second largest in Italy – with a nearby *Mithraic temple*.

HERCULANEUM (ERCOLANO)
(183 F6) *(㎿ J9)*

When Mount Versuvius erupted in AD 79 Pompeii was showered with lava rain and Herculaneum was smothered under hot mud. From Corso Ercolano, you can ascend to the Roman sports arena and enter the still not completely excavated town. *Nov–March daily 8.30am–5pm, April–Oct 8.30am–7.30pm | Corso Resina*

PAESTUM AND CILENTO
(186 B1–2) *(㎿ K9–10)*

At the southern arc of the Gulf of Salerno – in the harbour town that has recently received a facelift – these wonderfully preserved Doric temples dedicated to Hera and the fertility god of Ceres rise into view in the old Greek commercial town of Poseido. The Romans called it ★ *Paestum*. The Arabs destroyed the

the traditional paper from shops in Amalfi and Positano and admire its production in *Museo della Carta (March–Oct daily 10am–6.30pm, Nov–Feb Tue–Sun 10am–3.30pm | Via delle Cartiere 24 | www. museodellacarta.it)*.

In the mountains above Amalfi, perched on large rock and tucked away in lush vegetation, is the enchanting *Ravello*, famous for its music festival and very modern *auditorium*, Romanesque *cathedral* and precious villas such as the Arabic *Villa Rufolo* (13th century). From the ☆ terrace in the garden of *Villa Cimbrone* (with renovated charming hotel), there

town; its ruins lay under a thick layer of vegetation until 200 years ago. *Temple site daily 8.45am–1 hour before sunset, museum daily 8am–7pm, closed on 1st and 3rd Mon in the month).*

On the plain of Paestum is **INSIDER TIP** *Cilento* a beautiful, unspoilt coastline with ● sandy beaches, bays and grottoes – e.g. between Pisciotta and Palinuro or between Marina di Camerota and the Golfo di Policastro. Inland, the Monti Alburni and the Monte Cervati reach heights of almost 2000m/6562ft: the national park is a popular holiday destination for beach lovers and hikers, and offers attractions such as the Baroque cloister *Certosa di San Lorenzo (Wed–Mon 9am–8pm)* in *Padula*.

POMPEII (POMPEI) ★
(183 F6) (*∅ J9*)

What makes this town excavated from the hard lava stone so unique is not its build-ings but the insight it provides into every-day Roman life *(Nov–March daily 8.30am–5pm, April–Oct 8.30am–7.30pm | www.pompeisepolta.com).* Shops, bars, cob-bled streets worn with deep grooves from the wagons of the ancients Romans … The phallic symbols on the entrances were used to ward off evil spirits. Here are also the famous frescoes depicting scenes of the initiation of women into the cult of Dionysus in the *Villa dei Misteri.*

VESUVIUS (VESUVIO) ☙
(183 F6) (*∅ J9*)

An absolute must when visiting Naples is a trip to the still active volcano, Mount Vesuvius (1281m/4200ft) in the south-east of the city. A serpentine road leads from Ercolano to two fee-paying car parks (also accessible by bus). From here you can walk across the lava fields to the rim of the crater (20 min).

A lunar landscape: near the crater, Naples's fertile Vesuvius looks very barren

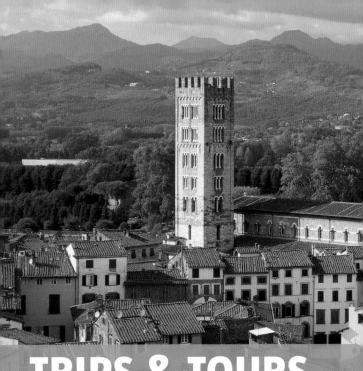

TRIPS & TOURS

The tours are marked in green in the road atlas, the pull-out map and on the back cover

1 ON THE PILGRIMAGE ROUTE TO ROME

The route of the medieval pilgrims from the Alps to Rome, takes you through some of the most beautiful Italian towns and countryside. The Via Francigena, the old Franconia road from central Europe down through Italy to Rome, is one of the great historical routes along with the route to Santiago. Covering 850km/ 528mi, it stretches along country roads from the Great Saint Bernhard Pass to Rome. A pilgrim in medieval times walked about 30km/19mi a day. But even today's motorised travellers should plan at least five to six days. Pilgrims on foot today will find it well-signposted along footpaths and there are plenty of overnight accommodation options. *www. viafrancigena.com, www.itineraria.eu, www.eurovia.tv*

The road over the Great Saint Bernhard Pass (2473 m/8144 ft) is usually open from May to the end of October. This road was first built by the Romans on their way to Gaul. Reports of a hostel here date back to the 8th century; the current (18th century) building, in a superb position among the majestically, snow-topped mountain peaks, is run by Augustinian monks who offer

A programme of Italian contrasts: a pilgrimage from the Alps via Siena to Rome and then off to the Abruzzo National Park

accommodation only to walkers and pilgrims, not to motorised travellers. On the SS27 main road, 12km/7.5mi north of Aosta is the town of Gignod where, in the part of the town called **La Clusaz**, there is a former pilgrims' and coach inn which today is a pleasant little hotel *(Budget)* with good food *(Moderate)*: **Locanda La Clusaz** *(14 rooms | closed Wed lunch and Tue | tel. 0 16 55 60 75 | www.laclusaz.it)*. Places

for pilgrims to visit in **Aosta → p. 35** are the Santa Maria Assunta cathedral and the monastery of Sant'Orso with its large craft market. The route continues along the SS26 through the valley of the Dora Baltea River with the impressive alpine mountain backdrop and past the **castles → p. 37** of the former feudal lords. The wayside crosses that used to serve as signposts for pilgrims can be found today in **Bard**.

The next places of interest are the two bishoprics of **Ivrea** and **Vercelli**, where the route comes out on to the fertile north Italian plains of the Po Valley, the Padania. In **Mortara**, at the centre of the rice fields of Lomellina, the pilgrims used to stop at the two medieval churches of San Lorenzo and Santa Croce, before continuing their journey to **Pavia** → p. 75.

In **Fidenza** on the Via Emilia, the stone relief on the beautiful Romanesque cathedral illustrates the efforts made by pilgrims. The bas-relief on the tower to the right of the façade depicts pilgrims of all social strata, those on horseback with pack animals, to those on foot wrapped in hooded cloaks (12th century). From Fidenza or **Parma** → p. 79 pilgrims made their way up the Taro Valley and over the Apennines southwards to Tuscany: this beautiful route (SS26) through picturesque countryside and the ever-changing mountain meadows and woods takes one through villages such as Talignano, Fornovo, Bardone, Berceto with impressive Romanesque churches. Crossing the Cisa Pass (1093m/3586ft)

the traveller enters Tuscany at **Pontremoli**, where San Pietro church contains a labyrinth symbolising the pilgrimage to the Holy Land.

Passing the impressive Romanesque church of **Sorana**, the route goes via Aulla through the Magra Valley to Sarzana and continues against the backdrop of the marble mountains via Carrara, Massa and Pietrasanta and down to Lucca. **Pietrasanta** → p. 105 in particular, with its cathedral square lined with cafés, its art galleries and sculpture workshops (Carrara marble), invite the traveller to linger. For the pious pilgrims, **Lucca** → p. 90 was an important stop, even in medieval times the cathedral's large black figure of Christ, the Volto Santo, was revered (nowadays, too, every year on 13th September with an atmospheric candlelight procession). The route then goes across the marshes of Fucecchio and continues to Castelfiorentino, Certaldo and **San Gimignano** → p. 103, all of which have largely retained their medieval town centres. In **Abbadia Isola** near Monteriggioni (picture book

'Manhattan of the Middle Ages': the impressive towers of San Gimignano

example of a medieval fortified town) are the remains of a large Cistercian abbey. One important destination on the route to Rome is Siena → p. 100 with its relics, churches and inns and, above all, the once enormous hospice and hospital Santa Maria alla Scala opposite the cathedral, nowadays a fascinating museum complex. The following ● INSIDER TIP▶ section of the route, through the Arbia and Val d'Orcia, takes one through some of the most beautiful landscapes in Italy with its wide open spaces, its gentle hills and its tranquillity. Places of particular interest include the medieval towns of Isola d'Arbia, Buonconvento (not far from here is the large monastery Abbazia di Monte Oliveto Maggiore) and San Quirico d'Orcia, which has a wonderful medieval cathedral. From here a little detour is recommended to Sant'Antimo, a Romanesque abbey located in wonderful surroundings on the ancient pilgrim route and a must for those wanting to follow in the footsteps of medieval spirituality. At Monte Amiata → p. 103 the Abbadia San Salvatore used

to provide pilgrims with accommodation and assistance.

Acquapendente (cathedral crypt is worth a visit) on the border to the Lazi region, is also located on the pilgrim route. A peaceful agricultural area of meadows, woods, maize fields, vineyards and olive groves accompanies the traveller to Lago di Bolsena → p. 121, whose clear water invites you to swim. In the lakeside town of Bolsena, a Roman pilgrim celebrating Eucharist in the 13th century apparently experienced a miracle; blood began to flow from the host – a revelation of transsubstantiation in which bread and wine become the body and blood of Christ – an event which inspired the Festival of Corpus Christi and the building of Orvieto cathedral.

The route continues southwards via Montefiascone to Viterbo → p. 120, the former residence of bishops and the Pope, and from there to the Etruscan tuff stone town of Sutri with its rock-hewn sanctuaries. In medieval times it is believed to have had a flourishing shoemaking trade: after all, with the Holy City and its seven pilgrims' churches only a day's walk away, visitors wanted to arrive in respectable footwear.

2 THE APENNINES – THE 'GREAT ROCK' OF ITALY

The centre of Italy is not characterised by a landscape of hills as in Tuscany but rather by the rugged magnificence of the Apennines, the range of mountains that stretches like a backbone down the entire country. In the heart of the Abruzzi it reaches its highest point, the massif of the Gran Sasso d'Italia known more familiarly as the 'big rock'. This route, which starts or finishes in the Abruzzo towns of Teramo and Chieti, leads through the Abruzzo National Park, through the hillside town of L'Aquila and

Piana di Tivo: sheep graze here in summer, in winter it is a playground for skiers

through the mountains of Maiella, partly on steep, winding roads, and partly across wide open plateaus. It introduces the visitor to a unique landscape replete with harsh yet grandiose natural beauty and rare fauna as well as traces of ancient life. For this tour covering about 350km/217mi, you should set aside at least two days.

From Teramo the main road SS80 goes to L'Aquila. First of all, it crosses the hills to Montorio al Vomano (worth a visit here: the parish church on the piazza of the old town centre, above the town). In the background, the Gran Sasso massif rises up to its two highest peaks: Corno Grande (2912m/9554ft) and Corno Piccolo (2655m/8711ft).

The Valle del Vomano now becomes narrower, wilder and more tortuous. After passing a tunnel and a small reservoir, it is worth taking a little detour through the Gola del Vomano a wooded gorge, then to Pietracamela at 1167m/3829ft, a starting point for tours in the national park and to the grassy slopes of the Piana di Tivo, a good winter skiing area. On the way back to the SS80, just below Pietracamelas

take the secondary road via Intermesoli and Fano Adriano with their wonderful old houses. The SS80 climbs again through the Valle del Vomano valley between the two lakes, the picturesque little Lago di Provvidenza and the more formidable Lago di Campotosto a bit higher up, until it finally reaches the Passo di Capannelle (1299m/4262ft). Descending towards L'Aquila, the landscape changes from wooded slopes to deeply eroded limestone cliffs.

Before reaching L'Aquila, there are two sights worth visiting: the remains of the Roman amphitheatre of the ancient town of Amiternum (turn left as the main road forks to Rieti), and the impressive Romanesque San Michele church, whose crypt and catacombs survived attacks in the 16th century, situated at San Vittorino on the SS80 after L'Aquila. The landscape has now broadened to the Conca di L'Aquila, the 'basin', and the industrial installations indicate the approach of the capital Abruzzo → p. 106, which is worthy of an extensive visit.

The route continues along the SS5 following the valley of the Aterno, the most important river of the Abruzzo, and comes to the main towns on the broad, high plateau Rocca di Cambio (1433m/4701ft) and Rocca di Mezzo (1329m/4360ft), all the time accompanied by the beautiful backdrop of the mountain chain of the Gran Sasso. Tourism, above all winter sport, has developed here with numerous ski-lifts along the slopes of Campo Felice. The route descends now to Ovindoli with its old town centre. It is the starting point for mountain tours to the peaks of Monte Sirente (2349m/7707ft) and Monte Velino (2487m/8157ft). The slopes of Monte di Magnola (2220m/7283ft) are a skiing area. A nice place to stop is the picturesque village of Rovere (towards Rocca di Mezzo) north of Ovindoli, at the Albergo diffuso Robur Marsorum consisting of 16 comfortable rustic rooms located in and around the old village centre *(Via Antonio Milanetti | Tel. 0862 917249 | www.robur marsorum.com | Moderate)*. The route descends the valley through dark pine woods and the narrows of San Potito to the wide plain Piana del Fucino at 600m/ 1969ft. Until the 19th century, the plain was a lake (once the third largest in Italy) and a highland moor which reclamation transformed into agricultural land.

In Celano the mighty castle, Castello Piccolomini (worth visiting for its Museum of Sacred Art), rises high above the town, and to the south-east is the wild, romantic gorge, Gola di Celano. From Celano you should take the SS 83 southwards skirting the plain of the drained Fucino Lake, which is bordered on the left by rough karst formations with their early cave dwellings.

At Gioia dei Marsi the road climbs again and winds its way through the mountains of the national park up to the Passo del Diavolo (1400m/4593ft), the watershed between the Tyrrhenian Sea and the Adriatic. Following the course of the river

through woods and meadows you reach Pescasseroli → p. 111, the national park's tourist centre.

The S 83 leads via Opi to Villetta Barrea. Here a very worthwhile little detour (round trip: a good 50km/31mi) takes you to Scanno, **INSIDER TIP** one of the wildest, unspoilt sections to a particularly beautifully maintained Abruzzo mountain town. Returning to the SS83, in Civitella Alfedena you can visit the interesting wolf museum, Museo del Lupo *(daily 10am–1pm and 2.30pm–5.30pm)*. The route then takes you along the Barrea reservoir and via Alfedena to Castel di Sangro with its medieval town centre. Here in the hamlet of Santa Liberata-Casadonna there is the surprising Relais Reale offering high standard gourmet cuisine *(6 rooms | closed Mon and Tue | Tel. 0 86 46 93 82 | www.ristorantereale.it | Expensive)*. Here also are the rather scattered holiday resorts of Roccaraso and Rivisondoli. Of particular beauty is the little Baroque town of **INSIDER TIP** Pescocostanzo (1395m/ 4577ft) with its basilica and its traditional art and craftwork. You might want to stay here at the Albergo Archi del Sole *(20 rooms | Porta di Berardo 9 | tel. 08 64 64 00 07 | www.archidelsole.it | Budget– Moderate)*. On the way to Fara San Martino, a detour near Palena takes you towards Monterodomo (round trip about 35km/ 22mi) to the extensive remains of the Roman city Juvanum situated at 1100m/ 3609ft *(with museum Thu–Sun 10am– 1pm and 4pm–7pm)*.

Continuing along the SS84 through the Maiella mountain range, you come to Fara San Martino, well known for its location at the foot of the rough limestone rock faces and for its pasta. A final, exciting stretch of the winding, mountainous road SS263 leads to the lovely Guardiagrele → p. 110, and from here the SS81 takes you to Chieti → p. 110.

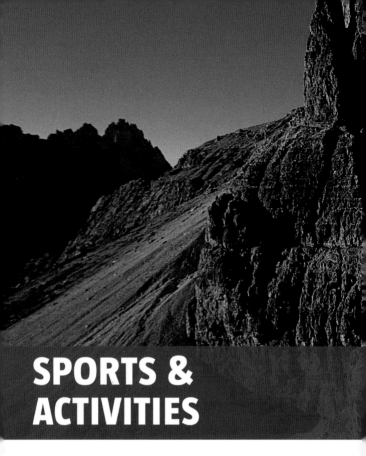

SPORTS & ACTIVITIES

Few other European countries can claim the geographical diversity of Italy: towering Alpine mountains, large lakes, gently rolling hills, rugged terrain and thousands of miles of beautiful coastline. The choice of sports and activities is equally diverse.

The trendsetter is the 'fitness and fun' industry on the Adriatic around Rimini and Riccione, the California of Italy. The wide sandy beaches are ideal for beach volleyball. Many bathing areas focus on health activities, with gyms, sport programmes and beach competitions. The nearby mountains, whether Alps or Apennines, offer a range of outdoor activities, from paragliding to rafting, ski or mountain bike tours.

BIRDWATCHING

Once the country of the bird hunters, Italy has become a paradise for ornithologists: the protected estuary landscapes of the Po *(www.parcodeltapo.it)* and Isonzo *(www.isoladellacona.it)* rivers along the northern Adriatic are home to hundreds of birds, some of which are quite rare. Bird watching tours are offered at the visitor centres and nature oases and there are also many walks you can do on your own.

From birdwatching to surfing and skiing: Italy's geographical diversity is reflected in its wide selection of outdoor activities

CYCLING

Cycling is a popular sport in Italy and at the weekend the cyclists hit the roads in large groups. Although there are very few cycle tracks, there are loads of brochures with proposed tours. In the towns, especially those in the Po Valley, such as Milan, Ferrara, Ravenna and Mantua, you can hire bikes in many hotels or at the station and use them to INSIDER TIP explore the restricted traffic zones of the old centres. Popular mountain bike areas are the Finale area in Liguria and the Tuscan Emilian Apennines where the terrain and difficulty level varies. You will also find rental bikes in the seaside resorts, for instance along the Adriatic, for tours in the Po Delta nature reserve or along the beach promenades.

DIVING

The coastal areas particularly suited to diving are in Liguria around the peninsula of Portofino and on the coastal section of the Cinque Terre. A good spot is along the upper Adriatic, the craggy Trieste coast near Castello di Miramare. Further south in the Marche, divers flock to the rocks of Monte Conero near Sirol. In Lazio the San Felice promontory of the Circeo nature protection area near Sabaudia is popular with divers. The Isole Tremiti archipelago is a highlight in the south, including the tip of the heel at Santa Maria di Leuca as well as the sea off the peninsula of Isola di Capo Rizzuto and at Scilla on the Strait of Messina. A fascinating experience is in Campania, a dive in the INSIDER TIP grottoes of Palinuro and off the Sorrento Peninsula – or you can dive down to the INSIDER TIP ruins of the Roman villas on the seabed off Baia not far from Naples.

GOLF

The Italians caught golf fever some time ago, and there are lovely courses around the country (e.g. in *Val Ferret* in Aosta Valley). *www.greenpassgolf.com* provides detailed descriptions of the courses.

HIKING

You can walk through Italy from north to south on the *Sentiero d'Italia* trail. There are good connections along the entire Alpine chain from the Aosta Valley in South Tyrol to the Carnic Alps in Friaul. Deserted hiking trails pass over the Piedmontese Alps and down to the Ligurian Sea *(www.mountainzones.com)*. The ✹ mountainous coastal area of Liguria offers stunning hiking trails through verdant Mediterranean maquis, with breathtaking views of the sea. The marked hiking routes in the mountains of the Monti Sibillini national park, between Umbria and the Marche, offer a spectacular scenic experience. That is also true of the ★ *national parks* of the Abruzzo and the Monte Pollino between Calabria and Basilicata, Sila and Aspromonte, all stunning mountainscapes. The tourist offices can help by providing the addresses of experienced mountain guides and of organised group tours. The mountains also offer new hiking trails with historic themes, e.g. the *pilgrimage route Via Francigena* from the north to Rome, the Apennine crossing along the German-American frontline in the Second World War, the *Linea Gotica,* or walking in the footsteps of St Francis of Assisi through central Italy.

MOUNTAINEERING & ROCK CLIMBING

The entire chain of Italian Alps offers challenging climbing tours, especially those with summits of 4000m/13,120ft in the Aosta Valley. *Vie ferrata*, protected climbing routes with iron hooks, ladders and wire cables pass through the Dolomites and make it possible even for non-mountain climbers to scale the precipices. And in Finale Ligure free climbers get together to explore the cliffs above the sea.

PESCATURISMO

A tip is *pescaturismo:* in fishing areas you can help bring in the catch or there are deep sea fishing trips on offer. This often culminates in a nice fish meal. Information is available from the tourist boards.

THERMAL SPAS

Traditional spa resorts have undergone a facelift and now offer a wide range of health and beauty treatments. Italy, a country that once had many active volcanoes has a large number of well-known thermal spas. The most famous thermal spas include those in the Euganean Hills with its Abano Terme, the spas of Tuscany, especially Montecatini Terme, and naturally the island of Ischia. *www.benessere.com/terme/italia*

WATER SPORTS

The top destination for water sports fans is Lake Garda, where the winds in the northern section make it popular with surfers. But there are also surfboard rental companies in all of the tourist areas along the coast and it is possible to rent surfboards in the large holiday resorts, too. The Ligurian coast is particularly popular, especially around Albenga and Noli, the Conero on the Adriatic as well as the Lazio coast near Sabaudia and Fregene. Sailing is possible all along the coast, and there are plenty of marinas (where sailing courses are offered).

WINTER SPORTS

The entire Alpine range has an established infrastructure. Most of the larger Alpine ski resorts offer a snow park for the snowboarders and freestylers, or ice palaces for the ice skaters. You will find beautiful cross-country skiing trails in the valley of Gran Paradiso in the Aosta Valley, in South Tyrol, in Trentino and in the Carnic Alps. There are also good ski areas further south, e.g. in the Apennines along the Abetone massif around Sestola or further south in the Abruzzo near Pescasseroli. The best place to go for ski tours in unspoilt countryside is the Piedmont Maritime Alps (e.g. the Maira Valley).

The northern area of Lake Garda is a popular destination for windsurfers

TRAVEL WITH KIDS

Italy in the summer with the children promises warm Mediterranean waters, wide sandy beaches on the Adriatic or in the south and – especially along the northern Adriatic – large water and amusement parks.

Many hotels offer a discounted price for children *(www.italyfamilyhotels.it)* and almost all restaurants have a menu with smaller portions. Children may also enter the larger state museums free of charge. For an active family holiday try **INSIDER TIP** exploring the lagoons along the northern Adriatic in a comfortable houseboat: the *Idrovia Veneta* waterway connects the spectacular Venice Lagoon with the quiet canals of Marano and Grado, with their rich birdlife and lidos: *www.leboat.co.uk.*

THE NORTH-WEST

ACQUARIO DI GENOVA ●
(179 D5) (*ΩΩ D4*)

This is Italy's most exciting and popular aquarium, located in the old harbour: *Nov–Feb Mon–Fri 9.30am–7.30pm, Sat/ Sun 9.30am–8.30pm, March–June and Sept/Oct Mon–Fri 9am–7.30pm, Sat/Sun 8.45am–8.30pm, July/Aug daily 8.30am– 10pm | 19 euros, children (aged 3–12) 13 euros, free for under 3 | Porto Antico | Ponte Spinola | www.acquariodigenova.it*

Photo: Aquarium in Genoa

Ötzi, the glacier mummy, stone monsters in the Baroque park, long-nosed Pinocchio and dripstone caves: all perfect for the little ones!

THE NORTH-EAST

MUSEO ARCHEOLOGICO DELL'ALTO ADIGE IN BOLZANO (180 C2) (*ω F2*)

'Ötzi', the famous mummy, now resides in Bolzano. There are also special family rates at selected times. *Tue–Sun 10am–6pm | adults 9 euros, children (aged 6 and older) 7 euros, under 6 free, family ticket 18 euros | Via Museo 43 | www.iceman.it*

PO VALLEY AND LAKES

ACQUARIO DI CATTOLICA LE NAVI (181 D6) (*ω H5*)

The futuristic architecture from the 1930s resembles a fleet; located on Cattolica beach, it is home to an aquarium with lots of different species of fish. *April–June, Sept daily, in winter Sat/Sun 9.30am–4.30pm, mid June–Aug daily 10am–9.30pm |*

19 euros, children (under 12) 14 euros, under 1m/3ft free | Piazzale delle Nazioni 1 a | www.acquariodicattolica.it

AQUAFAN IN RICCIONE
(181 D6) (*ØŊ G5*)

There is one attraction after another along the Adriatic coast, one of which is this enormous water park. *June–mid Sept daily 10am–6.30pm, longer on selected evenings | 28 euros, from 3pm 16 euros, children (aged 6–11) 20 euros, free on 2nd day | Via Pistoia | www.aquafan.it*

AQUALAND IN JESOLO
(181 D3) (*ØŊ G–H3*)

Offering cascades, slides, rafting tours and Caribbean landscapes, this aqua park is regarded as one of the most spectacular in Italy. *End May–beginning of Sept daily 10am–6pm | 28 euros, 1–1.40m (3–4.5ft) 24 euros, under 1m (3ft) free | Via Michelangelo Buonarroti 15 | Lido di Jesolo | www.aqualandia.it*

GARDALAND
(180 B3) (*ØŊ F3*)

Italy's most famous amusement park is based on the Disneyworld concept. *April–mid June and mid–end Sept daily 10am–6pm, mid June–mid Sept daily 10am–11pm, Oct and Dec Sat/Sun 10am–6pm | 35 euros, children (under 11) 30 euros and free for children under 1m/3ft | Castelnuovo | Ronchi | www.gardaland.it*

MIRABILANDIA IN RAVENNA
(181 D5) (*ØŊ G4*)

This enormous funfair is regarded as the main competitor to Italy's Gardaland. *April–June and 1st half of Sept daily 10am–6pm, July/Aug 10am–11pm, mid Sept–mid Oct Sat/Sun 10am–6pm | 34 euros, children (under 11) 28 euros, free for children under 1m/3ft and on second day | SS Adriatica 16, 162km/100mi | www.mirabilandia.it*

INSIDER TIP ▶ GIUSEPPE MEAZZA STADIUM IN MILAN (179 D3) (*ØŊ D3*)

If there is no game on, you can look round Italy's largest football stadium. *Daily 10am–6pm | 13 euros, children (aged 6–18) 10 euros, free for children under 6 | Via Piccolomini 5 | Entrance Gate 14 | www.sansirotour.com*

CENTRAL ITALY

PARCO DI PINOCCHIO IN COLLODI
(182 A1) (*ØŊ F5*)

Statues of characters from the story of little Pinocchio, set in beautiful gardens. *8.30am–sunset | 11 euros, children (aged 3–14) 8 euros | Via San Gennaro 3 | www.pinocchio.it*

ROME AND THE APENNINES

BIOPARCO IN ROME ☺
(182–183 C–D4) (*ØŊ G8*)

In the verdant vegetation of this nature reserve, you will find i.a. Siberian tigers, apes and rare turtles. *April–Oct daily 9.30am–6pm, otherwise until 4pm | 13 euros, 11 euros for children under the age of 12, free for children under 1m/3ft | Piazzale del Giardino Zoologico 1 | www.bioparco.it*

CASINA DI RAFFAELLO IN ROME
(182–183 C–D4) (*ØŊ G8*)

In the urban park Villa Borghese, children (aged 3–10) can run about, play and make things in this beautiful large children's activity centre. *Tue–Fri 9am–6pm, Sat/Sun 10am–7pm | 7 euros | Viale della Casina Raffaello/Piazza di Siena | www.casinadiraffaello.it*

PARCO DEI MOSTRI IN BOMARZO
(182 C3) (*ØŊ G7*)

In a dense forest, the 'monster park' on the edge of Bomarzo near Orte in north Lazio

Spinning through the air in Mirabilandia near Ravenna

is home to bizarre and eerie, weathered stone monsters from the 16th century. *Daily 8.30am–1 hour before sunset | 10 euros, children (aged 4–13) 8 euros, free for children under 4, www.parcodeimostri.com*

RAINBOW MAGICLAND ☺
(183 D4) (ⓜ H8)

Established in 2011, southern Italy now has its own Disney-style amusement park, just outside Rome an enormous funfair with fun pools, wonderland, entertainment and evening parties. *Daily mid April–mid June and 1st half of Sept 10am–6pm, July 10am–10pm, daily Aug 10am–11pm, Oct Sat/Sun 10am–6pm | 35 euros, children (under 10) 28 euros, under 1m/3ft free | Via della Pace | Valmontone-Pascolaro | www.magicland.it*

SOUTHERN ITALY

DRIPSTONE CAVES

Extending along Italy's boot are some of the largest dripstone caves in Europe, subterranean chambers full of stalagmites and stalactites that have an enchanting beauty. Among the most spectacular caves (in addition to huge *Grotta Gigante*

near Trieste) are the *Grotte di Frasassi* and *Grotta Grande del Vento* in the Marche not far from Fabriano, in the mountains of Cilento in Campania the *Grotte di Castelcivita* (**(184 B5) (ⓜ K10)** | *tours Easter–Sept daily 10.30am, noon, 1.30pm, 3pm, 4.30pm and 6pm, March and Oct 10.30am, noon, 1.30pm and 3pm | 10 euros, children (aged 6–12) 8 euros, under 5 free | www.grottedicastelcivita.com).* In the boot heel in Apulia the *Grotte di Castellana* (**(185 D4) (ⓜ M9)** | *mid March–Oct daily tours) 9.30am–4.30pm or 7pm | short tour 10 euros, children (aged 6–14) 8 euros, long tour 15 and 12 euros | www.grottedi castellana.it).*

ZOO SAFARI IN FASANO
(185 E4) (ⓜ M9)

Watch lions lazing around in a landscape that resembles the African savannah. The theme park *Fasanolandia* is part of the safari park *(individual attractions 2 euros extra)* with funfair attractions, dolphin show etc. *March–Oct daily 9.30am–4pm (Aug to 4.30pm), Nov–Feb Sun 10am–3pm, zoo safari and Fasanolandia 22 euros, only Fasanolandia 8 euros, children under 4 free | Via Zoosafari | www.zoosafari.it*

FESTIVALS & EVENTS

PUBLIC HOLIDAYS

1 January; **6 January**; **Easter Monday**;
25 April *Liberation Day;* **1 May**; **2 June**
Republic Day; **15 August** *Assumption Day;*
1 November *All Saints' Day;* **8 December**
Immaculate Conception; **25/26 December**
Christmas Day

FESTIVALS & EVENTS

FEBRUARY/MARCH

▶ *Carnival* is celebrated in Piedmont's
Ivrea with a food fight, the ▶ INSIDER TIP
Battle of the Oranges, in Venice with
spectacular masquerades, and in Viareggio
with satirical floats depicting political
leaders

MARCH/APRIL

Poignant Easter processions, especially
impressive is the ▶ *Good Friday procession* in Taranto (Apulia) and Chieti
(Abruzzo), as is the Virgin Mary's emo-
tional reunion with her resurrected son
in Sulmona on Easter Sunday (Abruzzo):
▶ INSIDER TIP *La Madonna che Scappa
in Piazza*

MAY/JUNE

15 May: ▶ ★ *Corsa dei Ceri* in Gubbio
(Umbria): three teams race huge statues
of the village's patron saints up Mount
Ingino – spectacular!

May–mid June: ▶ *Maggio Musicale
Fiorentino:* international music festival
week in Florence *www.maggiofiorentino.
com*

Corpus Christi: ▶*Procession* and colourful
floral carpets of flowers i. a. in Bolsena and
Genzano near Rome, in Spello (Umbria)
and in Campobasso (Molise)

SUMMER (JUNE–SEPT)

End of June–mid July: ▶ *Festival dei Due
Mondi* in Spoleto with theatre, dance and
music events

End of June–end of August: ▶ INSIDER TIP
I Suoni delle Dolomiti: on mountain meadows below the peaks of the Dolomites of
Trentino awe-inspiring concerts. *www.
isuonidelledolomiti.it*

July: ▶ *Heineken Jammin' Festival:* international rock and pop stars appear at
the festival in San Giuliano near Venice,
www.venezia.net/heineken-jammin-festival
Beginning July–end of Aug: The world

Carnival processions, medieval tournaments and top-class music festivals: Italy is in a festive mood all year round

famous ▶ *Arena di Verona Opera Festival* in Verona's Roman arena

Beginning of July–mid Sept: ▶ *Ravello Festival:* First-class concerts and more against the backdrop of the Costa Amalfitana. *www.ravellofestival.com*

2 July and 16 Aug: ▶ *Palio di Siena:* Italy's most famous and – for reasons of animal welfare – controversial horse race on the beautiful piazza

Mid July: ▶ *Neapolis Festival,* southern Italy's most important rock-pop festival in Naples, *www.neapolis.it*

Mid July: ▶ *Pescara Jazz* and ▶ *Umbria Jazz,* are two of the best jazz festivals among the numerous jazz festivals during the Italian summer. *www.pescarajazz.com* and *www.umbriajazz.com*

Mid July: ▶ ★ *Arezzo Wave Love Festival:* the five days best groups in the new rock-pop trends play in the Arezzo stadium, a world-class festival. *www.arezzowave.com*

August: In the height of the summer, a vast array of events such as gourmet festivals and on 15 August ▶ *Ferragosto,* a fantastic firework display

Second half of August: The bohemian set meets for ▶ *Notte della Taranta* in Salento in Apulia

In the last two weeks of August, international street ▶ *buskers* entertain in the squares in Ferrara. *www.ferrarabuskers.com*

3 September: ▶ ● *Trasporto della Macchina di Santa Rosa:* in honour of their patron saint, 100 men carry a 30m/98ft tower through the medieval streets of Viterbo

OCTOBER

▶ *Barcolana:* thousands of sailboats take part in Europe's largest amateur regatta in the second week of October in the Gulf of Trieste in the northern Adriatic

LINKS, BLOGS, APPS & MORE

LINKS

▶ www.italia.it/en/home.html Italy's official portal for tourism is packed with information about the different areas as well as plenty of practical information to help you organize your trip. You can also click on an interactive map of Italy and make a virtual tour of some of the main towns you wish to visit

▶ www.italia-magazine.com Italia is an online magazine with tips on travel, holiday homes, Italian cooking and even information about buying a property

▶ short.travel/ITA1 The getyourguide portal allows you to book excursions, museum visits, special city tours, wine tasting, cookery courses, sports activities and much more in locations all over Italy

▶ www.wimdu.co.uk Simple, chic, cosy and stylish private apartments can be found all over Italy and can be rented inexpensively using this site for one night and more

BLOGS & FORUMS

▶ www.beppegrillo.it/en Satirist, actor and activist Beppo Grillo successfully draws attention to corruption and misuse of power with his political satire. He launched the political party *movimento 5 stelle* (5 Star Movement). His blog is popular all over the world!

▶ blog.napoliunplugged.com Bonnie Alberts, journalist and photographer, blogs from her adopted home of Naples; included are sections on the nightlife, shopping and information about upcoming events

▶ www.parlafood.com The personal blog of Rome-based American food historian, sommelier and journalist Katie Parla with lots of great insider tips about her personal favourites: restaurants, pizzerias, wine bars, ice cream shops, and bakeries

▶ www.travelpod.com/s/italy?st=user Travel portal, with community blog entries, pictures and videos describing journeys in Italy (and searchable by town or area) also links to all the main tourist attractions

Regardless of whether you are still preparing your trip or already in Italy: these addresses will provide you with information, videos and networks to make your holiday even more enjoyable

VIDEOS & STREAMS

▶ www.youtube.com/watch?v=HHWBL9_alKs A brilliant five minute clip 'Europe and Italy' by the comic book artist and animator Bruno Bozzetto that demonstrates in a few minutes just how different the Italians are from the rest of Europe

▶ www.learnitalianpod.com A free online resource that teaches Italian grammar, pronunciation and practical Italian phrases for use in everyday situations through the means of podcasts that you can download

▶ www.dailymotion.com This video catalogue has a beautiful film about every place in Italy that is on the Unesco World Heritage List

▶ vimeo.com/33976434 In this video, Francesco Paciocco presents his impressions of Milan – people, squares, visual angles, moods, moments – in a wonderfully dense and not touristy sequence of combined images. An excellent video town portrait

▶ www.eyeonitaly.com/podcast Podcast in English that focuses on culture and travel in Italy, also with regional and city podcasts

APPS

▶ Italy Guides Helpful city guides about many Italian towns available as apps for iPhone and iPad Touch

▶ AroundMe A free app as a travel companion, which locates your exact position via satellite and displays the nearest hotels, restaurants, banks, pubs, etc.

NETWORK

▶ www.partyamo.com You can get to know people living or staying in Milan using this network portal. People meet regularly for an aperitif, a game of badminton or brunch on Sunday

▶ www.homeforhome.co.uk Portal used to organise the global exchange of private apartments for holiday purposes. There are numerous offers in places such as Rome, Florence, Venice, and Naples

TRAVEL TIPS

ARRIVAL

If you are travelling to Italy by car from the UK, an attractive route is to go via Dijon to Chamonix and then head for the Mont Blanc Tunnel into the Aosta Valley. In good weather an alternative to the tunnel is the Grand St Bernard Pass from Switzerland. Coming from Germany and Austria the route would be via the Brenner Pass motorway in the Italian South Tyrol. There are also numerous passes (some subject to toll), many of which cannot be used in the winter. In the summer, they offer spectacular views, but require considerably more travelling time.

There are direct rail connections to Italy from European cities via the UK France, Switzerland, Germany or Austria www.raileurope.co.uk and www.fsitaliane.it/homepage_en.html. Car transporter trains are a comfortable, but not cheap in the season alternative. You can also travel to Italy by train on the Eurostar and TGV – and it is a comfortable and inexpensive alternative (www.seat61.com). The average travel time from London to Milan is nine hours.

The main international airports in Italy are: Milan, Turin, Bologna, Genoa, Venice, Trieste, Pisa, Florence, Rome, Bari and Naples. British Airways (www.britishairways.com) offer regular flights from the UK to Italy and you can also fly direct with Alitalia (www.alitalia.com) and with low coast airlines such as Easy Jet (www.easyjet.com). In North America the following airlines all have direct flights to Rome: Delta Airlines (www.delta.com) from New York, American Airlines (www.aa.com) from Chicago and Air Canada (www.aircanada.com) from Toronto.

CAR HIRE

Car rental companies have offices at all the international airports and train stations (credit cards mandatory!). You will pay about 80 euros a day for a standard car, or from about 300 euros per week. Enquire about special holiday and weekend rates. It is usually cheaper if you book in advance.

CUSTOMS

UK citizens do not have to pay any duty on goods brought from another EU country as long as tax was included in the price and they are for private consumption. The limits are: 800 cigarettes, 400 cigarillo, 200 cigars, 1kg smoking tobacco, 10L spirits, 20L liqueurs, 90L wine, 110L beer.

RESPONSIBLE TRAVEL

It doesn't take a lot to be environmentally friendly whilst travelling. Don't just think about your carbon footprint whilst flying to and from your holiday destination but also about how you can protect nature and culture abroad. As a tourist it is especially important to respect nature, look out for local products, cycle instead of driving, save water and much more. If you would like to find out more about eco-tourism please visit: www.ecotourism.org

From arrival to weather

Holiday from start to finish: the most important addresses and information for your trip to Italy

Travellers from the USA, Canada, Australia or other non-EU countries are allowed to enter with the following tax-free amounts: 200 cigarettes or 100 cigarillos or 50 cigars or 250g smoking tobacco. 2L wine and spirits with less than 22% vol. alcohol, 1L spirits with more than 22% vol. alcohol content.

Travellers to the United States who are returning residents of the country do not have to pay duty on articles purchased overseas up to the value of $800, but there are limits on the amount of alcoholic beverages and tobacco products. For the regulations for international travel for U.S. residents please see *www.cbp.gov*

DRIVING

A driving licence and vehicle registration documents are obligatory and the green insurance card and international travel cover are recommended. The speed limit in built-up areas is 50km/31mi, otherwise 90km/55mi, on motorways 130km/80mi or when it is raining 110km/68mi, on dual carriageways 110km/68mi. Even during the day, you have to put your headlights on when driving outside of towns. The legal blood alcohol limit is 0.5. You have to have high-visibility jackets for the driver and passengers in the car.

Except for a few stretches in southern Italy, you have to pay tolls on all the motorways. Dual carriageways *(superstrade)* are free of charge. In order to avoid queuing at the toll stations, you can pay with all major credit cards.

Many of the city centres are pedestrianised or have restrictions for vehicles; you have to buy tickets to use most parking bays. You can buy scratch parking tickets and

CURRENCY CONVERTER

£	€	€	£
1	1.20	1	0.85
3	3.60	3	2.55
5	6	5	4.25
13	15.60	13	11
40	48	40	34
75	90	75	64
120	144	120	100
250	300	250	210
500	600	500	425

$	€	€	$
1	0.75	1	1.30
3	2.30	3	3.90
5	3.80	5	6.50
13	10	13	17
40	30	40	50
75	55	75	97
120	90	120	155
250	185	250	325
500	370	500	650

For current exchange rates see www.xe.com

magnetic parking cards at kiosks and tobacconists. Cameras are increasingly being used to monitor the streets going into the pedestrianised town centres, called *Z.T.L. (zona traffico limitato)*. Your hotel will help by providing you with a vehicle pass. When smog levels are particularly high, towns may prohibit cars in emission classes 1, 2 and sometimes even 3, as well as older diesel vehicles without a particle filter. This is indicated on large displays on the streets into the town. Drivers of the vehicles in question have to leave them outside the centre and continue with public transport. You continue with public transport; in most cases there is a P+R system. The centre of Milan interior is an 🕐 environmental zone, and the above-mentioned emission classes need an *Ecopass* to enter the town, which drivers can obtain from the same places that sell tickets for public transport e.g. tobacconists or multi-storey car parks. Petrol stations sell *super 95 senza piombo* or *gasolio* (diesel). Except on the motorway, petrol stations close at lunchtime (12.30pm–3pm) and on Sunday, but there are many self service machines in such instances.

EMBASSIES & CONSULATES

UK EMBASSY IN ROME
Via XX Settembre 80/a | tel. +39 06 42 20 23 33 | www.gov.uk/government/ world/organisations/british-embassy-rom

USA EMBASSY IN ROME
Via Vittorio Veneto 121 | tel. +39 06 46 74 1 | italy.usembassy.gov

For the contact details for consulates in other areas, please refer to the above websites.

EMERGENCY SERVICES

Emergency number *(Pronto Soccorso)* free from every public telephone:
– Police *tel. 113*
– Fire brigade *(Vigili del Fuoco) tel. 115*
– Ambulance *tel. 118*
– Breakdown service *tel. 80 31 16*

INFORMATION

ITALIAN STATE TOURIST BOARD (ENIT)
– *1 Prince Street | London W1B 2AY | tel. +44 20 7408 1254*

– *630 Fifth Avenue, Suite 1565 | New York, NY 10111 | tel. +1 212 245 48 22*
– *175 Bloor St. East, Suite 907 – South | Toronto ON M4W 3R8 | tel. +1 416 9 25 48 82*
– *www.enit.it*

EASY ITALIA
That is the name of the new service number available to tourists from 9am–10pm if they have any questions or problems: *tel. 0039 39 03 90 39*

HEALTH

At hospitals or the local health authority ASL *(Agenzia Sanitaria Locale)*, European residents should present their European Health Insurance Card EHIC. Additional travel insurance is advisable and, of course, for non-EU residents essential. Remember to ask for receipts for any treatment that you have to pay for, so that you can apply for a refund from your own health authority upon your return home. The ambulance emergency services *(pronto soccorso)* are generally swift, good and uncomplicated.

INTERNET CAFÉS & WI-FI

There are internet cafés everywhere (2–6 euros/hr); in the larger towns, you will also find some cafés with Wi-Fi access. That also applies for most of the hotels, many of which at least offer wireless Internet connection in the bar, reception and lounge area, some free of charge, some by means of a fee password from reception. The same is also true of the waiting and bar areas at airports and at larger train stations as well as some motorway service stations, especially in the north.
The municipalities of Rome *(www.roma wireless.com)*, Milan and Bologna are

actively developing the network access in the city centres and in the public parks. You can find addresses via *www.wi-fi-italia.com* and *wi-fi.jiwire.com*.

MONEY & CREDIT CARDS

Banks usually have ATM cash dispensers *(bancomat)*. Almost all hotels, petrol stations and supermarkets, as well as most restaurants and shops accept major credit cards.

MUSEUMS & SIGHTS

The opening hours of the museums have become far more visitor-friendly in recent years and almost all of the state museums are open during the lunch hour. In the summer, the opening hours may be extended until much later in the evening. Closing times are indicated in this guide, but the ticket office often closes earlier. The entrance price ranges from 4–10 euros, occasionally with an additional charge for reservations. The state museums *(musei nazionali)* are also free of charge for EU citizens under 18 and over 65, and young adults aged between 18 and 25 only have to pay half price. The *Settimana della Cultura* takes place in April each year, during which all state museums can be visited free of charge.

OPENING HOURS

On weekdays, grocery shops usually open from 8.30am–1pm and from 5pm–7.30pm, all other shops, boutiques, supermarkets and department stores normally open from 8.30am–12.30pm and from 3.30pm–7.30pm. All of the shops are closed on one afternoon of the week. In tourist areas, the shops and boutiques stay open late

at night. Churches are usually open every day from 8am–noon and from 3pm–6pm.

PHONES & MOBILE PHONES

The international dialling code for Italy is *+39* and the area code is part of the number and must always be dialled (including the zero). Dial *+44* for calls from Italy to the UK and *+1* from Italy to the USA and Canada. Mobile numbers start without a zero.

BUDGETING

Coffee	£1–£1.20/$1.60–$2	*for a cappuccino at the bar*
Ice cream	£1.60/$2.60	*for one large scoop*
Wine	from £2.40/$4	*for a glass at the bar*
Museums	£3.30–£8/$5–$13	*for entrance*
Petrol	c. £1.40/$2.30	*for 1L Super*
Beach	from £11.50/$18	*Daily rental for sunshade and lounger*

To make calls from a foreign mobile telephone it is cheaper to use an Italian prepaid card. They are sold in tobacco shops for 5–10 euro. For frequent callers it is worthwhile buying a rechargeable SIM you can then have an Italian number and the charges for incoming calls are dropped. When buying a SIM you have to have proof of identity, a contact address and a mobile phone. There are only a few public telephones that use coins. Telephone cards *(carta telefonica)* are available in bars, tobacco shops and post offices.

POST

Stamps are available from post offices and tobacconists (*tabacchi*). Post offices are generally open Mon–Fri 8.20am–1.20pm, Sat to 12.20pm.

PRICES

At the bar, an espresso will cost you about 1 euro, but if you sit down at a table to drink it, it may well cost you twice as much or even three times as much.

PUBLIC TRANSPORT

Trains (*www.fsitaliane.it, www.trentitalia.com*) and buses are relatively inexpensive. The trains are more punctual than their reputation, but often crowed. The ultra-fast new trains Frecciarossa and Eurostar, which are increasingly replacing normal trains, connect the major towns: they are considerably more expensive and you have to book a seat. There is a local network to the smaller villages and more remote regions, e.g. with Trenord to Lombard valleys, with the Vinschgauer train to South Tyrol's Vinschgau Valley, with Ferrovie Sudest through Salento in Apulia. You can take bikes on many of the local trains. You have to stamp your train ticket in the orange-yellow machines on the platform before boarding the trains. In addition to

WEATHER IN ROME

	Jan	Feb	March	April	May	June	July	Aug	Sept	Oct	Nov	Dec
Daytime temperatures in °C/°F												
	11/52	13/55	16/61	19/66	23/73	28/82	31/88	31/88	27/81	21/70	16/61	12/54
Nighttime temperatures in °C/°F												
	4/39	5/41	7/45	10/50	13/55	17/63	20/68	20/68	17/63	13/55	9/48	5/41
Sunshine hours/day												
	4	4	5	7	8	10	11	10	7	6	5	4
Precipitation days/month												
	8	9	8	8	7	4	2	2	5	8	10	10
Water temperatures in °C/°F												
	14/57	13/55	13/55	14/57	17/63	21/70	23/73	24/75	23/73	20/68	18/64	15/59

the Italian railway, there is also the fast and comfortable private railway Italo *(www.italo.it)*. Cities such as Rome, Milan and Naples have underground trains and large bus networks.

TIPPING

A service charge is normally included, but waiters, chambermaids, porters etc. are naturally pleased if you reward them for friendly service. Five to ten per cent is usual in restaurants.

WEATHER, WHEN TO GO

The holiday resorts are all hopelessly crowded in August. Prices hit the roof and you will often be forced to book at least half-board. Whilst the towns and museums are relatively empty during the summer, they burst at Easter and over long weekends. A good time to go is May/June and September/October, although a lot of hotels close at the end of September. You can check the weather online at: *www.tempoitalia.it*

WHERE TO STAY

AGRITURISMO

An increasing number of farms in Italy are renting out rooms, holiday flats and pitches for motor homes and tents. They are often elegantly restored country homes, which are priced accordingly. One excellent website with many illustrated offers is: *www.agriturist.it*. The AA Association publishes a Caravan and Camping Guide each year for Europe and Alan Roberts 'Best Campsites in Italy' guide is also recommendable. Other good websites: *www.agriturismo.org.uk*, *www.agriturismo.it*, for holidays on farms in South Tyrol *www.roterhahn.it*, 🕒 organic farms *www.agriturismibiologici.net*.

BED & BREAKFAST

There are numerous listings for private accommodation at attractive rates on the following websites *www.bbitalia.it/en/* and *www.bed-and-breakfast-italy.com*

CAMPING

You can find useful information about the best campsites at *www.camping.it/english*

HOLIDAY HOMES

You can find details of properties by contacting the local tourist board or by browsing *www.italia.it/en/home.html* and *www.homelidays.co.uk*. A good website for holiday homes in southern Italy is *www.nonsolocasa-italy-travel.com/*. Good accommodation is also available at *www.cilento-travel.com/en.html*. You can read about a nice selection in Tuscany at *www.holidayhomestuscany.com*. And one special tip: The renovation and redesign of private accommodation in old villages, hamlets and old town districts into holiday accommodation is referred to as *albergo diffuso*: *www.alberghidiffusi.it*.

HOTELS

In the tourist areas by the sea or in the mountains, you often only get rooms with half or full board during the high season – and the prices rise sharply in July/August.

A few good search portals are *www.booking.com*, *www.trivago.it* and *www.initalia.it/en/*. The Lega Ambiente (Italy's environmental organisation) lists a whole range of particularly environmentally friendly hotels: *www.legambienteturismo.it*.

HOSTELS

Youth hostels, Backpacker hostels and cheap hotels are listed under *www.aighostels.it/en*, *www.hostelsclub.com* and *www.hostelitaly.com*.

USEFUL PHRASES ITALIAN

PRONUNCIATION

c, cc	before e or i like ch in "church", e.g. ciabatta, otherwise like k
ch, cch	like k, e.g. pacchi, che
g, gg	before e or i like j in "just", e.g. gente, otherwise like g in "get"
gl	like "lli" in "million", e.g. figlio
gn	as in "cognac", e.g. bagno
sc	before e or i like sh, e.g. uscita
sch	like sk in "skill", e.g. Ischia
z	at the beginning of a word like dz in "adze", otherwise like ts

An accent on an Italian word shows that the stress is on the last syllable.
In other cases we have shown which syllable is stressed by placing a dot below the relevant vowel.

IN BRIEF

Yes/No/Maybe	Sì/No/Forse
Please/Thank you	Per favore/Grazie
Excuse me, please!	Scusa!/Mi scusi
May I ...?/Pardon?	Posso ...? / Come dice?/Prego?
I would like to .../Have you got ...?	Vorrei .../Avete ...?
How much is ...?	Quanto costa ...?
I (don't) like that	(Non) mi piace
good/bad	buono/cattivo/bene/male
broken/doesn't work	guasto/non funziona
too much/much/little/all/nothing	troppo/molto/poco/ tutto/niente
Help!/Attention!/Caution!	aiuto!/attenzione!/prudenza!
ambulance/police/fire brigade	ambulanza/polizia/vigili del fuoco
Prohibition/forbidden/danger/dangerous	divieto/vietato/pericolo/pericoloso
May I take a photo here/of you?	Posso fotografar La?

GREETINGS, FAREWELL

Good morning!/afternoon!/ evening!/night!	Buon giorno!/Buon giorno!/ Buona sera!/Buona notte!
Hello! / Goodbye!/See you	Ciao!/Salve! / Arrivederci!/Ciao!
My name is ...	Mi chiamo ...
What's your name?	Come si chiama?/Come ti chiami
I'm from ...	Vengo da ...

Parli italiano?

"Do you speak Italian?" This guide will help you to say the basic words and phrases in Italian

DATE & TIME

Monday/Tuesday/Wednesday	lunedì/martedì/mercoledì
Thursday/Friday/Saturday	giovedì/venerdì/sabato
Sunday/holiday/ working day	domenica/(giorno) festivo/ (giorno) feriale
today/tomorrow/yesterday	oggi/domani/ieri
hour/minute	ora/minuto
day/night/week/month/year	giorno/notte/settimana/mese/anno
What time is it?	Che ora è? Che ore sono?
It's three o'clock/It's half past three	Sono le tre/Sono le tre e mezza
a quarter to four	le quattro meno un quarto/ un quarto alle quattro

TRAVEL

open/closed	aperto/chiuso
entrance/exit	entrata/uscita
departure/arrival	partenza/arrivo
toilets/ladies/gentlemen	bagno/toilette/signore/signori
(no) drinking water	acqua (non) potabile
Where is ...?/Where are ...?	Dov'è ...?/Dove sono ...?
left/right/straight ahead/back	sinistra/destra/dritto/indietro
close/far	vicino/lontano
bus/tram	bus/tram
taxi/cab	taxi/tassì
bus stop/cab stand	fermata/posteggio taxi
parking lot/parking garage	parcheggio/parcheggio coperto
street map/map	pianta/mappa
train station/harbour	stazione/porto
airport	aeroporto
schedule/ticket	orario/biglietto
supplement	supplemento
single/return	solo andata/andata e ritorno
train/track	treno/binario
platform	banchina/binario
I would like to rent ...	Vorrei noleggiare ...
a car/a bicycle	una macchina/una bicicletta
a boat	una barca
petrol/gas station	distributore/stazione di servizio
petrol/gas / diesel	benzina/diesel/gasolio
breakdown/repair shop	guasto/officina

FOOD & DRINK

Could you please book a table for tonight for four?	Vorrei prenotare per stasera un tavolo per quattro?
on the terrace/by the window	sulla terrazza/ vicino alla finestra
The menu, please	La carta/il menù, per favore
Could I please have ...?	Potrei avere ...?
bottle/carafe/glass	bottiglia/caraffa/bicchiere
knife/fork/spoon/salt/pepper	coltello/forchetta/cucchiaio/sale/pepe
sugar/vinegar/oil/milk/cream/lemon	zucchero/aceto/olio/latte/panna/limone
cold/too salty/not cooked	freddo/troppo salato/non cotto
with/without ice/sparkling	con/senza ghiaccio/gas
vegetarian/allergy	vegetariano/vegetariana/allergia
May I have the bill, please?	Vorrei pagare/Il conto, per favore
bill/tip	conto/mancia

SHOPPING

Where can I find...?	Dove posso trovare ...?
I'd like .../I'm looking for ...	Vorrei .../Cerco ...
Do you put photos onto CD?	Vorrei masterizzare delle foto su CD?
pharmacy/shopping centre/kiosk	farmacia/centro commerciale/edicola
department store/supermarket	grandemagazzino/supermercato
baker/market/grocery	forno/ mercato/negozio alimentare
photographic items/newspaper shop/	articoli per foto/giornalaio
100 grammes/1 kilo	un etto/un chilo
expensive/cheap/price/more/less	caro/economico/prezzo/di più/di meno
organically grown	di agricoltura biologica

ACCOMMODATION

I have booked a room	Ho prenotato una camera
Do you have any ... left?	Avete ancora ...
single room/double room	una (camera) singola/doppia
breakfast/half board/	prima colazione/mezza pensione/
full board (American plan)	pensione completa
at the front/seafront/lakefront	con vista/con vista sul mare/lago
shower/sit-down bath/balcony/terrace	doccia/bagno/balcone/terrazza
key/room card	chiave/scheda magnetica
luggage/suitcase/bag	bagaglio/valigia/borsa

BANKS, MONEY & CREDIT CARDS

bank/ATM/pin code	banca/bancomat/ codice segreto
cash/credit card	in contanti/carta di credito
bill/coin/change	banconota/moneta/il resto

USEFUL PHRASES

HEALTH

doctor/dentist/paediatrician	medico/dentista/pediatra
hospital/emergency clinic	ospedale/pronto soccorso/guardia medica
fever/pain/inflamed/injured	febbre/dolori/infiammato/ferito
diarrhoea/nausea/sunburn	diarrea/nausea/scottatura solare
plaster/bandage/ointment/cream	cerotto/fasciatura/pomata/crema
pain reliever/tablet/suppository	antidolorifico/compressa/supposta

POST, TELECOMMUNICATIONS & MEDIA

stamp/letter/postcard	francobollo/lettera/cartolina
I need a landline phone card/ I'm looking for a prepaid card for my mobile	Mi serve una scheda telefonica per la rete fissa/Cerco una scheda prepagata per il mio cellulare
Where can I find internet access?	Dove trovo un accesso internet?
dial/connection/engaged	comporre/linea/occupato
socket/adapter/charger	presa/riduttore/caricabatterie
computer/battery/rechargeable battery	computer/batteria/accumulatore
internet address (URL)/e-mail address	indirizzo internet/indirizzo email
internet connection/wifi	collegamento internet/wi-fi
e-mail/file/print	email/file/stampare

LEISURE, SPORTS & BEACH

beach/bathing beach	spiaggia/bagno/stabilimento balneare
sunshade/lounger/cable car/chair lift	ombrellone/sdraio/funivia/seggiovia
(rescue) hut/avalanche	rifugio/valanga

NUMBERS

0	zero	15	quindici
1	uno	16	sedici
2	due	17	diciassette
3	tre	18	diciotto
4	quattro	19	diciannove
5	cinque	20	venti
6	sei	21	ventuno
7	sette	50	cinquanta
8	otto	100	cento
9	nove	200	duecento
10	dieci	1000	mille
11	undici	2000	duemila
12	dodici	10000	diecimila
13	tredici	½	un mezzo
14	quattordici	¼	un quarto

NOTES

FOR YOUR NEXT HOLIDAY ...

MARCO POLO TRAVEL GUIDES

ALGARVE
AMSTERDAM
ATHENS
AUSTRALIA
AUSTRIA
BANGKOK
BARCELONA
BERLIN
BRAZIL
BRUGES, GHENT &
  ANTWERP
BRUSSELS
BUDAPEST
BULGARIA
CALIFORNIA
CAMBODIA
CANADA EAST
CANADA WEST
  ROCKIES
CAPE TOWN
  WINE LANDS,
  GARDEN ROUTE
CAPE VERDE
CHANNEL ISLANDS
CHICAGO
  & THE LAKES
CHINA
COLOGNE
COPENHAGEN
CORFU
COSTA BLANCA
  VALENCIA
COSTA BRAVA
  BARCELONA
COSTA DEL SOL
  GRANADA
CRETE
CUBA
CYPRUS
  NORTH AND
  SOUTH
DUBAI
DUBLIN
DUBROVNIK &
  DALMATIAN COAST
EDINBURGH

EGYPT
EGYPT'S RED
  SEA RESORTS
FINLAND
FLORENCE
FLORIDA
FRENCH ATLANTIC
  COAST
FRENCH RIVIERA
  NICE, CANNES &
  MONACO
FUERTEVENTURA
GRAN CANARIA
GREECE
HAMBURG
HONG KONG
  MACAU
ICELAND
INDIA
INDIA SOUTH
  GOA & KERALA
IRELAND
ISRAEL
ISTANBUL
ITALY
JORDAN
KOS
KRAKOW
LAKE GARDA

LANZAROTE
LAS VEGAS
LISBON
LONDON
LOS ANGELES
MADEIRA
  PORTO SANTO
MADRID
MALLORCA
MALTA
  GOZO
MAURITIUS
MENORCA
MILAN
MOROCCO
MUNICH
NAPLES &
  THE AMALFI COAST
NEW YORK
NEW ZEALAND
NORWAY
OSLO
PARIS
PHUKET
PORTUGAL
PRAGUE

RHODES
ROME
SAN FRANCISCO
SARDINIA
SCOTLAND
SEYCHELLES
SHANGHAI
SICILY
SINGAPORE
SOUTH AFRICA
STOCKHOLM
SWITZERLAND
TENERIFE
THAILAND
TURKEY
TURKEY
  SOUTH COAST
TUSCANY
UNITED ARAB
  EMIRATES
USA SOUTHWEST
VENICE
VIENNA
VIETNAM

- PACKED WITH INSIDER TIPS
- BEST WALKS AND TOURS
- FULL-COLOUR PULL-OUT MAP
  AND STREET ATLAS

ROAD ATLAS

The green line ___ indicates the Trips & Tours (p. 146–151)
The blue line ___ indicates The perfect route (p. 32–33)

All tours are also marked on the pull-out map

Photo: Rimini harbour

Exploring Italy

The map on the back cover shows how the area has been sub-divided

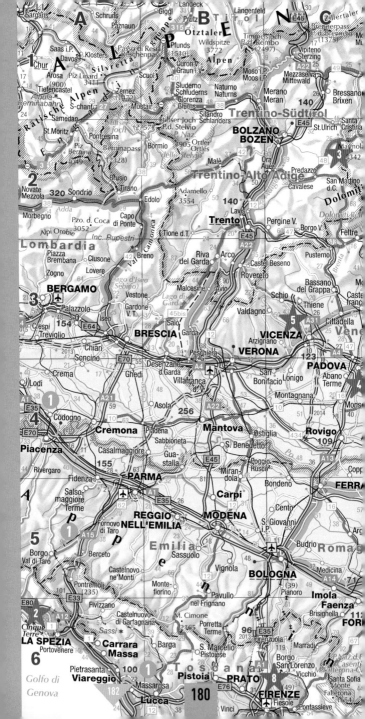

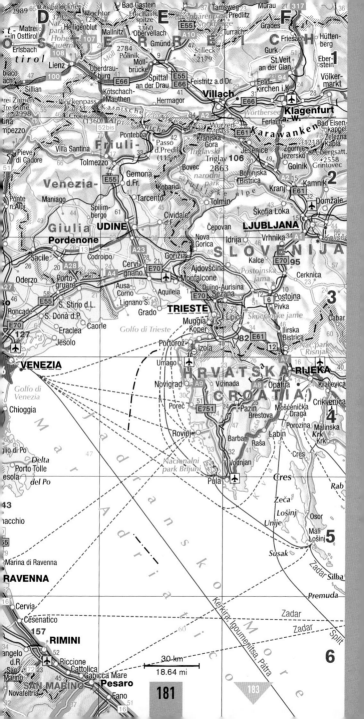

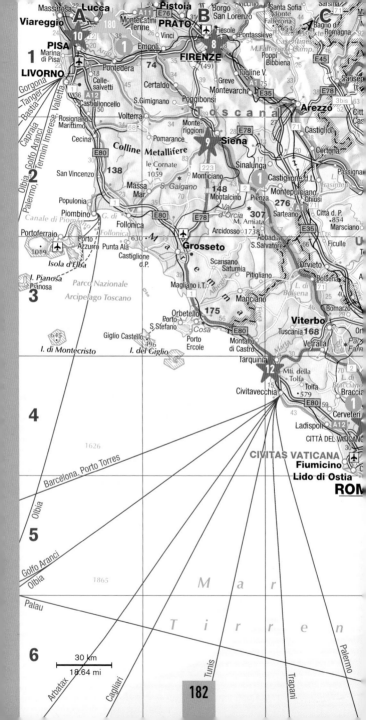

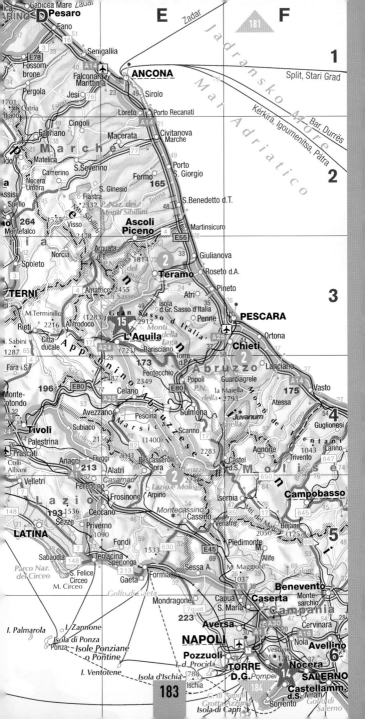

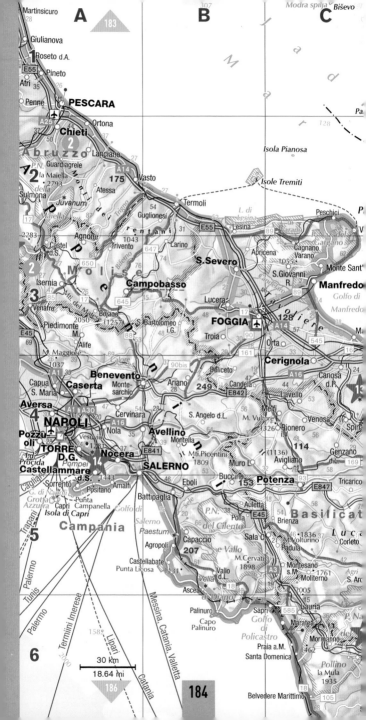

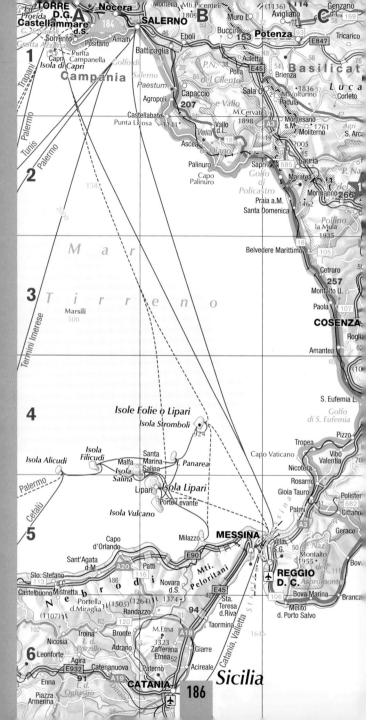

A

TORRE D.G.A.
Castellammare d.s.
G. di Napoli
Sorrento
Grotta Azzurra
Positano
Punta Campanella
Capri
Isola di Capri
Amalfi
Campania
Golfo di
Salerno
Paestum
Agropoli
Capaccio
207
Castellabate
Punta Licosa
Velia
Ascea
Palinuro
Capo
Palinuro

Montella
Mti.Picentini
1809

B
Nocera
SALERNO
46
Eboli
Battipaglia
P.N.
del Cilento
Sala G.
M.Cervati
1898
Vallo
d.L.
18
Diano
Sapri
585
Golfo
di
Policastro
Praia a.M.
1462
Santa Domenica

Muro L.
Buccino 153
Auletta
Polla
Padula
Montesano
s.M.
Moliterno
2005
Lauria
Maratea
Mormanno 266
Pollino
la Mula
1935

Avigliano
(1136)
C
Genzano
169
Tricarico
Potenza
E847
93
58
Brienza
Basilicat
Luca
Corleto
1836
M.Volturino
1761
S. Arca
Agri
N. Na

Mar
Tirreno
Marsili
500

Belvedere Marittimo
18
105
Cetraro
257
Montalto U.
Paola
107
COSENZA
Rogli
Amantea
62

Termini Imerese

Palermo

Isole Eolie o Lipari
Isola Stromboli
924
Isola
Filicudi
Isola Alicudi
Santa
Marina
Salina
Malfa
Isola
Salina
Lipari
Isola Lipari
Porto Levante
Isola Vulcano

I. Panarea

Milazzo
MESSINA
Villa
S.G.
Montalto
1955

S. Eufemia L.
Golfo
di S. Eufemia
Pizzo
Tropea
Capo Vaticano
Vibo
Valentia
76
Nicotera
Rosarno
Gioia Tauro
Palmi
Polister
682
Cittano
Gerace

**REGGIO
D. C.**
Bova Marina
Branca
Bov
Aspromonte
106

Palermo
Cefalù
Capo
d'Orlando
Sant'Agata
d.M.
A20
Sto. Stefano
113
d.C.
Castelbuono
Portella
d.Miraglia
(1107)
Troina
L. d.
Pozzillo
Nicosia
Leonforte
Agira
E932
Catenanuova
91
Enna
Piazza
Armerina
L. d.
Ogliastro

Patti
116
Novara
d.S.
1374
Randazzo
120
Bronte
Adrano
M.Etna
3323
Zafferana
Etnea
Paternò
A19
CATANIA
186

Portella
d.Miraglia
(1505)(1264)
E45
Sta.
Teresa
d.Riva
Taormina
Giarre
Acireale
Sicilia

Mti.
Peloritani
Sto. Stefano
Novara
d.S.
42
94
Catania, Valletta

Nazi
dell
111

Sta.
Teresa
d.Riva
1646

Melito
d. Porto Salvo

Altamura
Gioia d.Colle
Fasano
D
E
99
Ostuni
F
Canale d'Otranto
Vlorë
E843
Alberobello
379 53
Matera
88
Mottola
Puglia
Martina Fr.
Ceglie
Messapica
E55
Brindisi
Kérkira
Igoumenitsa
185
1
Laterza
100
Massafra
65
Mesagne
Penisola
Salentina
Sami, Patra
TARANTO
E90
7
Francavilla F.
Squinzano
Bernalda
30
39
7ter
LECCE
sticci
106
Metaponto
Manduria
Veglie
101
16
Policoro
Porto Cesareo
Nardò
Galatina
Martano
16
Otranto
E90
Golfo
Gallipoli
Maglie
104
275
S. Cesarea
Terme
2
Ugento
44
Tricase
di Taranto
Marina
di Leuca
Capo S.Maria
di Leuca
Trebisacce
Alb.
2154
Jetrio
54
E90
Rossano
170
Cariati
ongobucco
Punta Alice
3
1708
Campana
Naz.
ella Sila
Ciro
E846
S.Giovanni
in Fiore
Strongoli
i l a
46
107
Cotronei
Neto
109
Crotone
Cutro
Catanzaro
60
Isola di C.R.
Golfo di
Capo Rizzuto
2747
Catanzaro Marina
4
Squillace
Soverato
alle C.
Calabria
Monasterace
Marina
5
Mare
Ionio
2000
3358
Ionian
Sea
6
30 km
18.64 mi

187

KEY TO ROAD ATLAS

Highway, multilane divided road - under construction Autobahn, mehrspurige Straße - in Bau		Autoroute, route à plusieurs voies - en construction Autosnelweg, weg met meer rijstroken - in aanleg
Trunk road - under construction Fernverkehrsstraße - in Bau		Route à grande circulation - en construction Weg voor interlokaal verkeer - in aanleg
Principal highway Hauptstraße		Route principale Hoofdweg
Secondary road Nebenstraße		Route secondaire Overige verharde wegen
Practicable road, track Fahrweg, Piste		Chemin carrossable, piste Weg, piste
Road numbering Straßennummerierung	E20 11 70 26	Numérotage des routes Wegnummering
Distances in kilometers Entfernungen in Kilometer	**259** 130 129	Distances en kilomètres Afstand in kilometers
Height in meters - Pass Höhe in Meter - Pass	1365 •	Altitude en mètres - Col Hoogte in meters - Pas
Railway - Railway ferry Eisenbahn - Eisenbahnfähre		Chemin de fer - Ferry-boat Spoorweg - Spoorport
Car ferry - Shipping route Autofähre - Schifffahrtslinie		Bac autos - Ligne maritime Autoveer - Scheepvaartlijn
Major international airport - Airport Wichtiger internationaler Flughafen - Flughafen	✈ ✈	Aéroport importante international - Aéroport Belangrijke internationale luchthaven - Luchthaven
International boundary - Province boundary Internationale Grenze - Provinzgrenze		Frontière internationale - Limite de Province Internationale grens - Provinciale grens
Undefined boundary Unbestimmte Grenze		Frontière d'Etat non définie Rijksgrens onbepaalt
Time zone boundary Zeitzonengrenze	-4h Greenwich Time -3h Greenwich Time	Limite de fuseau horaire Tijdzone-grens
National capital Hauptstadt eines souveränen Staates	**ROMA**	Capitale nationale Hoofdstad van een souvereine staat
Federal capital Hauptstadt eines Bundesstaates	**Firenze**	Capitale d'un état fédéral Hoofdstad van een deelstat
Restricted area Sperrgebiet		Zone interdite Verboden gebied
National park Nationalpark		Parc national Nationaal park
Ancient monument Antikes Baudenkmal	∴	Monument antiques Antiek monument
Interesting cultural monument Sehenswertes Kulturdenkmal	✳ Chambord	Monument culturel interéssant Bezienswaardig cultuurmonument
Interesting natural monument Sehenswertes Naturdenkmal	✳ Gorges du Tarn	Monument naturel interéssant Bezienswaardig natuurmonument
Well Brunnen	⌣	Puits Bron
Trips & Tours Ausflüge & Touren		Excursions & tours Uitstapjes & tours
Perfect route Perfekte Route		Itinéraire idéal Perfecte route
MARCO POLO Highlight	⭐**1**	MARCO POLO Highlight

INDEX

This index lists all towns and destinations featured in this guide.
Numbers in bold indicate a main entry.

INDEX

CREDITS

WRITE TO US

e-mail: info@marcopologuides.co.uk

Did you have a great holiday?
Is there something on your mind?
Whatever it is, let us know!
Whether you want to praise, alert us
to errors or give us a personal tip –
MARCO POLO would be pleased to
hear from you.
We do everything we can to provide the
very latest information for your trip.

Nevertheless, despite all of our authors'
thorough research, errors can creep in.
MARCO POLO does not accept any
liability for this. Please contact us by
e-mail or post.

MARCO POLO Travel Publishing Ltd
Pinewood, Chineham Business Park
Crockford Lane, Chineham
Basingstoke, Hampshire RG24 8AL
United Kingdom

PICTURE CREDITS

Cover photograph: Tuscany, Cortona, red Fiat (Laif: Madej)
Artissima: Elena Biringhelli (18 centre); U. Bernhart (132, 138/139, 140); DuMont Bildarchiv: Bernhart (59), Nagy (114, 119), Spitta (110, 150, 161, 163), Wrba (2 bottom, 36, 66/67, 79); R. Freyer (front flap left, 12/13, 30/31, 43, 113, 117, 160); R. M. Gill (70, 82); J. Gläser (28 right); R. Hackenberg (61); Hangloosebeach: Luca Valentini (19 bottom); H. Hartmann (47); Hilton Molino Stucky Hotel (18 top); Huber: Borchi (6), Gräfenhain (2 centre top, 7, 34/35, 44), Hallberg (3 centre, 106/107), Klaes (146/147), Ripani (99), Scatà (143), Giovanni Simeone (15, 105), Spila (3 bottom, 122/123); ©iStockphoto.com: lazortech (18 bottom); M. Kirchgessner (front flap right, 23, 26/27, 30, 40, 62, 64, 100); H. Krinitz (29, 31, 49, 50, 90/91, 152/153); N. Kustos (103); Laif: Amme (156/157), Celentano (108), Galli (38, 124, 126, 128), Madej (1 top), Sasse (17, 130), Zanettini (162 top); mauritius images: Alamy (2 top, 5, 9, 10/11, 20/21, 25, 68, 72, 159, 176/177), CuboImages (4, 28 left), ib (Kutter) (89); D. Renckhoff (57); J. Richter (3 top, 84/85, 86); M. Schulte-Kellinghaus (148/149, 160/161); O. Stadler (77, 155); T. Stankiewicz (54, 81, 135, 137, 144, 145); M. Strobel (162 bottom); Vesuvio Trekking (19 top); H. Wagner (8, 32, 93, 94, 97, 121); T. P. Widmann (2 centre bottom, 52/53); E. Wrba (75)

1st Edition 2014

Worldwide Distribution: Marco Polo Travel Publishing Ltd, Pinewood, Chineham Business Park, Crockford Lane, Basingstoke, Hampshire RG24 8AL, United Kingdom. E-mail: sales@marcopolouk.com
© MAIRDUMONT GmbH & Co. KG, Ostfildern
Chief editor: Marion Zorn
Author: Bettina Dürr; editor: Nadia Al Kureischi
Programme supervision: Anita Dahlinger, Ann-Katrin Kutzner, Nikolai Michaelis
Picture editor: Gabriele Forst
What's hot: wunder media, Munich
Cartography road atlas & pull-out map: © MAIRDUMONT, Ostfildern
Design: milchhof : atelier, Berlin; Front cover, pull-out map cover, page 1: factor product munich
Translated from German by Sarah Trenker; editor of the English edition: Margaret Howie, fullproof.co.za
Prepress: M. Feuerstein, Wigel
Phrase book in cooperation with Ernst Klett Sprachen GmbH, Stuttgart, Editorial by Pons Wörterbücher

DOS & DON'TS

A few tips to help you avoid the typical tourist mistakes in Italy

DO BE VIGILANT

You must keep your eyes open for pick-pockets on public transport. When you are wandering through the town, always keep your handbag and camera on the side away from the street. The safest method is to wear a waist bag. At the hotel, you should ask if there are guarded garage facilities.

DON'T BUY FAKES

Even if you are an avid bargain hunter: do not buy anything – cheap Ray Bans, Gucci handbags, Louis Vuitton purses – from the *vu cumpra*, street hawkers from Senegal or Somalia that ply the pedestrian zones. The goods are never the real thing and, as it is illegal to purchase them if caught, you can be fined up to 3000 euro.

DON'T ORDER PASTA AS A MAIN COURSE

It might be all right to fill up on a plate of pasta in a cheaper restaurant or tourist trap and then simply pay and go. In better-class restaurants, however, there is an unwritten law against this. In Italy, pasta is a *primo piatto* and is followed by a main course of meat or fish. If you need a snack, a sandwich – *a panino* – or a couple of tramezzini at the bar are a good idea.

DO BE PATIENT

In Italy – especially in the south – you will discover that the Italians have a completely different concept of time.

This often means that you seem to have to wait for no particularly good reason. On the other hand, people have a lot more time and that can result in some very nice encounters and sometimes lead to some wonderful solutions to your problem.

DO DRESS APPROPRIATELY

In Italy it is expected that appropriate clothing (no shorts, no skimpy tops) be worn in churches and places of worship. It is also best not to walk around talking and taking photographs while religious services are in progress.

DON'T ORDER ANYTHING WITHOUT ASKING THE PRICE

In many cases, it is advisable to ask the price in advance, e.g. before you take a taxi, when you make a room reservation, before having your car repaired, or when ordering a Tuscan steak, *fiorentina,* where prices are often indicated per 100 g *(etto).*

DON'T PICK LEMONS OR FIGS

Especially in southern Italy, you will often pass gardens with trees full of figs, lemons and oranges. You should resist the temptation to pick them, rather wait until you meet someone at the farmhouse or working in the orchard and then you can ask permission. The people are usually all too proud of their products and happy to give away a few pieces of fruit.